LUMINOUS JEWELS OF LOVE AND LIGHT: Volume 2

By

Richard Shiningthunder Francis

ISBN: 1-4033-8844-X (e-book)
ISBN: 1-4033-8845-8 (Paperback)
ISBN: 1-4033-8846-6 (Hardcover)

This book is printed on acid free paper.

1stBooks - rev. 02/18/03

DEDICATION

To Ada Maria Francis, the most welcome and celebrated Love of my life,

And to Pat Fields, a Soul of immeasurable and awe-inspiring compassion,

And to Ann Blufeather, who made this whole life possible,

This book is dedicated with deep, truest, and most heartfelt Love.

ACKNOWLEDGMENTS

Sir Isaac Newton is reputed to have said, "I can see so far only because I stand on the shoulders of giants." For anyone following the Way of Love, this is also certainly true. So, gratitude is due to these spiritual luminaries from many traditions, but who all share a common worldview, and who know what is really important. These people of the communion of Love include Jesus, the Buddha Gautama, Solomon, Lao Tzu, Patanjali, Francis, Kwan Yin, and innumerable others, many of whose names will tragically never be known, for they cultivated a fine antiegotism. To you all, venerable sisters and brothers, profound gratitude from a full and loving heart.

Among the others who have made our publishing work possible through their profound interest, excellent input, and amazing gifts of love are the following, in alphabetical order:

Ann Blufeather, whose gentle Soul and kind generosity and Love made this life possible. You lived as a being of tenderness, and left this world like a fearless warrior— the very best of both worlds. May we all learn from your fine example how to live, and how to die.

Barb Cole and Jim Plants, who gave us our first computer, and changed our lives forever, very much for the better! You have made so much of our subsequent work possible, and have shone the Light of Love into countless hearts. May you walk in the blessing of the great Spirit forever, both in this life and after you step into the Milky Way.

Mary "Maribee" Butler, whose tender friendship, kindness, and goodness are matched only by her sharp intelligence and equally sharp eye. Thank you very much for your proofreading and taping, opening the doors of the inner Spirit to those who would not otherwise have a chance to walk into the Light.

Doctors and nurses of St. Elizabeth North and South Hospitals in Covington, Kentucky, and those fine physicians, nurses, and aids at Christ Hospital in Cincinnati, Ohio. Love uses every one of you in a great, spectacular but often quiet Way, every day. May your lives be filled with health, happiness, abundance, and Love.

Dominic and Noeleen Ellickson, where friendly compassion and remarkable generosity made the publication of this work possible. May love shine on you forever.

Pat Fields, about whom enough good could never be said or written, a true angelic Soul. By your life, you have taught more than a thousand books. You walk immersed in the Light of sweet Love. May blessings and Love overflow in your kind, joyful heart forever, both in this life and in the Homeworld. Hapi says, "betht budth fer ever."

Maria Francis, Soulmate and Love of my life, whose courage, wisdom, and tenderness are unequalled. A thousand books, a hundred lifetimes, could never begin to express what you mean to me. You are the best human being whom I have ever met— and I've met the best! You mean everything to me, and our Love is the holiest joy of life.

Tom Gustin, whose brilliance and profound spirituality are both deeply recognized and appreciated. You are a real messenger of Love. You've shown extraordinary and remarkable strength and kindness in years of selfless service to our shared Master, the Lovemind. May the blessings of deepest Love and tranquility rain upon you like the spring showers.

Karen "Aurora" Ludwick, whose Love is "crystallized" in forms of beauty that are as ancient as yesterday and as new as tomorrow. May the energies of Love fill your heartmind and world with joy and bliss. May contentment come to you, and satisfaction subtly sidle up to you like a warm companion. May you live forever in deep peace.

Frank Merriman, a powerful, lasting friend and an excellent and superb teacher, who has accomplished great things by investing in other people. You have given so much from a heartful of generosity and selfless giving. You are a real blessing from heaven, a gift of cosmic Mind, for many, many people.

Greg Sexton, whose skills and talents have renovated our lives. Your kindness, as well as your many abilities, have proved to be extraordinary in every way. You have brought Love into many, many lives, and have shown the extraordinary strength of character created by only Spirit. May Love bless you every day.

Shirley Sexton, whose elegant refinement changes everyone she knows for the better. May Love continue to guide and smile upon your life, as you have touched so many with your bright mind and tender heart, both of which are of inconceivable value to the Lovemind. Keep up the excellent and superb work of helping and healing people.

Isaiah Toran, my longlost brother, whose beautifully creative mind enriches our entire planet. What an instrument for the Lovemind you are! Love is always bringing to birth new and beautiful creations through your heartmind. You are a bringer of beauty into our often gray world, and you fill the galaxy with bright colors and sweet melodies.

******

******

Any questions or comments about this book or its contents can be sent to:
rmfrancis@juno.com.

******

To you all, my friends, may your lives be filled to overflowing with peace and Light. May your hearts overflow with Love. May your lives overflow with true and lasting success and joy. May you all live forever in compassion, bliss, and tranquility.

******

May whatever merit is generated by this book be shared with all hearts everywhere. May all hearts everywhere flow and glow with the infinite Light of illimitable, immeasurable Love. May all hearts find happiness.

TABLE OF CONTENTS

Author's Preface: Holibooks: Ancient Classics of Mystical Literature

Topsy-turvy, upside-down, inside-out. This is the quasipsychedelic world of mysticism. Volume 1 (Parts I and II) of *Luminous Jewels* captured much of the strange essence of Mindmysticism. It was a lightning "nickel tour" through history, religion, psychology, and philosophy. Volume 2 here presents selections from three illuminated, illuminating classics.

The mystic sees all three as sacred guides. (This speaks well of the universality of mysticism.) She recognizes common themes in Jesus and Lao Tzu and the Upanishadic mystics, knowing that they are spiritual brothers under the skin.

Part III of *Luminous Jewels*, the first of three classics presented here, is a specimen of the most excellent in mystical literature. It is a fresh version of the Gospel of John. (It is not technically a "translation," but a rendition and commentary. "The Gospel of Universal Love" was originally published as a separate smaller book, in 1987.) It is a sentence by sentence commentary on every word of Jesus in this Gospel.

Early Christians followed the supreme Way, the Way of Love. They practiced Love as tolerance, openheartedness, and kindness. They were never nitpicking fanatics or extremists. They did not have any dogmas. They cared nothing for doctrines. They were committed to loving each other, and all. This— not doctrinal conformity— gave the great gift of unity without uniformity. All that was required to be a "Christian" was to embrace the Way of everyday Love, and to adopt the inner Christnature (Lovenature) to "save" you from the lower nature. This Love was manifested as compassion, kindness, goodness, service, etc. "Christians" were not just members of a separate religion. All people— including Hindus, Taoists, and Buddhists— who had embraced fully, and identified with, this Lovenature were seen as sisters/brothers in the larger, most generic "Christian" community. Everyone who loved, and saw the Essence of Love as the Center of the Mind, was welcome in this communion. For "Christ," also in its larger and generic sense, did not refer specifically only to the historical man Jesus. It referred to the deepest level of the unconscious Mind, called the "Lovenature" or "lovemind." (See

"Chart of Mind." on page 126) This deepest level of the Unconscious was Spirit or God. For John says in his first epistle, "You have all received a Christing from Him." (1Jn. 2:20) What, then, did this generic "Christ" mean? It meant a permanent state of enlightenment. It meant that one had awakened to the true nature of reality, and turned her entire life over to the direction of the Lovemind deep within the psyche. So, "Christ" was a rough synonym with "Tao," "Brahman," or "Buddha," as those terms were used in other cultures.

Early Christians, who often called themselves "gnostics" (A Greek word for "mystics"), were by no means xenophobic. They were friendly and open to prechristian or nonchristian faiths. The ancient texts of the Nag Hammadi Library prove that they were completely open towards, and very tolerant of, traditions other than their own. In this, they stand in bold and daring contrast to their fearfilled and suspicious, often unkind, counterpart "Christians" in the modern world. There were no foolish "tests of fellowship," to determine whether you were the "right kind" of Christian.

Christians spoke with a polyphony that celebrated their diversity. They had multiple cosmologies within the one faith. They did not brand fellow Christians who believed differently as "heretics," worthy of damnation and murder. They did not burn each other at the stake, or drive swords into one another. They did not yet suffer from the disease of hateful divisionism.

"Gnostic" is from the Greek *gnosis*, now an English word too. What is gnosis? It is a spectacular, moving, electrifying Mindexplosion of Lovelight that changes your life forever. But what, exactly, is known during gnosis?

You are exposed to bottomless Mind. The Mind is no longer "your" Mind. Instead, it is a shared Mind. It is vast, oceanic, a bottomless and immeasurable "sea" of Light and Love.

People called this illimitable Source of Lovelight Supermind, Superconscious, Superlove, Ultramind, Ultralove, Brahman, Tao, great Spirit, holy Spirit, God, and by other names through the millennia.

This inner God is not a "person." Only in undeveloped, unsophisticated, or backwards cultures is It personified (presented as an inflated human being, in a process called "anthropomorphism"). By contrast, the most enlightened luminaries from every tradition have not presented this ultimate Reality as separate from the rest of Mind or creation. And, because you also have a mind, if this Reality is unified with all Mind, It is also united with you. In fact, It dreams up the entire world through your mindnervoussystem. 1

The Gospel of John is a superlative mystical revelation. What is revealed is a God of continuous interaction with people. This God is not in the sky, but "in" the person. It is a God of purest Love and forgiveness. So, It is astonishingly different from the traditional Jehovah of the ancient Hebrew culture. Jesus is startling in his description of a God Who has nothing in common with the wargod already ancient in his time. In so redefining God, he implicitly denies Jehovah. That is, in fact, one of the reasons that the religious leaders despised and feared him.2

John presents a gnostic God. What is a "gnostic God"? It is a God known not through the temple, through laws and Scriptures, ceremonies or joining the "chosen people." It is a God known within, a God touched within the sanctuary of the heartmind.

This gnostic Christian Gospel splendidly and unquestionably elucidates the mysticism of Jesus. Only a mystic could speak of God "in" the Self, or "in" other people. Only the Spirit of the eternal, nonphysical Christ could speak of being "in" his disciples. (If a physical man said this, it would be total nonsense.) Jesus' repeated references to unity also highlight lucid mysticism. In John, chapter fourteen, it is this deep, eternal, nonphysical Lovenature that says, through Jesus, "I am the Way, the truth, and the life." It was also this same deep Lovemind, in every heart, that said through Jesus, "No one comes to the Father except through Me." (14:16)

In fact, in 17:3, he stated, in prayer: "This is timeless life, to know You ..." The word used in this verse for "know" is a form of the word gnosis. (Remember that the generic word "gnostic" was simply a Greek synonym for "mystic.")

---

1 . For a fuller discussion of this cosmic view see my *Journey to the Center of the Soul: Mysticism Made Simple* (Liberty Township, Ohio; Love Ministries, Inc., 2002)

2 . For more information on many of Jesus' possible nontraditional teachings, see my *The Mystic Gospels of Jesus the Christ* (Liberty Township, Ohio; Love Ministries, Inc., 2002)

This does not indicate that Jesus was a formal "cap G" Gnostic. The "cap G" Gnostics were Christian groups developed after his death, and some of these were cultlike. (Some were superioristic, had strange doctrines, and were organized.) But it does identify him as a generic "small g" gnostic.

By as early as 200 AD, the Christian church had divided into two warring camps, each seeking the detached heads of the other— the Gnostic Christians and the Orthodox Christians. These believers were separated by bitter hatreds and vicious bigotries: The Orthodox passionately despised the Gnostics, damning them to hell. They confusedly included the "small g" gnostics in with the "cap G" Gnostics and ended up hating and killing just about everybody!

In no time, they began atrocities and brutal barbarities against the disapproved Gnostic and gnostic Christians. The result was a war within "Christ's domain." The Orthodox were strangers to tolerance, which they saw as dangerously weak, evil, and even demonic. "Compromise," as for modern fundamentalists, was a "bad" word, a yielding to the devil.

Heresiologists (specialists in "damnable heresies") sought out and ruthlessly tortured and butchered the Gnostics and gnostics. Not that the Gnostics hurt others. They were compassionate, nonviolent people. But they believed the "wrong" things. And the insecure Orthodox, who by now had become bloody monsters, found this intolerable!

Suddenly, by definition, you could be a butcher, a tyrant, a murderer, a monster, if you only believed the "right" teachings. You could still be recognized then as a "Christian." But the most compassionate, tender, moral, and honest person could never be a "Christian" if she believed the "wrong" things about Jesus, the Bible, or God. This mindless, mechanical standard was used to measure her value even if she spoke with reverence and Love about Jesus Christ. The entire Church fell into this backwards, harsh judgmentalism, starkly disobeying the Master of Love.

The Gnostics were not as demoniacally extreme as the Orthodox. But the organized, "cap G" Gnostics were not perfect either. One goal that they did try, without total success, to implement was to keep Christian gnosis alive as the coreteaching of Christianity. So, we do owe them for that.

Towards nonchristians, they adopted a friendly and nonthreatened attitude that also marked their Founder and Masterteacher. All through their millennia-long history, Christian and other mystics have always been outstanding for their openness to, and tolerance of, other spiritual traditions. For all mystics— whether they emerge from Buddhist, Hindu, Taoist, Sufi, Kabbalist, gnostic, or nature-based faiths— are brothers and sisters under the skin, and they know it!

So, Part IV of *Luminous Jewels* is the second great mystical classic presented in this book. It is a representation of mysticism from another tradition. This is Taoism. It is much less alien and cryptic than it used to be. The word "Tao" is becoming part of the language even of popculture. The Taoist masterpiece included here is both prechristian and nonchristian. It is a classic of mystical literature, written about 500 BC, in China. It's Chinese name is *Tao Te Ching* (pronounced roughly, "Dow duh jing"), often translated, "Way of Virtue."

We have taken the liberty of giving it a completely original name that we believe represents its truest essence. For by the mysterious Chinese word *Tao*, the ancient mystical sage-writer seemed to mean what is now called "great Mind," and the word *Te* was the manifestation or expression of this Mind. (The Chinese *Ching* simply means "book.") So, the title of the classic, as rendered here, is the unconventional "The Book of the Great Mind and Its Expression."

It is a remarkably simple text. It can be read in an evening, but might take ten thousand years to understand. It is the foundation for "Taoism"— a very popular worldview. At one time, it ranked as one of the world's major religions. It is a purely mystical path, probably followed now more in the Western world, ironically, than in its motherland of China.

While the Gospel of John emphasizes Love and gnosis, the Taoist classic highlights cooperation, flowing, nonresistance, and trust. Since there is a Power, called "Tao," (pronounced "dow") that already regulates all things, the Taoist does not stress herself by trying to control everything. Of course, you don't want to let go of control when operating a chainsaw. But in the West, we have far too often tried to control far too much. We have tried to control the earth and her ecosystems, and have nearly killed, or at least, ruined her. In the same way, Lao Tzu (pronounced "lah-oh dzuh"), the legendary writer of this book, writes of the cosmos, "If you try to change it, you will ruin it." (Chapter 29)

This mysterious Power is the one that lifts the sun into the dawn, and produces green shoots in springtime. It unfolds the rose, causes sweet rain to fall, and is, right at this moment, beating your heart and turning fruits and vegetables into flesh and bone! This ultimate nanotechmaster controls every important event in your life. It is major intelligence, creating order and structure in all of nature, from the hexagonal form of snowflakes to the arrangement of atoms in a cell. Indeed, this Tao is the Source of atomic architecture and molecular geometry. It expresses through mathematical design and breathtaking precision in the arrangement of stars in galaxies. But as the wise Taoist masters, and mystics from all traditions knew, the verifiable existence of precision in the cosmos does not imply the archaic, primitive notion of a God "out there" anywhere.

Still, this immense, inignorable mathematical order gives every evidence of being Mind, with both intelligence and will. Masters say that it is supremely spiritual Mind, and that It dwells in "your" unconscious Mind. This makes arguments about a "big daddy" somewhere in outer space appear clumsy, childish, and petty. This old whining, tremulous argument smacks of dullness and ignorance.

Taoism is all about learning to live as one who trusts this amazing Mind more than the pathetic human attempts to control and/or modify the cosmos. After all, if there is a brilliant Mind in control of everything, including the major events of your own life, then you can safely abandon frenetic, kinetic attempts to control everything. You can drop them as superfluous baggage, lay aside meddling, manipulation, coercion, and enforcement. You are here to live well, with compassion, not to change the whole world. Of course, there are things which it is your responsibility to control. But they are few indeed, not even in the same universe with the hypercontrol impulses that dominate the average person. People drain lifenergy, and make themselves quite sick, worrying about things that they cannot control— and actually trying to control them!

Not that the enlightened Taoist is an absolute fatalist. As the kung fu masters demonstrated, in an offshoot of Taoism, if friends are attacked, they should be defended. If Love calls, the master or student of Taoism responds. An enlightened sage is not a passive quietist, not an inactive, lazy bump on a log. She is neither a "couch potato" nor a cybernetoid "mouse-potato." Mystics have been among the most active, creative, productive people, because Love kept them busy.

Love overrides the constructive inactivity (*wu-wei*) of the master. Indeed, Tao is universal Mind, and that is Love. The sage always responds actively, even enthusiastically, to any calling or direction of Love. That prevents total paralysis. Complete stasis is never mistaken for high spirituality. Complacency or apathy is *never* a part of true spirituality. And neither is consistent, unrelenting inactivity.

Both Christian and Taoist mystics are called upon always to respond actively to the guidance of Love in their lives. In chapter 13 of his classic, the master Lao Tzu recommends that we "love the world," as does Jesus, in another context. [Jesus recommends *not* to "love the world" as *kosmos* (Greek) or "natural order." But he does not here mean the "world" of people and sentient life. Both Jesus and Lao Tzu agree that we should indeed "love" this "world."] Love is never silent, never absent, but we must learn to listen to it. This art we perfect by cultivating the "third ear," the talent of learning to listen to our own deeper Mind (Soul). For it is through the Soul that Spirit (God, Love) can speak. Jesus calls us openly to embrace Love as our guide and our God. Jesus stirred up a hurricane of controversy two thousand years ago, with this same explosively controversial message, and it still has not died down. He said, "I came to light a fire on earth," and that fire, that passion, still burns brightly and warmly in the heartlove of his followers. As for Jesus, he is not a particle less controversial today than he was before he was tragically murdered for his message and his God.

Astonishing, baffling, surprising, controversial— these do not begin to scratch the complex surface of the Mind called "Jesus Christ." Indeed, you could easily go through several lists of adjectives, and not even approach the full effects of a single moment with this man, or Spirit, called "Jesus Christ." A thousand adjectives would fail miserably to capture his infinite, indescribable Essence. He was, among so many roles, master psychologist, supreme Lover, ultimate spiritual Seer, and miraculous mystic. He became, during his life, the full incarnation of cosmic Mind, and so, himself became indescribable and immeasurable. Now, so far from us in history, he has been molded into all things, according to all interpretations. It is because he has been seen through so many filters, lenses, and colorations that Christians have never stopped fighting and warring about the Prince of Peace. Catholics say that he would obey the pope; Jehovah's Witnesses say that he would sell *Watchtower* magazine, Mormons that he would wear "holy underwear."

Hideous interpretations have been conjured from the dark, damp basement of the subconscious. Jesus is the final mass-murderer, the rapist of the world, in some ghastly interpretations of the Revelation to John. He has been remade in the gruesome, nightmarish image of the ancient wargod worshipped by those who murdered him— Jehovah.3

The ghoulish legend of the Jehovah-myth has been used to rationalize and justify every form and intensity of rape, torture, and murder— even by those who claim to follow the Master of Love.

Still, happily, all Christians have not fallen for this illusion, this gigantic historical error. Dialog and discussions have evolved peacefully and wondrously among various religions which all claim Jesus as their source. These have progressed constructively, even creatively, in the joy, wonder, and Love that Jesus said would mark all those who truly followed him. These peace-filled communications have blossomed as new syntheses and understandings. Some Christians, indeed, have gone so far into the Mind of Love that they have begun to recapture some of the delightful playfulness, innocence, sweetness, and charm of nature itself.

While Christians of Love, known as Jesus-Christians, have always been widely and wisely open to people of every other tradition— Jewish, Islamic, Buddhist, Hindu, and earth-based— traditional, Orthodox Christians have a tough time with this. They find universal tolerance uncomfortable, and universal salvation positively damnable and heretical. That will never do, for them. They have a monopoly on the Lord of the cosmos, similar to the one in which the ancient Hebrews believed. The result of this Christian exclusivity is that no one can ever speak on a level playing-field with, as the equal of, a Christian.

---

3 . See my *Jehovah Goodbye: the "New Theism" of Love* (Liberty Township, Ohio; Love Ministries, Inc., 1999)

Earliest Christians were not a separate religion, but were all the people of Love gathered from every tradition. Paul simply organized the church into an administrative structure for convenience. He had no idea that it would someday mushroom into a gigantic, unresponsive, powerbased, loveless bureaucracy. It was, in retrospect, the worst move in his long career. As a former Pharisee, he still believed in organizing religion, but, even he probably realized much too late, this should never have been done with the Christian community. For when it became an organization, it ceased to be a community or family. The sense of warm sister/brotherhood became lost and cloaked in questions of "right doctrine" and "membership." The earliest Christian "churches" were not buildings, but small groups of people, who met in houses of believers. (The Greek word for "church" was *ekklesia* in the Christian Greek Scriptures, and never once referred to a building. It was used to refer only to members of the sister/brotherhood of early Christians.)

A major exception to the shut-tight exclusivity of some Christians has been some compromise with Judaism. This is a good thing, for it promotes dialog and productive interpollenation between faiths. But most Christians friendly to Jews— and I am friendly to all people and cultures, including the Jewish— go altogether too far. To create peace, and even brotherhood with Hebrew culture and tradition does not mean that Christians should simply toss away as garbage what is truly unique within their own faith. Compromise and elasticity are good; but trying to turn your faith into the faith of the other is not a healthy approach. Christianity struggled long and hard to break away from its Jewish roots. And so long after they have been severed, those roots cannot and should not grow back together again.

Does a real Christian ever have the right to be antisemitic? Of course not. Love calls her away from such rampant stupidity. She can fully respect and even admire the Jewish people for their genuine contributions to history. The problems begin with the blithe assumption that the ancient god of the Hebrews *must necessarily have been* the same God worshipped by Jesus and Christians.

While mystics among the Jews have always known that the essence of their "Yahweh" was Love, this is not at all true of the common god venerated by the ancient Israelis. It is not at all true of the god taught in the Hebrew Scriptures. To be an enlightened being, a being of Love, necessitates full and unconditional abandonment of the Jehovah-myth, because it is a false god.

But it is every bit as stupid and shortsighted to hold modern Jewish people responsible for the actions of their ancestors as it would be to hold us all responsible for the behaviors of Neanderthals. Antisemitism is just another bigotry, always rooted in the least educated (and educable) of people. It is just hatred; there is no polite way to say it. It is moronic and imbecilic to try to rationalize, "I hate the Jews because I love Jesus." How bass-ackwards is that?

Jesus commanded the Love of *all people.* He made no exceptions for people of skinshades, and no religious exceptions. Did Jesus have problems with Jews? Yes. But if we refuse to love them because of that, his problems will not be with *them.* Then, he will have major problems with *us*, and our stubborn unforgiveness. Hatred in all forms is simply indefensible; and bigotry is one of the worst and lowest forms of hatred.

Still, divisive fundamentalism— as destructive in Christianity as in Islam— guarantees that manifold interpretations of Jesus will be with us for a long time. It is within neither the power nor the right of any adult to force any other adult to change. We must all be allowed to grow at our own pace.

Disagreements of many varieties will be shackling the Christian world for decades to come. Cooler heads rarely prevail in such knee-jerk matters as doctrine. These conflicts have stunned and stunted the Christian church for centuries. Many of the most vicious clashes are about the true nature of the simple man from Nazareth. How refreshingly simple it is to read his Way of "Love plus nothing." For Love is all that he asked of his friends. He did not even provide a corpus of intellectual teachings or doctrines. So, it is absurd to claim that he demanded conformity to one.

Jesus was mystery incarnate. He was the very embodiment of radical controversy. The religious of his day, the fundamentalist Jews, regarded him as a rebel and renegade, a worthless and dangerous heretic. It was because his God, and his religion, were so different from the traditions of Scripture that the traditionalists and Scripturalists murdered him. He was, they lied, in their terror, simply too dangerous to live. The man from Nazareth created a blasting windstorm of lightning and controversy from his first word.

And here we are, in the twenty-first century after his life and death, still wrestling with the same old (ancient) Mystery: Was Jesus even a "man" at all? Or, was he the Lord of the cosmos? Or, was he, in some unclear way, both? Such questions drive us relentlessly into the very heart of the Mystery.

For the mystic, that Mystery is the Core of Mind. Even the synoptic Gospels, not written for gnostic Christians, indicate a mystical Nucleus of Mind, usually called "Spirit." Indeed, it would have been impossible to have written about Jesus and to have deleted his nucleus of Lovelight. This was the Core of his mysticism. He was what he was, after all, because he had touched, in very deepest Mind, the inner Mystery.

That is, he had touched the Mind of Love. But what the synoptics imply obliquely, John states explicitly: God was "in" Jesus, and both Christ and God would be "in" Jesus' followers. It is crystalclear in John that divine nature (Lovenature or Lovemind) interfaces, and even overlaps, with human nature. The synoptics hint at greater Reality, but John rips away the veil, boldly and dramatically portraying Jesus not as a freak, but as a model. In John, Jesus says, "The things that I do, you also will do, and things greater even than these." (John 14:12) If this is so, then the Core of human nature is nakedly exposed as Spirit. Divine nature, somehow, *is* human nature.

As important as the historical presentation of Jesus is, all early Christians agree that the imperative which compels faith is not just the appearance of the man Jesus. Those who made this error formed, and still form, the cult of Jesus, not the faith of Christ.

Christianity arose, in fact, precisely because that human being, Jesus, died. Some Christians believe that this was a historical event. The author has no problems with this, although many components in Jesus' life were symbolic. For example, what was symbolized by the Resurrection was the eternal, timeless Spirit of Christ that lives on forever in all persons. (The man Jesus had lost his entire identity in, become one with, this Spirit of Love.)

****

History has *nothing to do with essential spirituality.* Arguments about history just tend to divide people into hateful camps and religions. So, the spiritual person largely avoids the snares of bickering about history.

****

The "believer" or "follower of Jesus" is not the person who has committed certain doctrines to memory. Nor is it the person who falls mindlessly at the feet of Jesus, as though he were an idol (a physical object of worship). No, the believer believes and the follower follows. Actually to follow Jesus, one must have had an awakening similar to his own— a unitive theophany, in which borders and boundaries separating the "human being" from Being Itself dissolve and vanish. In this "entheognostic" (inner Godknowing) event, the human mind slips into the divine Unconscious, like the poetic "dewdrop slipping into the shining sea." In sum, the "believer" is what early Christians called themselves— a gnostic.

A gnostic is, most simply, one who has discovered that only Mind has reality, and that the Core of all Mind is infinite Love, dreaming up the world. This gnosis is often weakly connected to its English cognate, "to know." But gnosis is not just knowledge, as in datagathering. No, gnosis is a very special kind of knowing, with a very special Object that is known. For gnosis is a direct, immediate, overwhelming knowing of deepest inner Mind (the Superconscious within the Unconscious) as God. This experience cannot fully be described by, or reduced to, mere words.4

It was a form of the Greek *gnosis* that Jesus used in John 17:3, when he said, in prayer, "This is timeless life, to know You, the only true God, and the One whom you have beamed forth, Jesus Christ ..." So, "timeless life" was equated and synonymous with "knowing God." A more succinct summary of the mystical view would be impossible. This is in essence and sum, the mystical event in a nutshell. To have had the "knowing" of gnosis is to have entered an altered state of being called "timeless" life— a phrase usually mistranslated as "everlasting life."

---

4 . See my companion volume to this book, *Luminous Jewels of Love and Light* Volume 1 (Liberty Township, Ohio; Love Ministries, Inc. 2002), for a general introduction to mysticism and a thousand selections from people who, in the Way of love, have experienced gnosis.

The promise of Jesus to his followers was *not* "everlasting" life, because all life is already, intrinsically everlasting. Instead, he promised the "timeless" life. What is this timeless life? As implied, it is a life separate from the everyday world or reality of time, and thus, of space. (Space and time exist only relative to each other, as Einstein showed.) So, it was a life that existed independently of matter, of the entire "physical" cosmos. It is purely a life of Mind, and occurs in the Mind, where all *metanoia*, or transformation, occurs. This was a Mindlife of pure and continuous communion with the inner Spirit of Love. So, it was a life of deep tranquility, bottomless bliss, and immeasurable compassion. As Paul later stated, "The fruit of the Spirit is love, joy, peace..." (Ga 5:22)

The Gospel of John is the mystic record, as contrasted with the historic record, of the Christ. That is, it indicates the Reality ("truth") that is beyond mere words. It points to the mystical awakening, gnosis, as the Root and Fountain of all spirituality. God lives and moves and has his being "within" the human psyche. To touch this inner Reality is to enter a Mindworld which is more real than the passing lightshow of the "material" world. John makes it much more crystalclear than Matthew, for instance, written for Hebrews, that God is *not* the Hebrew wargod Jehovah. (Indeed, it is for this heresy that Jesus is ultimately murdered.) The God of Jesus is no parochial or local god who is "owned" by a particular nation. He is the God of all, even of pagans. Jesus even says, in one verse, that a worshipper of the pagan Jupiter has shown greater faith than the Jews: "Nowhere in all Israel have I found so great a faith..." he says. The God of Jesus does not live on a mountain called Sinai. Indeed, Jesus makes clear, his God does not live even among the clouds, or stars. He lives, Jesus says over an over, "in" Jesus and "in" his followers. This God cannot be known with only the mind, through the dull, mechanical, insipid study of the Bible.

No, this God can be known only through gnosis, through the entheognostic touch. This God is, unlike Jehovah, Love Itself. So, He/She can be known only through and in each act of Love. This Love is breathtakingly universal, beautifully unconditional, and without trace of ego or self. For, in entheognosis, at its peak, the self utterly vanishes into Love, and only Love remains. It is not the "self loving," but is "Love loving." And the very peak of entheognosis is

"Love loving Love," through and in all beings. The self then is metamorphosed into the Self of Love. After the experience, one "comes back down" to the normal everyday world as an incarnation of Love. Ego-identity is abandoned, and one's new identity is Love or God. When Mary Smith touches entheognosis, she is no longer Mary Smith, but the Mind, Soul, or Spirit of whom Mary is the vehicle or mirror.

Thus the scandalous declaration of every mystic, "I am God." This burns the ears of traditionalists, Scripturalists, dogmatists, and fundamentalists. But it was Jesus who made this claim, and either Jesus is a model fully to be imitated, or he is not. But in saying, "I am God," the mystic does not mean to imply that she has become God *in totality*. This claim would be an absurdity. Rather, she means that she has become God *in nature*. This means that her mind has been fully replaced by the Mind of Love, the Spirit. After the experience of becoming the incarnation of Love, she is only part human. For she is also part divine (Spirit). Her Love for God has become so massive that she becomes totally "lost" in this Love, where, everyone would love to be lost. Ultimately, her very self is absorbed by, vanishes into, this Lovemind, this Lovegod.

So, the mystical paradigm emphasizes intimacy with God, the inner and deep knowing (gnosis) of pure Love. But only by a consuming obsession with Love can this God be known. Knowing God is no pursuit of the hobbyist or partimer. For many, religion is what you do when you are too bored, or guilty, to do something more valuable or productive. The mystic sees cosmic Love (God) as her magnificent obsession. And she would have it no other way.

****

Every act of Love is an act of worship. Every act of Love is an act of healing. Every act of Love is an act of true spiritual growth.

****

For by Love alone are we transformed into the divine likeness. Paul wrote, "With unveiled faces, we reflect like mirrors the glory of the Lord, from glory to glory, until we are actually transformed completely into the Image that we reflect." (2 Cor. 3:17) This is the perfect blend of human with divine nature, until, in time, the human is completely eclipsed by the splendor of the divine.

Exactly as God revealed divinity (Lovenature) in the humanity of Jesus, so we are all called to this elevated and noble path. We are all the Logos (expression) of the one Mind, in incarnation. Indeed, as John says, in 1:1, God is *the same as God's expression*, meaning that we are all God. Or, to use the words of Peter, we are all "partakers of the divine nature." (2 Pet. 1:4)

This is how it works: What begins as God's (Mind's) undifferentiated expression (*Logos*) grows, in time, into the full reflection of perfect splendor and glory (Love). At this state, it is the *Khristos* or "Christ."

In passing, we should note that the "Christ" is *not* the same as the Jewish *mashiahh*, or "messiah." The "messiah" was a prophetic superstition among the Jews. He was a hero/warrior/avenger who would come, with blood and storm, and overthrow the Romans, and establish Israel as a new political state. In retrospect, some of the Hebrew converts to Christianity saw Jesus as the "Messiah," but this was a claim imposed upon him. It was one which he never claimed for himself. Indeed, in my *The Mystic Gospels of Jesus the Christ,5* he explicitly denies it. The messiah would be a bloody warrior, full of fire and violence, intent on revenge against the enemies of Israel. Jesus was none of this. So, his claim to be the "Christ" was *not* a claim to be the Jewish messiah, as it was later misinterpreted.

Among the earliest Christians arose a powerful faction called the "judaizers," whose goal was to try to transform Christianity into a splinter group of Judaism. Christians, they argued, were simply modified Jews, not a separate religion. Incredibly, many still buy into this illusion. But all of history has demonstrated just how foolish and shortsighted they were. Paul and other gnostic Christians resisted the Judaizers, and ultimately won the war for Christianity. It was the Judaizers who, nevertheless, were able successfully to promulgate the superstition that Jesus fulfilled Hebrew prophecies, and hence, was the Jewish messiah. But real Jews are still looking for the messiah

---

5 . This is a "quasi-fictional" account of some of the "lost words" or teachings of Jesus. It contains the "Gospels" of Judas, Andrew, Simon, and Mary Magdalene (Liberty Township, Ohio; Love Ministries, Inc., 2002)

and, knowing their religion better than anyone else, completely rejected Jesus in this role.

But is not the grecogenic (Greek-originated) word "Christ" just a translation of the Hebrew word "messiah"? It can be, but wordmeanings can be radically transformed by time, context, and circumstance. The word "Christ" came to mean an entirely new concept in Christianity than what the Hebrew "messiah" had ever meant in Judaism.

Both are conceptually related to "anointed." This goes back in history to a rather messy process in which a king or prophet was "anointed" by having oil smeared on the top of his head. (Our word "ointment" shares a root with "anointed.") The word "messiah" did not refer exclusively to one person in history. The kings of Israel, for example, were called "messiahs." But in time it evolved into the limited meaning of the one hero and master warrior sent by Jehovah to slaughter the enemies of Israel.

The word "Christ," in the Christian ("Christ-like") community came to represent, not one person, but a state of awakening or enlightenment. "Christ" was not the last name of Jesus. It indicated the condition or state of being filled with "grace" (Greek, *charis,* another Christian innovation), and becoming an incarnation of Love. It was, in short, a gift of God. So, again, as explained in *The Mystic Gospels,* "Christ" was an honorific. It is much more similar to the Sanskrit *buddha* than the Hebrew *mashiahh.* And, as there were many "buddhas," not just one, so there were many Christs in the early church. Indeed, everyone who followed Jesus hoped ultimately to become a Christ. In symmetry with the ancient wisdom-phrase, "You are already the Buddha," the *Mystic Gospels* record the ancient Christian phrase, "You are already the Christ."

This is, in fact, the origin of the word "christening." In the Greek Christian Scriptures, John wrote in his first epistle, "You have an anointing from the holy One..." (1 Jo. 2:20) but in an accurate translation from the Greek, "You have a *christing* ..." would be more accurate. So, while it sounds bizarre to our ears to hear the phrases, "Jane Christ," or, "Charlie Christ," this re-identification was the final goal of the Unitive (mystical or gnostic) event. For human nature and divine nature live within each of us, in inverse proportion.

John makes no attempt to "translate" Jesus, fitting him into the social matrix of Hebrew, Grecoroman, or other traditions. In this approach of honest candidness, he differs from Matthew, who had to do some fast and fancy dancing to make the rebel Jesus look anything like a respectable Jew, and from Luke, who wrote for a more sophisticated cosmopolitan audience. John presents Jesus simply, unadorned, and honestly, as a mystic. He strips Jesus of all his Hebraic cultural accretions. Indeed, John presents the conservative Jews as the main challengers of early Christianity. They were always his adversaries. Although it is "politically incorrect" to say so, they undoubtedly were his most active opposers. Early Christians and ultraconservative Jews were at each other's throats as early as the time of Jesus. This dichotomy has as its basis the indubitable fact that Jesus worshipped a very different God than they. He rejected the parochial, jealous, grumpy, unforgiving Jehovah. Jehovah had no sense of humor, while the master teacher brought smiles and laughter by talking about "gulping down camels" whole, and of "camels squeezing through the eyes of sewingneedles." (He seemed to have a comedic sense that any story involving camels was bound to be funny, as well as unforgettable.)

Later, the grumpy old men who edited the Christian Greek Scriptures also totally lost any sense of humor. By the time that the modern Bible was compiled, these leaders had already fallen into the subtle snare of the Judaizers, starting again to see Christianity as an outgrowth of Judaism. ("Judaism," by the way, is pronounced "Jew'-dah-izm," not "Judy-izm," as if it were the worship of "Judy.") These gruff, curmudgeonish, grim Christian editors deleted every reference to Jesus' ever having smiled or laughed. But that certainly doesn't mean that he did not.

John writes honestly. But who is his intended audience? It is obviously the large portion of the early church that defined itself as "gnostic."

John writes also as a person who has himself touched the gnostic state. He implies, as do all mystics, that the difference between Jesus and Jesus' followers is not a matter of *kind*. That is, Jesus is not a superfreak; he is decidedly not a different species, either physically or mentally, from other humans. Instead, the difference, however wide the gulf may appear, is only one of *degree*.

xxvii

True, Jesus is "alien" relative to the fundamentalistic culture in which he arose. But all mystics— and, for that matter, all moderates— would be. Why on earth, one asks, would Jesus come to be born in Israel? In India, for example, he would have been recognized for the great mastersage that he was, and would have been welcomed by both secular and religious leaders as a great guru. Instead, Jesus' Soul chose to incarnate in the most spiritually backward culture and religion on the planet. It was he, after all, who said, "The sick are the ones who need a doctor."

Jesus is "alien" relative to the "average" human being. For he is a being of the deepest Mind (Spirit), not of the body. Jesus knows, unlike most, that he is not his body. Even more importantly, he realizes that he is not the ego associated with that body. Who, then, is he? He is a temporary incarnation of the Lovegod or Lovemind— the deepest Corelevel of the Unconscious. He has stripped off the persona of the ego Jesus, and knows himself to be Supermind playing the role, donning the mask, of Jesus.

He has, in short, become the full master of his interior universe. And since there is *no* "exterior" universe, except as dreamprojection of the interior, he masters his own world.

But *he does not do this as a magician.* Miracles do not happen because Jesus *wills* them. As part of his agreement with the Spiritmind, he has already given up all egodesires or personal will. He cannot want anything. He, as Jesus, cannot even do anything. That explains the mystery of his words, "I do nothing." (John 5:19, 30)

Miracles do not occur by his own will or direction. They just happen in his presence. So, Jesus is a "theurgist"— a mystic who has allowed egodeath, and then taken one further step: She allows Power (Love) to flow through her into the world. So, every mature mystic develops into a theurgist.

Does this occur because the theurgist wants it personally? If so, does that deny her desireless mysticism? Let's get this straight: A mystic does not give up *all* desires. Instead, she surrenders and drops all *personal* desire. She is always and continuously open to the Flow of the desires of Love, called collectively the "will of God." In wanting or desiring Love to flow forth into the world, the mystic does *not* yield to egodesire. Instead, she does precisely what her path tells her to do: She surrenders entirely to what Love wants, the will-desire of Love or God.

Thus, the theurgist wants the Power to flow through her, but she does not seek to direct it with her ego. According to *The Mystic Gospels,* Jesus was quite as surprised as anyone when a miracle occurred in his presence. He also said, in these texts, that one cannot *perform* a miracle, but can only *permit* one to occur. Miracles are not controlled or regulated by the conscious mind or its will (desire).

But even after Jesus "dies" into Spirit, he still uses such words as "I" and "Me." Does this imply that the ego is still there? No. For when, after his transfiguration into Love, he uses these words, it is the Spirit, the highest Self, speaking through him. That is why, in versions of even the conservative King James Version of the Bible, he refers to the Self with a capitalized "M" in the word "Me." Thus, when he says the oft-quoted but misunderstood, "I am the Way, the Reality, and the life," these words are not to be understood literally as originating with, or referring to, the man Jesus. (Jn. 14:6) He also said, "Do you not believe that I am in the father, and the father is in Me? The things that I say... I do not speak of My own origin, but the father who remains in Me is doing his works." (14:10) Here, he has come fully to see his behavior as divine. To see his motivating thoughts as divine is only a micrometer behind. So, he set the example: While fully human, living within the framework of a physical body, he was also fully divine. Within his Mind, he had become God or Love. It was this deepest Self who said through Jesus, "I and the father are one." (10: 30) Yet his human part still existed, as for example in 14:28, "The father is greater than I."

Jesus is mastered by no greed, no lower passions, no self. He serves only the one Master within, the Lovemind, Lovegod, or Lovenature, according to his own principle, "You cannot serve two masters." He is the full interface, the medium, between the human mind and the divine Mind. Both live within his mind. The Spirit that speaks through him is Itself Reality.

What does it mean to say that the Spirit is "truth" or Reality? It means that only Mind has absolute reality. Nothing in the entire world of the "material and external" cosmos has absolute reality. Things and objects have only *relative or temporary* reality. Why? Because they are fully dependent upon a mind in order to exist. If there were no minds to perceive the material cosmos, it would disappear. This Spirit, in a function/area of Mind called the "Creator," is the Fountain of all being. And Jesus, by disappearing into It, has found his deepest Self. He has completely lost his egoself which has disappeared into his Spiritself. This is the meaning of his enigmatic words, "He who seeks to save the self will lose it, but he who loses the self for My sake will find it."

He has remembered, discovered at last, that he is the pure expression of the one Mind, the Logos. This is the nucleus of the Mystery recorded by John. Clearly, John does not write for the mystophobic majority, but the scarce mystophilic minority. And those who have followed the former, popular path have been thoroughly mystified, if not terrified, by the bewildering Gospel, the mystic's favorite— the Book of John.

A more complete understanding of the Mystery— the single most important— comes from the Gospel of John. For we can never derive from the synoptics what can be mined from the mystical "jewels" of John. We are also very fortunate that there are so many fine, excellent, and superb translations into English of this classic of mystical literature. Even so, an absolutely literal rendering of the book might be as useless as a literal translation of the classic to follow this one. (That is Part IV, "The Book of the Great Mind and Its Expression.") A literal rendering would be too choppy, staccato, barren, dry, bewildering, and incomprehensible, to convey all the richness of the knowing of deepest Mind (Spirit, *Tao*).

True, a single sentence can electrify the fibers of your whole being, if you are ready to hear its truth. But there is an almost sensual delight in being allowed to rest within the petals of the flower, to dwell upon and within the deep, sweet Mystery. You long to bathe in it, to soak in it, to have it pervade your bodymind and saturate your being, to immerse your Soul in it. In your mind, you also long to turn it over and over, like playing with a delicious chocolate on the tongue. You don't want to be rushed through it. As with a lovely work of art, you just want to stand and lovingly look at it, drink it in, see it from many angles. Until now, no work has sought to explore the multidimensionality of this mystical classic in the same way that has been done here, in "The Gospel of Universal Love." A degree of literalness marks almost all translations. And this is indispensable.

Only a semiliteral translation can be the basis for allowing the Mindspirit to soar beyond mere words on paper, to excite and electrify with the tender poetry of Spirit and Love. And as necessary and desirable as literal translation is, it does not allow one to soar into the new vistas and horizons permitted by paraphrase. It is safe, explored territory— a known quantity. It is a familiar, and populated area.

The Mystery, on the other hand, is bottomless. Mystical works can be understood ("known") only by mystics. But they should not, for this reason, be sealed away from the public in some elite or territorial vault. Instead, they should serve as a bridge or ladder to the higher states of being of which all persons are capable, and to which all are being called. The boundless, illimitable, and immeasurable can be only vaguely indicated through mere words, like seeing "through a glass, darkly," to use the mystic Paul's famous phrase. Fullest opening of the psyche to eternity is quite beyond the scope of the human intellectual mind.

The most that we can do is to approximate— very poorly. For words are poor vessels. We can create only the most pitiable indications of indirect, vague, and poor outlines of eternity and fathomless Love. Infinity mocks our words, even our highest, noblest, most lightfilled attempts to say anything meaningful about It. So, in all metaphysics and philosophy, we end up at that dark glass, full of obscurities, opacities, and distortions.

The Gospel of John, as splendid and glorious is its message, is also such a human document. So it, too, gives only imprecise impressions of the Illimitable. It too is obscure and vague. Like all other classics of mystical literature, it is open to a plethora of interpretations, more than one of which might be valid. So, the commentary here is only tentative and experimental. It is suggestion, not dogma. It encourages the reader to catapult creatively beyond the mere stiff text, the dead words. It stimulates personal creativity, perhaps personal revelation. So, especially in the immeasurable realm of spirituality, let us admit the common sensical observation that we do not, cannot, know everything. No one does. For anyone to claim that she has all the answers, due to reading the Bible, "inspired by God," is just sheer pride and prejudice. It is not courageously examining, but fleeing like a scalded cat from, eternal verities. So, no paraphrase of any mystical classic can ever be exhaustive or complete.

This, then, is the case with the present paraphrase and commentary. They are *not* fully descriptive, but only indicative. They are not carved into granite, but written upon water. We labor under no illusions that these words in any way pronounce the "final inerrant, infallible truth." In places, we break dramatically with some other versions, and in many other areas, are in full agreement. Still, much of the paraphrased material will be explosively controversial. And the commentary following is much moreso. Everything about the words, life, and nature of Jesus has always been radically arguable.

The paraphrases use the verses from the Gospel of John only as launch pads into the creative interpretations of mystical teaching. The introductory words of each verse are only paraphrases. They are not meant as literal renderings of that verse. Each sentence is then followed by commentary. The sentence is the backbone, the matrix-idea, but is often nothing more than a "start" button for a closely, or distantly, related mystical idea. So, what follows each sentence is *not a paraphrase, but a "nutshell" version of a related mystical teaching.* No claim is here made that the writer of John taught every elaboration in the commentary. Some of the commentaries seem to be what he was aiming for, but others are elaborations or embellishments that go quite beyond actual textual justification. We do well to keep in mind the old nostrum that "the letter killeth, but the Spirit giveth life." In these minicommentaries, we have striven only to capture the "spirit" or mystical essence, of the statements. [While we are on the subject, a technical note: Jesus was clearly, in the Greek text, talking to a number of people. But, in the minicommentaries, we have often used the singular rather than the plural "you" so as to be of more immediate access to the reader, as well as to make a stronger impression. This is also done deliberately to create a sense of personal relation with the Christspirit, as well as personal responsibility to respond to his call.]

This book, then, is not designed to be taken as if every word were the precise word spoken by Jesus. But this work is in full harmony with the descriptions of truth (Reality) which are the legacies of the luminaries of all mystical tradition. But also, like any other human work, it has had to flow through, and has been affected by, a relatively clear but unique mindnervoussystem. So, all hopes of perfection and infallibility have been abandoned.

Jesus is here presented as a mystic. Jesus was not a respected Jew, or rabbi. Jesus was not a Christian. Instead, he spoke words of a universal philosophy founded in Love. His special vision of the relationship between two inner natures— the human and the divine— marks him as mystical. So does his knowing that God was "in" him, and would be "in" his followers. As a master of theurgical mysticism, he reflected Power into the world. And he was by no means imprecise in his delineation and description of that Power. It was the "intimate Infinite," so close to his Loveheart that he called it "father." [In fact, he called it by a more informal term of address, using the word *abba,* which is more like our "daddy."] He taught no clear "doctrines" in the modern use of that word, but rather a way of life. (Early Christianity, like Taoism, was called simply "the Way.")

He expressed energetic feelings about this Power as Love, and its fullest expression in his life. Even the most "tame," or "diluted" translation of the Gospel of John has been unable to eradicate his mystical "oneness" with the "father" within. Incredibly, translators have made attempts to hide his mysticism. For one example, the *New World Translation,* the version of the Bible produced by the Jehovah's Witnesses, has repeatedly rendered the simple Greek preposition "in" as "in [union with]..." This is not only unwarranted, but completely indefensible and unjustifiable on the grounds of the Greek language itself. But it is simply a rather transparent attempt to hide Jesus' mysticism. For Jesus talked repeatedly about God's being "in" Jesus, "in" his followers, and even about his (Jesus') and the father's being "in" those disciples.

Fundamentalists insist on a totally transcendent God who is irreversibly separate from human nature and mind, and indeed from all creation. To speak of God "in" a person denies and contradicts this. It demolishes the whole idea of a God who is completely other, totally transcendental. It obliterates the popular Jehovah-myth, as Jesus did, and posits instead a wholly new image of God "within." But if God is really "in" the person's Soul or mind, that changes everything.

For one very important thing, it proves that you do not need a particular church or organization to get in touch with God, or even to receive instruction and knowledge. Most fundamentalists and nonmystics want to foster a crippling dependence on the "crutch" of some doctrines or dogma. Or, their intent is to foster and support a crippling dependence upon an organization or church. But if God can be consulted directly, as Lovemind, then no intermediary church or group is needed. That is precisely why the mystic so celebrates her sacred freedom. It is also why she is so hated and despised by fundamentalists. Her independence is inviolable; no one has the right to steal it away from her.

So, among antimystical elements, there has been a deliberate attempt to cover up and obscure the idea that the divine and the human coexist within the human heartmind. Specifically, the divine expresses as Love. This makes every act of Love a true act of worship. This, in turn, means that all meetings, Bible-study, songs, and public prayer can fall outside the domain of actual worship. And this scares the daylights out of cults and religions that need the regular financial support of members. If one can more truly worship God in her home than by attending meetings at a hall, then the entire structure of human administrations and complex economic religious systems begins to unravel. In mysticism, this idea does not lead to chaos or anarchy, but to a worldwide communion of good people united by the fact that they love each other. This is true unity, not the mere uniformity that marks cults, conformist religions, and unyielding political systems.

This view goes back to the early church. By the year 200, the Orthodox had begun to define "truth" in doctrinal rather than moral (ethical) terms. So, the most monstrous and hateful person could claim to be "Christian," and so be recognized, as long as she believed the "right" things. And the most beautiful, tender, sincerely loving person could be raped, butchered, and murdered as subhuman, unworthy even of life, if she believed the "wrong" things. The nightmarish history of a ghastly caricature of the Church grew from these weeds, planted so early. Every form of obscenity and atrocity was "okay" as long as its perpetrators believed the "right" things about the Bible. They were guaranteed an automatic "ticket" to heaven, in a salvation-process that was "fully automatic." And even the sweetest, wisest, most tender and kind people among the Buddhists, Taoists, Hindus and especially, gnostics were symmetrically on a one-way road to eternal hellfire. This "black and white" thinking is precisely symmetric with that of the most mad, Islamic extremist and fundamentalist.

In other words, the transformative effects of the holy Spirit were downplayed, or ignored. As a result of this ghastly misunderstanding, Love became peripheral, and even negligible. Doctrinal conformity evolved as the crown-jewels of an immoral, obscene Church. God was, in effect, alienated from the heart by translating him into a variation of the cruel Jehovah of the Hebrews' earliest traditions. Remaking the Lord of Love, Light, and forgiveness into a bloody, cruel wargod did much to rationalize the most bloody brutalities of a senseless and barbaric Church. And all that one had to do to "worship" this alien and transcendental god was to fall at the feet of the historical Jesus. All these crucial factors— doctrinalism, the external and unjust god, and the mechanical worship of Jesus— led to a kind of conspiracy by the forces of the lower nature. This blind and dangerous part of the human psyche won a complete historical victory within the Church, and all its leaders became thoroughly misled down the bloodsoaked path to the abyss of darkness.

Add to this list another cruel and dangerous lie: No one had any direct link-up with God. The only and exclusive way that God expressed was not through human heartmind capacities, but only through his organization, his Church. It became so bad that to claim to have had *any personal revelation from God* was damned as heresy. And heretics, as we all know, were murdered!

The Church then swung to other pendulum-extremes. A theology evolved in which the world, including nature, was itself largely damned as "unspiritual." Millions of lives were carelessly and callously trashed by the teaching that sex— once celebrated as the natural blossom of Love— was evil and satanic. (These rules were most often made by grumpy old men, bitter because they were no longer sexually active or attractive. They envied younger people.) The human body was said to be polluted and unclean simply because it was a material object. With psychopaths making the rules, the Church embraced psychoses as its guidelines. Stated more simply, the whole Church fell into insanity.

This mystic Gospel has nothing to do with churches, administrations, hierarchies, corruptions, money, power, or offices. It is all about the individual and her personal relationship with the Infinite within her own deepest heartmind. Love is the *sole criterion* by which oneness with God is evaluated. Church membership is not even mentioned. Indeed, in the first century, there was no such thing as an organized Church. Not a single church building existed anywhere. The only "church" (Greek, *ekklesia*) was a body of *people*, not doctrines. It was the mystical "body of Christ." These people were united, not by teachings, but by their acceptance of a Reality called the "Christnature." It lived deep in the Mind as the Lovemind, Lovegod, or Lovenature. This "body" is not an official organization. Instead, it is a loose network of cooperating, friendly people working together to increase Love in the world. There is no official "membership" or "joining," no ritual Communion or Baptism necessary. Nor is any other rite, ritual, or ceremony needed for a person to "join" this communion. In order to "join," all that one must do is devote timenergy to the improvement of Love. Anyone who consistently loves anyone else is already a "member of this family." When she stops loving, she is no longer a "member." It's as simple as that.

There are no formal memberships or membership-records. Statistics are not kept. This family of Love is generic, and must never devolve into a denomination, sect, cult, or even a separate religion. It contains or envelops all who have hearts of Love— whether their "labels" be Buddhist, Sufi, Hindu, Catholic, Protestant, Jewish, or even agnostic. It is this pursuit of unconditional, consistent Love alone that is important, that has any real spiritual value. This "family," or "communion" is the truest mystical "body of Christ." The communion of Love is a *network* of independent people, *not* an organization. The past has demonstrated *ad nauseum* that the pattern called "organization" is a dismal, inevitable failure. If you would like more info on the Universal Love Movement, drop a line to: rmfrancis@juno.com

This Preface threatens to go on and on, for its Subject is endless. But in Love, I will have mercy on my readers and friends, and bring it to an end.

*****

*****

TECHNICAL NOTES:

Ancient Greek, the tongue of the oldest extant manuscripts of John, is a tongue of both paradox and mysticism. It is also elastic, in the sense that a single word can have various synonyms, while many words ("love," for example) can be translated into a single English word. So, Greek can lend itself to many valid interpretations, which is precisely why it is such a very rich language. Further, every sentence can reflect multiple shades of meaning and emphasis. This allows for a wide diversity in rendering any text into English, as is obvious from the many fine translations of this classical text of mystical literature available in most good libraries.

This present paraphrase is not a translation from the original. Instead, it is a version or rendition. I call it the "Love-Luminosity" Version. It is an admittedly incomplete and imperfect attempt to convey an entire spectrum of meanings for every idea expressed. When a single Greek word is elaborated into several English words, it will be marked by a single asterisk.

At other times, an entire sentence will be restated or rephrased. This is to give alternative perspectives. It might fall within, or just outside, the literal statement in the document. This kind of restatement will be marked by a double asterisk. Finally, with the highest degree of elasticity, each sentence spoken by Jesus will be followed by a commentary. These statements represent expansion, embellishment, and interpretation. They are not meant, designed, or intended to be or to represent the actual statements of Jesus. Instead, they are, as honestly stated, mystical commentary. Each of these notes is marked by a triple asterisk. These highlight mystical dimensions, meanings, or applications.

This is only one vision of an illimitable, immeasurable Reality.

****

****

Part III: "The Gospel of Universal Love: The Mystic Evangel of John"

****

The Love-Luminosity Version

****

BEGINNING: THE ARCHELOG

Chapter 1. Verse 1. In the beginning was the Logos and the Logos was with God and the Logos was God. In the beginning was the Expression and the Expression was with God and God was the very Expression of God**. In the beginning was the Logos.** At the start [of creation], the expression [of God] existed.** In the origin [of all], the expression was.** From the beginning [of spacetime], expression [and conceptualization] existed.*** At the beginning, God's manifestation existed.*** Expression started everything.*** The universe existed in only potential until God described it to Him/Herself.*** The universe arose from a Mindconfiguration.*** All things began as reasoned ideas.*** With expression, the cosmos came into being.*** Expression of thoughtideas was the beginning.*** The creation of thoughtnames was the beginning of the worlds. All things were created by thought.*** God's expression, [not yet separate from God,] existed from the start of this universe.*** By encompassing the names, the Mind created universes within Itself.***

2. And the Logos was with God. The expression separated from divine Mind.** The expression existed simultaneously with [, but separate from,] God.** The expression of God interfaced with God.** Expression drifted from Mind.** The expression, still within God, was exteriorized by divine Mind.*** The expression of God was conceptualized as separate from God.*** The expression, still interior to God, was projected by divine Mind as if it were "outside."*** The expression was viewed as the "outer."*** The expression was seen as the "other."*** The expression of Mind, although *in* God, was also *with* God.*** God's expression existed mutually with the Mind.*** The expression was a perfect mirrorreflection of the divine Mind.*** The manifestation appeared to stand outside of God.*** The creative energy began to depart from its oneness with the Totality, or Reality.*** Reality, all within God, stood "beside" God in Dreamind.*** Expression began to divide from the expressing Mind, in Mind.*** God dreamed that there was a cosmos separate from, and thus beside, Him/Herself.*** Reality and expression began conceptually to separate.*** Expression appeared to divide from Mind or Reality.*** Nothing was separate from the Mind until It began to dream up separation.***

3. All things came to be through him. By means of creative, expressive Mindmanifestation, all the cosmos came into being.** All the universes came to be because of God's expression.** God's expression was the medium through which all came into being.** God's manifestation was the medium through which the cosmos came into being.** Through only the expression of God, all existence came into being.*** Nothing exists that has not come into being through divine expression.*** Manifestation is the lens of expression for the cosmic creation.*** The divine field of Mind was concentrated through creative expression in all.*** Expression was the interface where divine Mind touched the world.*** Divine Mind flowed into the world through creative expression.*** Expression was the point of contact between the creative Unconscious and the created world.*** Through the expression divine Mind was differentiated into all things.***

Nothing came into existence without him. Nothing was ever created apart from divine expression.** Everything was created as divine expression.** Every object was created by the expression of Lovemind.*** Nothing, in any experience, ever came into being apart from the divine creative expression.*** Everything has always been divine expression.*** Not a single thing ever came into being without the mediation of creative and divine expression.*** Nothing can exist that is not his manifestation. *** Outside of God's creative Mind, existence is impossible.***

4. And in him was life. All life is divine manifestation.** Every living creature is an expression of divine Lovemind.*** There can be no living creature in which the divine creative expression does not participate.*** God, through his own direct expression, creates the living universe.*** Only within divine Mind do all forms and varieties of life arise.***

And this life was the light of men. This life is what makes enlightenment possible.** Without this kind of life, people would never find enlightenment.** * That which makes perception (light) possible is the same Mind that gives life.*** Life is intrinsically Light, and that Light can be known by human beings.*** Life is Light, but people must come to know It.*** Light is life, and life Light, within people.*** Life is an interpretation of Light.*** Life holds the potential of full illumination.***

5. And this Light continued to shine in darkness, but the darkness did not know it. The Light of awareness [consciousness] shone in the creative void, but the cosmos remained empty and dark.*** Fullest enlightenment existed in Mind even before there was a cosmos.*** Light filled the Mind before It filled the world, and galaxies.*** Consciousness existed even before there was any object of awareness, anything of which to be conscious.*** The mystery of awareness existed even when the entire cosmos was dark and void.*** A Selfconscious Mind existed even when the universe was completely empty.*** The Light of Reality shines within the darkness of illusion, but the illusionworld allows no place for It.*** The Light of life is at the heart, the nucleus, of the darkness of death, but those who believe in death allow no place for It.*** The spiritual Light is the nucleus and Essence of the world of darkness.*** The Light of wisdom and Reality [truth] shines within the dense darkness of ignorance, but ignorance does not allow belief in It.***

But the darkness has never put it out [extinguished It, overwhelmed It, appropriated It, overcome It.*]...

*****

The narrative continues with chapter 1, verse 9:

For the Light is that which ignites [and illuminates*] every being who comes into the world. No one in the world is without this Light.** This Light is within everyone who has been born.** Whoever lives in this cosmos has this Light already.** Every creature within the "material" cosmos contains this Light within itself.*** Everyone who comes to this world [from higher universes] will be enlightened.*** The enlightenment-potential exists within everyone who has been born.*** The Light [of conscious awareness] awakens everyone to the true nature of Reality.***

10. He was in the world, and the world came into being through him. The perfect expression of God came into the very world that had come about through him.** God's perfect expression appeared within this world, the very world made possible by that flawless manifestation.** Perfect Mind manifested in the material universe.** The world springs into being from the inner Fountain of awareness, as the perfect expression.*** As perfect Mind came into being within the world, the world came into being through him.*** He cocreated

his world with God; then, by dreaming, his Soul entered that world.*** While in the world, the perfect Mindmanifestation saw Itself everywhere reflected in the world created by perception.*** The world is continuously created anew as perfect Mind enters it.*** Perfect Mind enters this world, but is not fully a part of it, for the world does not produce It.*** The world is formed by Mind's continuous participation in its formation.***

And the world did not know him. The material order does not know the Mind that produces it.** The material world [of nature] did not recognize the perfect Incarnation of perfect Mind.** * Perfect Mind became an alien within his own universe.*** The natural order was "separated" from his inner being.*** He, when he incarnated, was not recognized as the Master of the universe.*** The world of illusion never awakened to his Reality.*** The relative world was unable to fuse or meld with his absolute nature.*** The purely "material" world does not experience his gnosis.***

11. He came to his own, and they were unable to receive him. He came as a human being, and it was the human race who did not accept him.** He came to those who shared his own divine nature, but still they did not know him.** Even though he came in human form, people could not learn how to receive him.** He approached beings of his own creation, and yet they could not relate to his nature.*** He came to beings who had spiritual and divine natures exactly like his own, but they could not comprehend him.*** Within his own universe, he dreamed into existence beings who did not know how to respond to him.*** Others, products of his own perception, refuse to learn how to accept his divine nature.*** Even though he is, ironically, the dreamer of the people, they do not accept him.***

12. But to those who were able to take him into themselves, he gave the Power to become the children of God. Those who realized his inner presence, he gave Power, so that they could awaken to being the children of God.** Those who drew him [into their hearts as Love] were empowered to recognize that they were the children of God.** Those who absorbed his Lovenature were empowered to become products of the One.** Those who drew him into and from their deepest inner being were empowered to know that they were produced by the perfect Mind.*** Those who allowed his nature to blossom within themselves became, like him, the offspring of God's

"fathering."*** Those who absorbed into their inner nature the nature of his being received from him the Power to be generated or created by God.*** Those who were illuminated by his divine nature, and took him into their hearts, were given Power. They then recognized that they were projected by God.*** Those who allowed his nature to manifest from within themselves receive from him the knowing that they were produced by the divine Mind.***

These were the ones who believed in his name. These were the ones who believed in his identity.** These believed in his Self.** They believed that his Self was also their truest Self.*** These recognized that his identity was more important than their own, and that it was also their true identity.*** They believed that his Self was more real than their own.*** They identified fully with him.*** They believed that he was their deepest Self [Spirit].*** They lost their personal selves within a cosmic Self, *his* Self.*** They believed that his identity was real, but their own an illusion.*** They saw his identity as absolute [perfect Mind], and their own as relative.*** They believed in his divine nature, rather than in human nature.*** They shared in his identity.*** They lost their own identities in his.***

13. They were not born from blood and flesh. They have risen above their material bodies.** Their truest, deepest Self is not a body.** They recognized that they were not "material" or "animal," but spiritual, beings.** They disowned and rejected their merely "material" lives.** They knew themselves to be spiritual beings dreaming a "material" world.*** They recognized that they did not arise from earthly parents, but from the Spirit or Mind of God.*** Their origin was not the lower nature, but the higher.*** They are not products of earthlife.*** They are not the products of biology or genetics.*** Their deepest, truest life does not depend upon skin, or bodies, or the flow of blood.*** They are not bodies, produced by or of the elements.*** They have become much more than human beings.*** They are no longer body-dependent, but are spiritual beings.***

14. The Logos became flesh. God expressed in a lower nature.** God manifested as a lower kind of mind.** The perfect Mind surrounded Itself with a cloak of human nature.** The Godmind incarnated within a human framework.** The perfect Mind projected

and dreamed up a bodymind for Itself.*** The illusionworld was created by mindmanifestation, at lower levels.*** The Absolute entered the relative world.*** Perfect Mind expressed itself in the dreamworld of the lower nature.*** God manifested as a role in the play of the human stagedrama.*** God's manifestation enters the "material" world through the image-form of a "physical" body.*** The Mind expressed Itself as the perceptual world of the lower nature [i.e., sensuality and materialism].*** The Essence of perfect Mind became the essence of the world.***

He lived among us.6 God lived in us.** Christ lived in us.** Logos lived in us.** Perfect Mind lived in us.** The direct expression of God lived in us.** Divine manifestation lived in us.** Perfect Mind dwelled in us in human form, of which our own human forms are also a reflection.***

And we saw his splendor. And it was the splendor of a son of God. We knew his glory, and it was that of a being generated directly by God.** We touched his glory, and knew it to be the glory of the One.*** We sensed his Power, and knew It to be the Power of Mind.*** We perceived his lightfilled splendor, and knew it to be the Light of the One Whom God continuously generates within us.*** We touched his effulgence, and knew it to be the Light of Primary Mind.*** We sensed his radiance, and knew it to be that of One who is perfect.***

He was filled with grace and truth. The embodiment of perfect Mind was filled with cosmic Love, for that Mind was Reality.** He was filled with perfect forgiveness.** This Mind is filled with the awareness of Reality and perfection.*** He fully knows Reality, which he is, and the condition of stainlessness. *** He embodies Reality, is Its incarnation, and lives in stainless forgiveness.*** He is the incarnation of Reality, of Mind, filled with infinite forgiveness.*** He is everything that is real, a manifestation of illimitable Love.*** Fully aware of Reality, he is filled with Love.*** In his Mind, Love and Reality are one.*** Immeasurable Love and Reality are the Essence of his being.*** ...

---

6 This, unfortunately, is an apparently intentional mistranslation of the Greek, which says, literally, "He tented in us," conveying, obviously a very different message-- that of an *interior* Logos, Christ, or God.

*****

The narrative continues with Chapter 1, verse 16:

And from his fullness, everyone has received. He has filled all people with his own satisfaction.** All that he has, he shares with everyone.** Whatever fullness [of grace and Love] that he might possess, he generously distributes to all.** Everyone has been allowed to partake of that fullness of truth [Reality] and Love.*** No one has been excluded or left out of that truth and Love.*** Not a single living being exists outside of that state of Reality and Love.*** Every living creature arises from that Reality, that Mind.*** No being exists outside of ultimate Reality or absolute Love.*** Everyone in the cosmos exists in a state of grace and truth.*** Everyone is welcome to the fullness of divine nature.*** Everyone has a divine potential for perfect Love.***

Grace follows grace. Forgiveness creates forgiveness.** Love engenders forgiveness, which creates Love.** When grace is given, grace is received.** Where Love is expressed, there Love gathers.** More Love is given to the person who gives more.** There is no end to grace.*** Grace continues to appear in the heart.*** Grace is immeasurable, and comes to those who forgive others.*** Love and forgiveness multiply themselves.*** Forgiveness creates forgiveness.*** Gifted perfection thrives on Love.*** Love is bestowed upon the loving.*** Perfection, by grace, follows forgiveness and Love.*** Forgiving arises from selforgiveness, and a sense of inner wholeness.*** The state of grace is selfsustaining.*** Love nourishes Love.*** Love is drawn by Love.***...

*****

The narrative continues with chapter 1, verse 18:

No man has seen God. No one has seen the Absolute, Mind, Spirit, Coremind, Source, or Origin.* No human being has ever seen the Totality of God.** No one has ever been able to see infinity.*** The full experience of God is beyond ordinary human capacities.*** God's fullness transcends human comprehension.*** The full nature of God is beyond human conceptualization.*** The human nature cannot fully encompass the divine nature.*** God cannot be visualized with accuracy.***

The only-begotten God, who lives in the bosom of the father, has revealed him. But God has generated God, the heart of the father, and in this way, has revealed himself.** But God has generated God from his own heart, and has thus revealed himself.** God has created a mirrorimage of himself, and in this image has revealed himself.*** God has projected himself as God, and in this form has uncovered himself.*** God has given birth to his own likeness as God, and so, revealed himself.*** God has made a reflection of himself, and in this, has been revealed.*** God has placed the totality of himself in his expression, and so, has revealed himself.*** God has produced God in the world, as his only product, and in this, reveals himself.*** God is the center of God, and so he has come to be known.*** God directly produces only aspects of himself, his very being, and that is how he is known.*** God generates nothing but God, and this he does from his heart, and that is how he is seen.*** Since God gives birth only to God, everything is divine.*** God makes God from the Core of his own being, and so, makes his nature obvious.*** The "sons" of God are also God himself, produced by the Loveheart of the Father, who thus makes his nature manifest.*** God translates his Self by producing that Self, in various forms, from his own heart, and that is how he is revealed.*** God continuously produces his Self, out of his own heart, and comes to be known by his products.*** The unified God becomes the polymorphic God, from the essence of his tender heart, and that is how he is known in the world.*** God is one, and produces only one, but through that one is his heartlove revealed.*** God the one produces God the many, and in that way is revealed.*** The One Essence produces itself, from the Love of the heart, and in producing it is recognized.*** ...

*****

The narrative continues with chapter 1, verse 51:

[Jesus] said to him, "I tell you the truth: Later, you will see heaven opened, and messengers going to, and coming from, the son of human nature." "Later, heaven will open to your mind, and you will see those who bring messages to and from your human nature."*** "Later, you will see the heavenly dimensions of Mind open up and messages delivered to and from the human mind."*** "Higher spheres of existence will open, and communication between them and the human will begin."*** "Heavenly states will unfold within you, and you will know an exchange of messages between divine and human natures."*** "The nature of heavenly existence will open up before you, and information will move from you to deeper Mind, and from there to you."*** "Higher planes will open, and you will receive and give messages while still in human form."***...

*****

The narrative continues with chapter 2, verse 16:

[Jesus] said to those who sold doves, "Take these out of here. Don't make the house of My father into a store." "A temple should be a house of God, not a sales-area."*** "A place that is truly holy is not an appropriate place for the exchange of goods and money."*** "A temple is dishonored if it is used like a market, for buying and selling."*** "The whole world is the 'house' of My Father, but this place is supposed to be specially so, and is not the right place to sell."*** "A place that is supposed to be holy should not be defiled by greed."*** "A place that is supposed to be holy is not a market."*** "Spirituality is not a matter of buying and selling."**** "Spiritual places, and spirituality, are polluted by materialism."*** "Worship is corrupted by selling."*** "Selling even religious things is not worship."*** "Selling things even for religious uses turns the holy into the lowly."*** "Worship and sales should never be mixed."*** "Never combine the corruption of selling and money with the sacredness of worship."***...

*****

The narrative continues with chapter 2, verse 24:

But Jesus did not reveal his innermost being to them, because he fully knew the human nature of every person. He did not reveal the fullness of his Being to them, because he was aware of their weak human nature.** He did not display his full perfection to them, because he knew that their human nature would hold them back."**

25. He felt no need for human confirmation. He had no need of human recognition.** He did not need to impress them to validate himself.*** The quest for vanity was meaningless to him.*** Human attention, and approval, meant nothing to him.*** Having no personal self, he had no need to draw attention to himself.*** Having no self to

display, he never practiced selfdisplay.*** Not believing himself "separate" from others, he felt no need to attract attention from the crowd.*** The idea of human endorsement never crossed his mind.*** To gain fame never occurred to him.*** He saw fame as meaningless.*** Being himself his only spectator, he made no attempt to win admiration or attention.*** His Love, knowing the Self in all, made vanity impossible.*** Knowing his Self as the Owner of all, he knew that recognition could add nothing to his riches.*** ...

*****

The narrative continues with chapter 3, verse 3:

Jesus answered, "I tell you the truth: Unless a man is born again, he cannot see the kingdom of God." "Unless a person is reborn as a new person, her inner eyes will not be opened to see the inner cosmos where God rules."*** "Unless a person renounces her human identity, and takes up a spiritual identity, the inner 'kingdom' ruled by Love remains invisible to her."*** "Unless a person is reformulated and restructured as a totally different being, she cannot enter the 'kingdom' of God."*** "Unless a person dies to personhood, and lives as Spirit, she cannot come under the full rulership of Love."*** "Unless you experience metamorphosis, including a new beginning, you do not come under the rulership of Love."*** "If your identity is not completely transformed, you will not come into Love's guidance."*** "Until one starts life over again, as a new being, the inner rulership of Love will not seem real."*** "Unless one dies to the old self, and is born again as a new Self, giving control to Love will seem elusive."*** "Unless you are born from above, from higher Mind, you do not enter the domain ruled by Love."*** "Not until human nature dies, and Lovenature is born, do you truly move into the Mind ruled by Love."*** "Unless you become a new and interior being, apart from your body, you will not know the kingdom of Love."*** "You must stop identifying with the body in which you were born, and be reborn as a Mind, then, a Soul. Only then will you come under the rulership of Love."*** "Unless your being is reconstituted in a spiritual configuration, you will not live in the inner kingdom of Love."*** "Not until divine Lovenature is born in you, and you into It, do you know the heavenly dimensions of Mind."***

"It is impossible to know the inner kingdom in which Love guides every thought until you yield to the Way of a newborn baby."*** "The guidance of Love comes only to one who sees the self as newly born."*** "Often, a single birth on earth is not enough for one to learn all that she has to know; then, she must be born again."*** ...

*****

The narrative continues with chapter 3, verse 5:

Jesus answered, "I tell you the truth: Unless a person is born of water and Spirit, he cannot enter the kingdom." "Unless a person arises from fluidity and spirituality, she cannot enter the divine realm."*** "Unless a person is born into a cleansed state, she cannot enter."*** "Unless a person undergoes a spiritual baptism, she cannot enter the divine Mind."*** "Unless a person becomes cleansed, and receives new birth from the Spiritual Source, she does not really come under Love's control."*** "Unless a person is born from purity and the Spiritual nature, she does not enter divine dimensions of Mind."*** "Unless a person is born from the Fountain and Ocean of Love and Spirit, she does not enter the divine realm."*** "Emergence from the deepest 'waters' of inner Mind and Spirit will bring one under the true rulership of Love."*** "You must be dissolved in God as in water, and must become fluidly cooperative with the will of Spirit, before you come under the full control of Love."***

6. "Only flesh can come from flesh, and Spirit comes from only Spirit." "Only more of the lower nature can come from the lower nature. The higher nature can come only from the higher nature within you."** "The body comes from the nature of earth; the Mind emerges from spiritual nature." ** "The lower nature controls when you believe that you are a physical body. The divinenature controls when you know that You are a Soul."*** "As human bodies derive from other bodies, so only your interaction with the Spirit within can produce your spiritual nature."*** "Human nature arises naturally from human thinking. Divine nature arises from Love."*** "The mind of human nature produces a physical body. The spiritual Mind produces You as a Soul."***

7. "Do not be amazed that I said, 'You must be reborn.'"

8. "The wind blows wherever it wants. It moves according to its 'will.'" "Spirit is like wind. It can go anywhere It wants, do anything

that it wants."** "The Spirit is invisible, like wind. Like wind, It follows only Its own 'will'."** "Wind moves. But it is without form."*** "It moves, but is directed by nothing outside itself."*** "It is impelled only from within itself, not by any external force."*** "It moves, as a model, by an energy that comes from within itself."*** "It is totally free to roam anywhere [, like the being of Love.]"*** "It is moved by the Intangible and Indiscernible, as if an inner will were at work."*** "It is moved by a mystery, as if by will."*** "Wind possesses an inner principle of effortless movement, moved by only itself."***

"You hear only its sound." "You do not know or see it, or what moves it; you see only the result."*** "You see only its manifestations."*** "It is like the Spirit, quite invisible, known only by how it touches and affects others."*** "The only way that you can even know that wind is near is by sensing its effects; you hear it."*** "Although an invisible mystery, it reveals itself to your senses, as Spirit does."***

"But you know neither its origin nor its destination." "[As it is with Spirit,] you might not know Its Source, or Its ultimate plans."** "You have no idea how it originated [, as with Spirit,] and know not where it is going."*** "Both its Source and its goals are elusive."***

"It is the same with everyone who is born from the Spirit." "Everyone who is born from the Spirit is like this wind."** "These factors— going wherever it wills, not revealing its Source or destiny— apply to all who are born from Spirit."*** "Everyone who has a spiritual rebirth has these same characteristics."*** "Everyone born as Spirit shares these same qualities."*** "This is how you are when you have assumed a new identity or Self as Spirit."*** "The recreated, reborn being is also elusive and incomprehensible, invisible to most senses."*** ...

*****

The narrative continues with chapter 3, verse 11:
"I tell you the truth: We speak about something that we know." "We do not speak of theory, but of what we actually know."*** "These are not just ideas, but actual experience."***

"We talk about Something that we have actually seen." "Although It is invisible, we have seen It."*** "We have actually sensed the presence of this intangible Spirit."*** "We have actually touched and felt the movement of this Spirit."***

"And yet, you do not allow our evidence." "You cannot relate to, and turn away from, our experience because it is not your own."*** "What we say about the Spirit is outside of your reality."***

"You do not receive It." "You are not open to the reception of It."** "You are closed to It because you do not understand It."*** "You do not receive It because your intellect cannot know It."***

12. "If I have told you of things that happen on earth, and you have not believed, how will you believe if I tell you of heavenly things?" "If you believe things of the lower mind incredible, how will you be able to comprehend things of the higher Mind?"*** "If you cannot accept spiritual experience that touches earthly mind, how could you comprehend the deeper mysteries of heavenly Mind?"***

13. "No one has ascended to heaven but the one who descended from heaven— the human son." "The only part of being that can rise to heavenmind is that which has emerged from It— human nature."*** "Human nature originates with heaven, and so, must return there."*** "No human has come to earth who has not first been in heavenmind."*** "The ascent to heavenmind does not happen to anyone who has not first descended from heavenmind."*** "No human being will rise to the heavenly planes except those who have descended from them."*** "The path to interior heaven must be trod only by those who have fallen from it."*** "Human nature has fallen from grace, but it will return."*** "Human nature originates with heavenly nature, and so, will return to that elevated state."***

*****

The narrative continues with chapter 3, verse 15:

"Whoever believes in him will not come to nothing, but will exist in timeless life." "Who believes in this inner Lord will not perish, but will thrive in a timeless condition."** "The one for whom the Godmind is Reality will enter into timeless life."*** "Whoever believes in divine sonship will have timeless life."*** "Whoever believes that she is generated by timeless Mind will herself become eternal."*** "Who knows the self to be emanated by timeless Mind is a timeless Self."*** "Whoever knows the Reality of the divine Son within will never fade away, but exists eternally."*** "The one who knows inner Mind to be created by divine Mind will never disintegrate or dissolve, but will exist in timeless Mind."*** "The one who knows the Mind will never disappear, but will endure outside of time."***

16. "God's Love was so great that he projected into this world the only One Who fully embodies his nature, so that whoever believes in him will not perish, but live in timeless life." "God projected from his own deepest inner Mind, into the mind of each of us, the perfect incarnation of himself, so that, if we believe that he is real, we will have timeless life."*** "There is only one God, and that God has emanated into Mind the substance and essence of his nature; when we know That as Reality, we are no longer perishable, but have entered the state of timeless existence."*** "God, as perfect Mind, lives in each of us as the principle of sonship; when we believe that, we become the 'son,' and are no longer caught in the trap of time, perishing with the world, but are liberated into timeless life."*** "God is perfect, stainless Mind; the principle of sonship is the perfect reflection of that Mind in human nature; when that has become more real to us than the passing 'material' world, we are no longer caught in its current, and perishing with it, but are liberated to timeless life."*** "It is the great Love of God that lifts us from mere human nature into sonship; this is becoming a perfect incarnation of that same Love; when we receive this great gift, we are no longer one with the perishing world of time, but live one with him, in timeless splendor."*** "God's Love for the material universe is so great that he projected into it, through our minds, the very mirrorimage of his being, so that whoever believes in his supreme reality will not pass away with time, but is timeless."*** "Divine Love overflowed into the world, through our interior minds, in the form of the inner divine nature; whoever accepts this One as his/her true identity transcends the world of time, living beyond time."***

17. "For God did not send his son into the material cosmos in order to condemn it." "To judge the world is not the reason that God emanates the sonmind."** "To judge is not the function of sonmind."** "God, through the inner sonmind, does not judge the world."*** "God does not emanate the principle of sonship, divine incarnation, to condemn the natural world."*** "God's perfect reflection in Mind does not judge the world of matter."*** "God does

not send forth the Spirit into his children so that it can condemn or judge."*** "The perfect inner reflection of God does not condemn the world of matter and nature."*** "Real sonship does not condemn or judge the absolute value of the world."*** "No one in the world is condemned when you have become the son of God."***

"Instead, the entire material universe will be saved through him." "God's purpose and function is not to condemn or judge, but only to save."*** "God wants to save the entire 'material' cosmos, by lifting it into Love."*** "God will save the 'material' world by showing us that it is really a Mindworld."*** "Since the whole material world is filled with God, it is really a Godworld."*** "The world is of God, and nothing of God is ever lost."*** "All sentient beings will be saved when they have grown into inner sonship."*** "Whoever knows her role in the inner sonship will be rescued from ignorance and oblivion."*** "God saves the whole natural order by flooding it with the Light of Love."*** "God saves the whole world, not because it is good, but because he is good."*** "God welcomes the whole natural order into grace and salvation."*** "God saves the world from the illusion of separation."*** "When it knows him, the cosmos is saved from the lower nature."*** "God saves the natural order from the falsehood of illusory appearances."*** "When, through enlightenment, the cosmos comes to know only Godmind as Reality, then it is entirely saved."***

18. "For whoever believes in him is not judged." "Whoever believes in the reality of divine sonship does not judge even the self."*** "Who believes that Mind is more real than matter has ceased judgment."*** "Whoever knows God as Absolute does not recognize absolute evil, and hence, does not judge."*** "Who knows God does not judge, and so is not judged."*** "The one who believes that she possesses son-nature will never be judged."*** "To know the Reality of the inner son-nature is to rise above selfcondemnation."*** "Whoever becomes the inner son or incarnation will never be evaluated."*** "To believe in the absolute Reality of a good Self is to become absolutely good, to pass utterly beyond selfcondemnation."*** "To believe more fully in the identity of the inner sonship, more than the self, is to escape condemnation."*** "The self in apparent multiplicity can be compared and judged; but the Self of unity is incomparable, beyond judgment."*** "The one

who is unified with the One cannot be compared with another, and so, cannot be judged."*** "The one Mind is incomparable, hence, beyond all judgment."***

"But the one who does not believe exists in judgment already." "The one who is lost in the illusion of the many is always selfcomparing, selfcriticizing, and selfcondemning." *** "The one who does not know the reality of the sonship is caught in selfcondemnation, bound by illusion."*** "The one who does not recognize the Reality of sonship settles for the falsehood of the human self only; and noting its many imperfections, she judges herself."*** "One is judged only when in 'separation' or 'division'— both illusion."*** "Whoever accepts the primary unifying identity of the sonship passes beyond judgment, but she who does not remains in selfcondemnation."***

"He does not believe in the name of the only-begotten son of God." "This kind of person does not believe in the identity of inner sonship."*** "She has not accepted sonship as her higher identity or deeper Self."*** "Not believing in the complete melding or fusion of her self with this Self of sonship, she has not known."*** "The inner sonship nature is alone produced by the nature, and from the essence, of God, but is not recognized."***

19. "For the basis of judgment is this: Light has come into the natural order, but people have loved the darkness rather than the Light." "Judgment arises from the darkness of ignorance, and dissolves in the wisdom of Light."*** "People judge themselves because of clinging to inner darkness, but deepest Mind is Light, which flows forth into the natural order".*** "Light fills the natural order; but the people of darkness prefer their darkness, and so remain locked in judgment".*** "It is not that there is no Light in the natural order; there is. But people cling to darkness, and from this, judgment originates".*** "Light has infused the entire natural order, but people cling to shadows, selfcondemned".*** "The cosmos is suffused with Light, but people often 'see' only those places where It seems not to be."*** "The universe is all flooded with Light, but weak minds eclipse it, creating shadows; from this comes judgment."*** "The universe is bright with Light, but the human inner eye is accustomed to darkness, and so, creates judgment."*** "Everything and everyone is of the Light-nature; but ignorance creates darkness."***

"Everywhere is Light, but people locked in human or lower nature flee into the illusions of darkness and judgment."*** "The entire world is illuminated, but people often like to shut their eyes and create darkness, and judgment, within."*** "The world is bright; it is only human minds, with judgment, that are dark."*** "People judge themselves when they divide the cosmos into Light and an opposite which they call 'darkness.'"*** "What people judge to be 'darkness' is only a lesser Light, weakened in their minds because they do not believe in It."***

"What they do is wicked." "This behavior is harmful."** "This activity is not sane."*** "This resists Love or God"*** "This is the apparent opposite of goodness."*** "This is a denial of the allgood Reality."*** "This behavior goes against the cosmic current."*** "This resists the Flow of Mind, Light, and Love."*** "It is misaligned with the divine Mind."***

20. "For all who practice wicked things hate the Light, and do not come to the Light, for fear that their actions will be exposed." "The action of Light renews and re-creates the inner being in harmony with goodness, and so the ignorant are naturally repelled by It."*** "Those who indulge in deliberate, consistent harm towards self or others show that they are 'opposite' the Light. They hate It, for to come into illuminated Mind would expose them to themselves".*** "Those who live as denizens of darkness do bad; and they hate and avoid the Light, lest It expose them."*** "Those without understanding are accustomed to darkness; so the Light blinds and scorches them, and they are repelled by It, for they do not want to recognize their harmful and dangerous ways."*** "Those who resist the current of Reality avoid illumination and enlightenment, for they know that, if they become aware of the inner Light, their actions will be revealed as ignorance."*** "If they become enlightened, they will be seen to have devoted their lives to fraud, to illusion."*** "The human self fears the Light, for if it comes into Its brightness, it will fade away as illusion".*** "Human nature is terrified by the Light, for it is a creature of shadowmind."***

21. "But the one who lives the truth comes to the Light, so that his actions might be made manifest, and he may know that he acts within God." "The one who acts in Reality comes to the Light, so that his actions might be known as occurring within the Mind of God."**

18

"The one who lives from Reality comes to Light, that his activities might be known as having occurred in the divine Mind."** "When one acts in Reality, her actions occur in God, and she comes to the Light, so that she might know this."** "People of Reality are drawn to the Light, so that their actions might be seen to have their root in the Mind of ultimate Reality."** "The one who lives in Reality welcomes the Light, so that she might be made aware that her actions are not her own, but God or Light acting through her."*** "The one who acts in Reality acts as a vehicle of divine nature, and moves towards the Light."*** ...

***

The narrative continues with chapter 3, verse 31:

[John the Baptizer said,] "He who comes from above is above all." "Christ is over all."*** "The Spirit is above all."*** "God is over all."*** "The Spirit of Love has Power over everything."*** "The Spirit has precedence over everything."*** "Spiritmind controls the whole cosmos."*** "The same Mind that creates the cosmos has rulership over it."*** "The deeper Self has mastery of everything in this life."*** "Anyone who knows her origin to be in the transcendent Mindspheres has transcended everything."*** "Whoever traces her origin to Godmind has risen above the 'material' universe."*** "Whoever has been born from above, higher Mind, has found a position superordinate to the 'material' cosmos."*** "Whoever knows that her Source and Essence are in God finds the universe subordinate to the Spirit within."*** "If one knows her Origin to be above the 'material' world, then she has become a master."*** "The one who draws her total nature and being from the Lord of all then herself becomes the Lord of all."***

"He who is of the earth is also of the earthly nature, and so speaks of earthly things." "The body is from earthly elements and supports earthly nature. The one who believes that she is merely a body will speak of only earthly things."*** "People become involved in earthly activities because they resonate with the earthly nature. They want to speak of only earthly things."*** "She who traces her origin to this world becomes a pawn of earth and earthly nature. So, her conversation is [shallow and] worldly."*** "Most people are materialistic because they feel comfortable only with things of earth, and so are the puppets of their earthly nature. Their speech is filled with materialistic content."*** "She who draws her source and being from only the material reality becomes a slave to the lower nature, the unhappy slave to materialism."*** "People of earthenergy, because they feel that the earth is their true home, and origin, are capable of speaking of only material things."*** "Thoughts and words about shallow material things and events originate with people of the lower, earthly nature, who consider earth to be their source and home."*** "Those whose hope and future are only material rather than spiritual betray themselves."*** "The earthminded have only earthly views, standards, and reference points. They cannot conceive of anything beyond these."***

"But the one who originates with heaven is above all." "The person who knows that her Source is in infinite Mind is not controlled by the world."*** "The being whose inner nature is heavenly has transcended all 'material' things."*** "The one who sees herself as an expression of limitless Mind has moved beyond slavery to greed and lusts."*** "The one who recognizes that she originates with pure Lovemind starts to become Lovemind, the Master of everything."*** "She who comes from Mind cannot come from the world, and she melds with the inner Mastermind."*** "She who lives in heavenly states has risen above merely earthly concerns."***

"He tells about what he has seen and heard, but no one of the earthly nature accepts what he says." "When the one who has touched Light talks about the experience, people of the lower, earthly nature cannot relate, and so, reject her."*** "Ordinary earthly people reject her descriptions of what she has perceived."*** "Those of earthmind cannot conceive what she describes, and so turn away."*** "They are incapable of grasping her descriptions."*** "They reject what she says as impossible, meaningless, or insane."*** "They cannot accept her as 'normal.'"*** "Human nature knows no parallels to what she is saying."*** "What she expresses lies fully outside the range of words."***

33. "But anyone who does listen, and accepts, acknowledges that God is true." "But anyone who listens, and accedes, knows that divine Mind is Reality Itself."*** "Whoever accepts what she says accepts the Reality of divine nature, and the illusion of the human."***

34. "Anyone sent by God speaks the words of God." "Because her mind emanates from the inner depths of deepest Mind, she speaks the words of that Mind."*** "Love sends people to speak the words of Love."*** "When a person knows her Source and Home to be deepest inner Mind, she speaks, not her own, but Its message."*** "This is how you recognize that anyone is from God: She will speak the message of God."*** "The one who has seen that she originates in the great and infinite Mind will teach Love."*** "When one knows the Self to be a projection of inner bottomless Mind, she will speak Its message."*** "What the being in God says, in all situations, will reflect the Love of God."*** "What God says in her inner Mind, the one beamed forth by God will say outwardly."*** "When she touches inner God, she expresses God even as God expresses her."*** "If one realizes that she is a projection of the divine Mind into the world, then divine words flow through her."***

"For God does not give the Spirit by measure." "God does not measure spiritual wisdom, but gives it all, continuously, to everyone."*** "God does not give spiritual knowing in measured quantities. He offers it all, continuously, to all."*** "God does not parcel out the energy of Love, but gives it all, always, to all."*** "God gives the entire Spirit to everyone. People vary only in the capacity to receive."*** "God gives all Spirit all the time, but people vary in the measure which they can receive, accept, or hold."*** "When God grants the higher nature, he does not do so partially, but totally. Any limit is only the receiver's."*** "God's gift of the Spirit is limitless and immeasurable, boundless."*** "God gives all of himself to all, in all situations."*** "Love is unlimited, and an infinite Love flows continuously to every heart, all the time."*** "Infinite inner Mind never holds back anything."*** Bottomless inner Mind does not weigh, measure, or limit the Flow of the inner Spirit of Love, joy, and peace."***

35. "The father loves the son, and has placed all things in his hands." "The interior Source loves the individuated God, and trusts him with everything."*** "The generator loves the generated, and gives her all Power."*** "The Source loves the mind derived from It, and has entrusted everything with it."*** "The Creator loves the created."*** "The Dreamer loves the objects and persons of the dreamworld."*** "Out of Love, the inner Sourcemind grants trust to

the Selfmind, the Spirit to the Soul."*** "The Spirit, through Love, has turned over control of part of the formation of the personal world to the Soul."*** "The Generator and Nourisher of the universe has turned it all over to his worldactive mind."*** "The father gives as a gift all the beauties of creation to his mirrorreflection within humanity."*** "Through Love, the Projector of the cosmos gives everything to his projected image."*** "Love integrates the Unconscious Superconscious Mind with the Soulmind."***

36. "He who believes in the son has timeless life." "When you know your truer Self to be the deeper Self, the Soul, you enter timeless life."*** "When divine and human natures combine to create the son-nature in you, and you see that as your truer Self, you have entered timeless life."*** "Timeless life in the now is the reward of anyone who identifies with the son-nature over human nature."*** "To know that the son-nature is more real than the self is to move into the 'eternal now,' and thus, to step outside of time into timeless life."***

"But he who does not believe in the son will not see life." "The one who does not know the truer Self to be divine-human nature will not live the real life."*** "If one does not believe that God is one with deepest Mind, and then, fuse her own human nature with that divine nature, creating the inner son-nature, she will not know this timeless life."*** "The genuine, fullest life is not possible for anyone who does not believe in her son-nature."*** "The most real life, timeless life, is impossible for a person who does not accept her inner relationship with the divine Mind within."***

"For this person remains in the 'anger' of God." "For she is locked in the grip of frustration and anger. This comes from deep Mind, so she feels that it is from God."*** "Anger is a form of fear, Love's opposite, and so cannot originate with God. But God creates the harsh world, and this is interpreted as anger."*** "Anger, a negative relationship with creation, forms negativity towards the Creator, and blocks Love and relationship."*** "Anger makes her destabilized, disoriented, and turbulent."*** "The Spirit cannot express purely when It is blocked by anger."*** "The frustrations and anger of human nature sever her from natural relationship, Love, and unity."*** "When she must battle the projected fears of her past, this appears to be the 'anger' of God."*** "The created world can be so cruel that it is seen as God's 'anger.'"***

***

The narrative continues with chapter 4, verse 10:

Jesus answered, "If you knew what gift God gives, ... you would have asked him, and he would have given you living water." "He would have given you the living, loving force of Spirit."*** "He would have given you a state of purity."*** "He would have given you the 'baptism' of the Soul."*** "He would have purified you from within."*** "He would have given you Me, the Christ, as inner springs of life."*** "He would have given you the life-principle of Spirit."*** "He would have given you a cleansing, holy Mind."*** "He would have given you the Spiritual nourishment to sustain your inner life."*** "He would have given you the Power of heartmind to renew and refresh your inner life."***

***

The narrative continues with chapter 4, verse 13:

"Whoever drinks of the water I give will never thirst again." "Whoever partakes of spiritual water will be satisfied forever."** "Whoever partakes of cleansing Mind will never have to be cleansed again."*** "Whoever once quenches her thirst for Spirit will never thirst again."*** "Whoever is thoroughly purified by spiritual life-energy is pure forever."*** "The one who drinks from this inner Fountain will be satisfied forever."*** "Who drinks of this fresh inner spiritual substance will be permanently fresh."***

"For the water that I will give him will be a well of water within him." "The water that I give will become its own Source."** "This inner water will be selfrenewing and selfreplenishing."*** "This water will come from the very deepest Mind, as if from a deep well."*** "This water will come from an inner spring of the heart."*** "I speak of the water from a well so deep that it is sunk into the Mind of God, at the Center."***

"When it bubbles up, it flows into timeless life." "When it comes to the surface of Mind, and is recognized, then this spiritual force awakens to timeless life."*** "When it bubbles up to knowing, it brings the awareness of timeless life."*** "This water of spiritual wisdom, when recognized, brings one into timeless life."***

***

The narrative continues with chapter 4, verse 23:

"But the time is coming, and is already here now, when the true worshippers will worship the father in Spirit and in truth." "They will worship with the deepest Mind, with a knowing of Reality."** "They will worship deepest Mind with deepest Mind, knowing only It to be Reality."*** "After having themselves become real, they will worship the Source with deep Minds of Reality, and will know this Reality as the Source."*** "They will worship with spiritual identity and with real Minds."*** "They will worship Spirit as Spirit, so that Spirit will be both adored and adoring. And this Spirit is ultimate Reality."*** "Genuine worship of the Source flows only from the deep Mind of spiritual nature, and this is Reality."*** "To truly adore the Source, one must do this as a Spirit, recognizing spiritual Reality."***

"In fact, the father seeks this kind of worshipper." "The Source wants to be adored by Spirit, not just mind or word."*** "The Source seeks and entreats people to worship him /her in this way."*** "Knowing God as Source and Reality is the only real and genuine worship."*** "The Source responds to only this kind of devotion."*** "The Source extends Itself as the worshipper when this kind of worship occurs."*** "This kind of adoration is Godmind worshipping Godmind."*** "This kind of worship emanates from the deeper Mind, and adores the deepest Mind."***

"God is Spirit." "Spirit is God."** "God is deepest Mind."*** "God is Coremind."*** "God is Lovemind."*** "God is the deep Lovenature."*** "God is the Superconscious Mind within the Unconscious."*** "The spiritual nature within is God."*** "God is the indwelling Spirit."*** "God is spiritual Love."*** "God is That Which underlies all Mind."*** "God is the Essence of Mind."*** "God is the Power that motivates to Love."*** "God is the profound nucleus of Mind and being, the Center of the Soul.7"*** "God is the wisdomind that generates and orders the universes."*** "God is

---

7 . For an expansion of this concept see my *Journey to the Center of the Soul, op.cit.*

24

Reality (truth)."*** "God is the Mindmatrix of interconnection."*** "Godmind is the cohesive and integrating factor of existence."*** "God is the divine nature, of Light and Love."*** "God is active cosmic process and pattern."*** "God is mutuality, reciprocity, and oneness in Love."*** "God is the One, the single unified Mind behind all diversity."***

"And they who worship him must do so in Spirit and in truth." "They must worship with the deep Mind, and in Reality."**...

***

The narrative continues with chapter 4, verse 32:
[Jesus] said to them, "I have food to eat of which you do not know." "I draw My sustenance, not from this world, but from another Source, which you have not come to know."*** "That which gives Me My true life is not literal food, but the interior nourishment of Spirit, which you do not know."*** "Literal bread does not keep Me alive, but I have inner, invisible 'bread' of the sustaining Spirit. You have not come to know him/her."*** "Food has nothing to do with sustaining the real, inner life. That requires a finer nourishment, about which you know nothing."*** "I draw My life from a Source that is not known by you."***

***

The narrative continues with chapter 4, verse 34:
Jesus said, "My food is for Me to do the will of him who sent Me." "What gives Me life is the accomplishment of the will of the One."** "It nourishes me to fulfill the will of the father Who sent Me."** "What sustains Me is to fulfill the desires of the One Who projected Me into the world."*** "My nourishment is to do the pleasure of the One Who beamed Me forth into this world."*** "I draw My life-energies from harmonizing with the One, that his/her will might be My will."*** "I want nothing but to want what the One wants. That is what keeps Me alive."*** "To do only what he/she wants is My only Source of life and Power."***

"And I must complete his work." "I must bring his mission to completion."** "I must complete this assignment to perfection."** "I must finish his assignment to Me."** "I must surrender my total self."*** "I must do his/her will completely."*** "In doing only his/her will, I must hold nothing back."*** "In doing his/her will completely, I must abandon Mine."***

***

The narrative continues with chapter 4, verse 36:

"The one who is reaping is already getting his wages." "People are reaping situations now as the wages of activities in the past."*** "People even now are being 'paid' for the work that they have done."*** "Those who have sown the seeds of action are now reaping what has grown as their wages."*** "To reap the fruit of past actions is just wages."***

"And a harvest is being gathered for timeless life." "The ultimate goal is to harvest all the 'grain' for timeless life."*** "Ultimately, this harvest will determine the quality of your timeless life."*** "The timeless life of the Soul is what is affected by this harvesting."*** "Whatever harvest is gathered now will affect, in the end, Your timeless Self."*** "No matter what the harvest is now, in the end, it will become part of Your timeless life."***

"In time the one who sows will rejoice in oneness with the one who reaps." "The one who sows is the same as the one who reaps, and both roles are You; and in time, you will rejoice."*** "This is all leading to ultimate joy. For the one who sows and the one reaping are the same."*** "The sower and the reaper are different persons, but share the same Soul. After they realize their oneness, they will enter into joy."*** "The one who sows and the one who reaps are different manifestations of the same Soulbeing, and one day, they will reunite in joy."*** "The Soul sows the seed, and the same Soul later reaps the harvest, in a different life. But when they meld and fuse at the Soulevel, the result is joy."***

37. "This is why that saying, 'One sows, but another reaps,' is true." "Because the Soul expresses as two separate persons, the saying, 'One sows, and another reaps,' is true."***

38. "I sent you to reap where you had not worked before." "But you have reaped where you have not sown."** "I sent you to reap benefits which are not really yours, since you did not do the work of sowing."*** "But you have been able to reap even where you have not sown the seeds."*** "You get to reap even though your present selves did not do the sowing."*** "You've reaped, even though the

26

people whom you are now did not do the work."*** "The identities which you now have are different from those who did the work of sowing."*** "Those who actually did the work of sowing were other men, at other times, although you get to do the reaping."*** "Those who came before you had other names, and did the sowing, even though you can now do the reaping."***

****

****

CHAPTER 5.

The narrative continues with chapter 5, verse 14:

Later, Jesus found him in the temple and said, "See, you are healed." "You have been made whole."** "You have now become complete."**

"Sin no more, that something worse does not happen to you." "If you don't sin, you can avoid something even worse."** "Sin creates some physical problems. So, if you sin, something even worse might happen to you."*** "Remain in error no longer, or something worse might happen."*** "Do not continue to live in your mistaken way, so that something even worse does not befall you."*** "Do not miss the mark of inner wholeness, unifying your Self."*** "Do not continue to live in the illusion of separation from Your deepest inner Self."*** "Live no more in incompleteness, isolation, and separation, the illusion of fragmentation."***

***

The narrative continues with chapter 5, verse 17:

Jesus answered them, "My father keeps on working, and I keep on working." "Because the inner Source continues to work, I, Who am a perfect mirrorreflection of him, continue to work."*** "The inner Source works continuously, and that is why I work continuously: He works through Me."*** "My Origin functions without ceasing, and I perfectly reflect his ways."*** "The deepest Mind never stops working, and It works through Me."*** "God always works, and, as his perfect Mirror, so do I."*** "The One, Who generates My life, is continually active, and that is why I am also."*** "The Lord of Love and Light works without cessation, and, since I am the instrument of his will, so do I."*** "The Source of the universes never stops working. Since I am one with him, I cannot stop either."*** "He Who produces all things is a Source of continuous energy, and some of that is expressed as My work."*** "The Mind behind the universes never stops Its continuous creation. Since I am the vessel of that creation, I never stop either."***

***

The narrative continues with chapter 5, verse 19:

"I tell you the truth: Nothing that the son does arises from himself." "When you are acting out of the son-nature, all that you do arises from the higher Source."*** "The son-nature can do nothing under its own power."*** "Nothing done by the son-nature in you is selforiginated."*** "Everything that you do from your son-nature is from the Source of Love."*** "The one who knows the son-nature does nothing from the level of the human self."*** "The one who knows relationship with Lovemind, as son-nature, does nothing personal, or by personal initiation, will, or power."*** "The son-nature within the divine nature does nothing out of personal desires of the human nature."*** "She who knows herself as divine daughter obeys Love rather than self."***

"He does only what he sees the father doing." "Son-nature perfectly reflects divine nature."*** "The son-nature is the Lovenature's perfect duplicate."*** "The son-nature is created by the convergence of human nature with divine nature, and can do only the will of the One."*** "The son-nature is the absolute slave of the Lovenature, and can do only what it is told."*** "The son-nature never acts or speaks independently of the Lovenature."*** "All 'individual' action becomes divine activity."*** "In the son-nature, the personal blends with the divine."*** "The human Mind surrenders to the divine Mind within, and so its actions are of God (Love)."*** "All actions of the son-nature are actions of the indwelling and perfect One of Love."*** "The actions of the enlightened being are those of the Sourcemind."***

20. "For the father loves the son, and shows him everything that he himself does." "Lovemind, out of Love, shares with the son-nature everything that it contains."*** "Perfect Godmind reveals everything about Itself, what It is and what It has, to the son-nature."*** "Sourcemind reveals Its totality, out of Love."*** "Love is the unifying energy that reveals divinity to humanity."*** "Love is the overlap between Godmind and selfmind."*** "Because of Love, nothing of Godmind is concealed from the inner son-nature or sonmind."*** "The Source allows sonmind to behold him in all things."*** "The totality of Mind is open to one who knows the sonmind unifying her with Lovemind."*** "Infinite knowledge and

understanding are revealed to the sonmind through Love."*** "Cosmic awareness arises through divine Love."*** "Through Love, universal vision and consciousness arise and are revealed."*** "Love grants the sonmind a vision of Lovemind."*** "The divine Being is known fully when, through Love, It reveals Itself."***

"And he will show him greater works than these, so that you will be astonished." "Someday, the Sourcemind will reveal to the sonmind works that are astonishing."** "When you know the deeper levels of Mind, you will be astonished."*** "When you know Reality greater than this world, you will be astonished."*** "When you see that Sourcemind is greater than 'material' creation, you will be surprised."*** "When Sourcemind reveals Itself to sonmind, the result is astonishment."***

21. "For exactly as the father raises the dead, and gives them life, so the son gives life to anyone whom he wills to have it." "The Sourcemind gives life and mind to all, who without It would be dead. The son-nature can also give life and mind to others."*** "Through human nature, when it is enlightened to sonmind, life is given to others."*** "As life continues after 'death,' so life is generated by Mind, enlightened to sonmind."*** "Life flows *from* cosmic Mind, and *through* the sonmind."*** "The sonmind is a channel through which life flows to others."*** "The Sourcemind brings life forth from death. The sonmind invests life according to his will."*** "Cosmic Mind creates life after life, through death. So, the sonmind projected by that Mind reflects life into others."*** "Life neutralizes death through the harmony between Sourcemind and sonmind."***

22. "For the father judges no one." "Sourcemind evaluates no one absolutely."*** "Infinite Mind never condemns."*** "Cosmic Mind recognizes no absolute evil."*** "Sourcemind recognizes no absolute duality of good and evil, for Good has no opposite."*** "Love never evaluates beings or actions as absolutely evil."***

"But he has left all judgment to the son." "The son-nature, affected by human nature, still falls into judgment."*** "Sourcemind does not judge absolutely; but lesser Mindareas get caught in the delusion of absolute dualism."*** "Coremind knows all as one, and all as good, but Soulmind and humanmind both affect sonmind, so that it still practices judgment."*** "Evaluation of absolute evil occurs only in lesser Mind."*** "It is the mind in human nature that gives absolute value to evil."*** "Only the human part of the divine Mind condemns."*** "The lower aspects of divine Mind have the option to condemn."*** "Only the shadowmind practices condemnation."***

23. "It is necessary to honor the son equally with the father." "The son-nature should be reverenced as the father, for It contains him."*** "Equal respect should be given to both infinite Sourcemind and to its reflection in human nature, for both are the same."*** "Equal honor should be given to the Sourcemind and to Its perfect reflection in human nature."*** "Divine nature should be recognized and respected through the human nature."*** "Human beings must be seen and addressed as divine beings."*** "Human nature, at its zenith, becomes divine nature."*** "Divine Mind, Christmind, manifest in humanmind." *** "At its highest expression and fullest blossom, human nature becomes the perfect divine Self."*** "Divine humanity is human divinity."*** "To honor human beings is to honor the Sourcemind."*** "You cannot worship God without honoring human beings."*** "The Sourcemind in Its human form must be respected exactly as It is in formlessness."*** "The human manifestations of the divine are themselves divine."***

"He who does not honor the son does not honor the father who has sent him." "If you do not honor the divine-human nature, neither do you honor the Sourcemind which beams it forth."** "She who does not honor the divine within the human does not honor God, Who emanates both."*** "The true Love of human beings is the most genuine worship of God."*** "To love human beings is to honor God."*** "The only way to love God is to respect people."*** "God receives and accepts only that honor given to human beings."***

24. "I tell you the truth: He who hears My words, and believes in him who sent Me, already has timeless life." "The one who hears with understanding these teachings, and believes in the cosmic Mind that emanates Me, already has timeless life."*** "The one who hears My interior expression, and believes that the divine Mind that creates Me is real, has already entered the timeless state."*** "The one who responds to this message, and believes in the ultimate Reality of the inner Sourcemind that forms Me, has entered the timeless state."*** "The timeless, deathless state of the Soul is entered by anyone who comprehends this message, and believes in the deepest Core of Mind

that is my Origin."*** "Anyone who believes in the absolute Reality of the cosmic Mind that creates Me, and who knows these things, has come into the timeless life."***

"He will not come into judgment." "She will not be condemned."** "This person will not be evaluated in absolute terms."*** "This being transcends condemnation."*** "Having ceased judging others, neither is she judged."***"This kind of being has risen above cause-and-effect."*** "...has risen above birth-and-death."***

"For he has passed from death to life." "The death of her human self has created the resurrection of her Soul or Self."*** "Her death has resulted in a new life."*** "She has moved beyond the power of death, and now knows only the Power of life."*** "She has moved from a state that leads again to death, to one of continuous life."*** "For her, death is no longer a part of life."*** "She has passed beyond birth-and-death."*** "She no longer has to die anymore."*** "Death is recognized as illusion."*** "Death is unmasked as life."***"Death is the expanded blossom of life."***

25. "I tell you the truth: The hour is coming, and is, in fact, already here, when the dead will hear the voice of the son of God." "Even those who are 'dead' can hear the inner voice of the son-nature, and respond."*** "When divine and human nature converge and combine, even the dead respond."*** "Those whom you regard as 'dead,' are alive; and even now, they hear the inner call to become the son-nature."*** "Both now and in the future, the dead can hear the message to come into the sonmind."*** "Even those who are dead are invited into sonship."*** "Even the dead must give up the human nature to divinity, creating the son-nature."*** "Even death cannot silence the inner message of sonship. Even now, the dead are hearing it."*** "Inner wisdom is stronger than even death."*** "The Lovenature is stronger than death, and communicates within, even after death."***

"Those who hear will come to life." "They, after death, will come to life."*** "They will come to inner life."*** "They will come to life in another reality."*** "Their minds will come to life within cosmic Mind, which knows no death."*** "Those who know will arrive at the state of deathless life."*** "They will enter a life of seamless continuity."*** "They will emerge from the tyranny of the time-death state."*** "They will emerge from life-death duality into a cosmos where life has no opposite."***

26. "For exactly as the father has life in himself, he has given to the son to have life also in himself." "The life of Sourcemind originates from within that Mind; so the life of the sonmind will arise from the sonmind."*** "Heavenly nature is a Fountain of life, but so is its convergence with earthly nature, in the son-nature."*** "When the son-nature has merged and fused with the heavenly nature, so that the 'two' are literally one and the same, then the life of the Sourcemind will emerge into both natures."*** "Even though 'father' and 'son' are two modes of Mind, they share a common root, the Origin of life, in the Sourcemind."*** "As the life of the divine Mind is intrinsic, so is the life of the enlightened human psyche."*** "When the life of the human nature becomes divine, it derives from 'both' sources, human and divine, for they are one."*** "Human life, and sonship, arise from divine life, and are dependent upon nothing else."*** "When the human mind is enlightened, it is able to originate life-force in exactly the same way as the divine Mind does, for they are one."*** "In the divine Mind, the human mind also becomes a source of life."*** "Divine Mind gives to human mind the gift of giving life."*** "The selfsustaining, selforiginating divine nature is bestowed upon human nature."*** "Divine Mind superimposes Itself upon the human mind, and then, the human becomes the Source."***

27. "And he has given him authority to pass judgment as well." "Divine Mind has given sonmind permission to evaluate absolute values."*** "Divine Mind permits sonmind to judge because of its human input."*** "Sourcemind allows the human mind, as part of the sonmind, to grow through the ignorant practice of judgment."*** "The human mind is given the option of condemnation so that it might grow beyond condemnation."****"When human mind, within sonmind, sees the illusory world as separate, it still forms opinions of condemnation."*** "Human mind, even after joining with Sourcemind, still possesses the freedom to coalesce illusions and condemnation."***

"This is because he is the son of man." "This occurs because the son still has some of human nature within him."*** "Judgment occurs only because of lower, human, nature."*** "Judgment reflects, not divine, but human input."***

28. "Do not be astonished at this, for the hour is coming in which all those who are in the graves will hear his voice." "Don't be surprised, for even the dead can hear the inner voice of the sonmind, and this will happen to all of them."*** "Even those whom you call 'dead' are alive, and all of them, too, will respond to the call to sonship."*** "Someday, the call to enlightenment, and union with the divine Mind, will reach even all those who have already died."*** "The calling to sonship goes out to both the living and the dead."***

29. "Then, they will come forth. Those who have done good things will come to a resurrection of life, and those who have done evil, to a resurrection of judgment." "Then, the good will have an opportunity for a new life, and the evil, who have judged, will themselves return to being judged."*** "They will emerge from the deathstate— those in harmony with goodness finding their inner lives, and the evil returning to the world of dualism, separation, illusion, and judgment."*** "... those who sought alignment with divine Mind will find their real, timeless lives, while the ignorant will find their world to be a mirror of their own judgments."*** "... each is given exactly what he or she has given: the good, life, for they wished life for others, and the bad, judgment, because they judged others."*** "... the good will find inner life, but the bad, selfcondemnation."*** "Everyone— both the good and the bad— partakes in resurrection. The good use it to grow into ever fuller lives, while the bad fall prey to condemnation, and thus, are themselves condemned."*** "Real life is a product of goodness, while the life of illusion-judgment is evil."***

30. "Of myself, I can do nothing." "I do nothing as a 'separate person.'"** "Nothing comes from My human nature."** "Not a single thing that I appear to do arises from My self."** "Nothing comes from My human self."** "I am incapable of acting personally, apart from divine Mind."*** "I can do nothing outside of Sourcemind."***"I can do nothing separate from Lovemind."*** "Without a self, I cannot act selfishly."*** "Nothing that I do arises from me."*** "Nothing that I do arises from the human psyche."*** "I cannot possibly act independently of the cosmic Mind That indwells Me."*** "I am interwoven with the Creatormind, and so, do nothing of my self."***

"I judge only as I hear, and so my judgment is just." "I judge only as I hear [from the inner Sourcemind]..."*** "I judge only as I hear and sense the world, so my judgments are trustworthy."*** "Only the Sourcemind can rightly judge, and 'my' judgments are simply reflections of his."*** "I do not judge as a human mind. These judgments are not mine, but belong to the divine Mind, and, hence, are just."*** "I never judge; but the Sourcemind judges through me."*** "I do not judge the world, but only my thoughts about the world, and so, my judgments are accurate."***

"For I have no desire of my own, but only the desire of my father who sent me." "I have surrendered all personal desire..."** "I have no human desire, but only the desire of the Sourcemind."*** "I have no personal will, but seek only the will of the Sourcemind who beamed me forth."*** "I have no personal will, but the will of Love, which projected my being."*** "My will is only the will of the Sourcemind That made me."***

31. "If I testify about myself, then my testimony is not valid." "If I talk about my human self, my talk teaches nothing true."** "If I bear witness to the [virtues of the] human self, I teach nothing of value."** "If I talk about myself, then what I say has no ultimate reality."** "There is no validity in talking about the self."*** "A teacher who talks about herself is empty."*** "If I were to tell you only about my human self, what I would say would be worthless."*** "If I were to discuss my human nature, I would be talking about an unreality."***

32. "There is another that testifies about Me, however, and I know that his testimony is true." "The deeper Mind bears witness to Me, however, and I know that Its testimony is real."** "The Sourcemind talks about the Christ in Me, which I am, and his teaching is true."*** "When My being is confirmed by cosmic Mind, then do I partake of absolute Reality."*** "When the evidence of My Being arises from divine nature, then I know that it is true."*** "When Love says that I am, then I know that I truly am."*** "My reality is confirmed by only Love."*** "It is Love that makes me real."***

***

The narrative continues with chapter 5, verse 34:

"But I do not receive human testimony." "What people say about Me makes no difference."** "It does not matter."** "I don't need

35

it."** "If I do not impress people, that is unimportant."** "What people say about Me is of no value or concern."*** "Nothing real depends upon the confirmation by human beings."*** "I don't depend upon other people to define My Self or my value."*** "Human standards cannot contain or define Me."*** "I have no need of anyone to witness for Me or to testify for Me."*** "My Being is unaffected by human values."*** "I am untouched by what human beings think of Me."*** "Human evaluations of Me are worthless."*** "I do not allow people to form My Self."*** "My total Self is quite beyond the scope of human interpretation."***

"I say these things only that you might be saved." "I teach this to liberate you from your lower nature."*** "I teach this to rescue you from ignorance."*** "What I say is designed to prevent you from identification with only the human."*** "This message can save you from animality and materialism."***

***

The narrative continues with chapter 5, verse 36:
"For the work which my father has given Me to complete is My evidence and testimony." "The evidence of Who I am is My work."** "What bears important testimony to Me is My work."*** "My true Self and nature are evidenced by the activities that flow forth through Me."*** "My activities are My witnesses."*** "What I manifest through My being and doing is the true mirror of Who I am."*** "A being is known by her expressions, and I am known by Mine."*** "My expressions manifest My nature."***

"This evidence proves that the father has sent Me." "It proves that the Sourcemind has projected Me."** "It proves that I am an expression of the Sourcemind."**

37. "And the father himself, who has sent Me, has given testimony of Me." "The Sourcemind tells about Me, in your own mind, for it is he who has projected Me."*** "The Spirit bears witness to your Soul that I am he."*** "The Sourcemind of Love provides evidence that validates My reality."***

"You have never heard his voice, or seen his form." "You have never heard without distortion the message of the Sourcemind, and It has no form."*** "Your minds have never been quiet or still enough to hear his voice, and you have never seen a pure form of the

Formless."*** "To you, his wisdom is inaudible and his form invisible."*** "To you, he is imperceptible."*** "He is without meaning to you, for you are sensual."*** "Silent and formless, he is too subtle for your grasp."***

38. "For you do not have his Logos dwelling within you." "The perfect expression of Sourcemind does not live permanently within you."*** "His flawless manifestation is not allowed to live and thrive within your hearts."*** "The mirroreflection of Love does not live within you."*** "An unobstructed image of God cannot be nourished within you."*** "God's active manifestation has no place within you."***

"For you do not believe the One Whom he has sent." "You cannot believe the Absolute, for you do not believe even the One projected into your heart, the sonmind."*** "You do not believe the Spirit sent into your hearts."*** "You do not believe the expression (*Logos*) of Sourcemind."*** "You do not believe his eternal Essence, the Christnature."***

39. "You are always studying the Bible, because you believe that you can find timeless life by doing this, but this tells of Me." "You study only outer Scriptures..."** "You study ancient texts..."** "You study Bible-history..."*** "You are experts at quoting the texts, but you have missed entirely their message."*** "You have memorized the ancient Scriptures, but have ignored their central message of Sourcemind's revelation."*** "You are always quoting the Bible, but have missed understanding of the God of which it teaches."*** "Your faith is mere biblicism; it is mechanism and legalism."*** "Even your Bible talks about the father, although in an obscured form."*** "The purpose of all Scriptures is to tell about Me, inner Spirit, sonmind, and Sourcemind."*** "The only purpose of all valid Scriptures is to lead to a direct knowing (*gnosis*) of My Being."***

40. "And you will not come to Me, so that you might have life." "I, the Spirit, am the only Source of life, but you refuse to come to Me."*** "The Bible cannot give life, for life comes only from the Sourcemind, through Me."*** "You refuse to integrate your human mind with My Mind, thus discovering timeless and real life."*** "In your minds, you are isolated from Me, and thus, from life itself."*** "You insist that you are separate from Me, and thus, have no life in yourselves."*** "You do not taste of real life until you come to an

intimate knowing (*gnosis*) of Me."*** "When you do not commune with Me in your hearts, you are not really alive."***

41. "I accept no honor, credit, title, or validation* from people." "I have no interest in impressing people."*** "I am not interested in what people think of me."****"I have no need of human confirmation."*** "I do not need or want admirers."*** "I do not want human applause or approval."*** "Human evaluations are not my standard of selfworth."*** "People are not the source of My honor."***

42. "But I know that you do not have the Love of God in you." "Your minds and hearts contain no divine Love."** "Perfect Love has no place in you."** "Unconditional, universal Love does not live within you."*** "You have left no inner space for immeasurable Love to activate your hearts."*** "Your minds are too narrow, too contracted to allow for the infilling of Love."*** "You are so full of self that you have no room for Love."***

43."I have come in my father's name." "I have come here in the identity of my father."** "I come to you, not as a man, but as the Sourcemind."*** "I come to this reality not as a human mind, but as infinite Sourcemind in physical manifestation."*** "I have forsaken the illusion of personal identity, and have embraced the truest Self of the Spirit of Love."*** "I have come to display the living Reality behind all manifestation."*** "I have come as the Incarnation of the Mind of Love."***

"But you did not receive Me." "You did not receive Me into yourselves."*** "You refused to be open to Me."*** "You refused to assimilate My nature with your own."*** "You resisted full integration with Me."*** "You resisted integration with, or absorption into, the Mind of Love."*** "You refused to merge and blend your will with the will of Love."*** "You insisted on the illusion of separation from Me, and, hence, from Sourcemind."*** "You remained in the state of ignorance, darkness, and illusion."***

"If another comes in his own name, you will receive him." "If a teacher is filled with ego, you will accept him."** "If another comes embracing mere human identity, you will receive him."** "You admire those who want to make a name for themselves."*** "You are impressed with personal fame."*** "You like famous teachers more than Me."*** "You are foolishly impressed by teachers who serve their own egos rather than God."*** "You stupidly admire insecure people who seek personal fame."*** "You welcome and accept people who, filled with egotism, prove that they have no real spirituality."*** "You celebrate and applaud those who are most selfish and arrogant."***

44. "How is it possible for you to believe, when you are receiving confirmation from each other?" "How can you believe in the deeper Mind, the higher nature, when all you seek is human confirmation from each other?"*** "You cannot believe in inner greater Reality, because your search for outer validation cripples you."*** "You are spiritually stunted by your own quest for fame, and so, cannot believe."*** "Your need to find human approval and applause paralyzes any chance of spiritual growth."*** "Your belief in intrinsic selfworth is shattered by the need to hear others praise you."*** "Your need for fame betrays your inner emptiness."*** "Value found in human recognition is illusory and transient."*** "The applause of the crowd immediately dies, leaving nothing."*** "Only the treasure of genuine Selfapproval supports the timeless life, lasting forever."*** "The need to be approved by the crowd is a spiritual disease."*** "You will never know your truest Self if you define yourself in terms of what others think."***

"You do not seek the honor that arises from only God." "True, genuine, valid Selfaffirmation arises from only Sourcemind."*** "A truly positive Selfimage arises from only the inner cosmic Mind."*** "Really feeling good about yourself can come from only Love."*** "A real sense of worth and worthiness arises from only the inner Spirit."*** "Feeling good about yourself can come from only the inner divine Mind."*** "You have tragically, pathetically forgotten that you need nothing but divine approval."*** "The inner sense of value is everything."*** "Without real Selflove, all the approval in the world means nothing."*** "It is enough infinitely to be loved by the inner Master."*** "Only when you have forgotten infinite Love do you long for, become the slave of, tawdry counterfeits."***

45. "Do not think that I will accuse you before the father." "There will be no need for Me to accuse you before the father."** "The Spirit of Love does not make accusations."*** "Love does not condemn you."*** "The holy Spirit does not use blame, accusations, and guilt."*** "Christ does not accuse you of anything."*** "In the world

of the Absolute Mind, you are already perfect, and perfectly forgiven."*** "If you are accused, it will be by your own deeper Self, your Soul."*** "You might blame yourselves, and justly, for many actions. But the inner Spirit holds nothing against you."*** "The Spirit of Love, allcompassionate, allforgiving, will not accuse you."***

"Instead, you will be accused by Moses, in whom you trust." "Since you have broken your own religious laws, which you trust, your own conscience will accuse you."*** "You are accused by your own strict interpretations of religious laws."*** "The laws which you use to condemn others will condemn you, in your own deeper Mind."*** "You are accused only by what you believe in."*** "Strict and merciless legalism, of your own making, is what condemns you."*** "The laws of Moses were harsh and unforgiving, and you allow yourselves to be accused by these, which you trust." *** "You are accused by your own harsh standards of 'righteousness' and judgment, found in the unfair and cruel laws of Moses."*** "Because you trust in laws and obedience to make you 'good' and acceptable to God, you unconsciously accuse yourselves when you break those laws."*** "The unforgiving law leaves you feeling unforgiven."*** "If you believe that a harsh law is 'just,' then your own deeper Mind will judge you harshly."*** "The same rigid, inflexible law designed to make you 'righteous' now makes you unrighteous."***

***

The narrative continues with chapter 6, verse 26:
"I tell you the truth: You are not looking for Me because you saw the signs, but because you ate the bread and satisfied your hunger." "You do not seek Me because you saw the signs that I was enlightened, but because I gave you bread to fill your bellies."*** "You don't seek Me because you saw the signs, or want the Power, of God's Love. You just want more to eat."*** "You say that you are looking for Me, but this is simply to satisfy your greed for material gain."*** "You are trying to use Me not to find the divine nature, but to satisfy the lower one."***

27. "Don't work for only food that perishes, but for that which lasts." "Don't work for only material gain, but work for Love, and you will have lasting treasure."*** "Do not let greed master you, to

work only for the perishable rewards of the 'material' world. Work, instead, for the Spirit of Love."*** "Material things only turn to dust, but the treasures of Love are an investment in forever."***

"For this true food will be given in timeless life, given to you by the son of man." "Everlasting spiritual treasure is known only in timeless life, discovered by the human nature."** "Timeless life comes through, by rising above, your own human nature."*** "Ultimate Reality is known only in the state of timeless being."*** "Only in enlightenment do you find your true sustenance and nourishment."***

"For God the father has confirmed him [son of man]." "The Sourcemind has declared that the human nature is good."*** "God the Sourcemind has declared the human nature, although unreal, as a real teacher."*** "God does not deny the temporary existence of human nature. He bids us use it as a tool for learning."*** "God infuses human nature with Light and Love, making it son-nature."*** "When the divine Mind fills up human nature, it becomes more than human."***

"For God the father has imprinted him with the seal of his ownership." "The Sourcemind has impressed its own pattern upon the human nature, declaring that nature to be Its own possession."*** "Deep in the Mind, Sourcemind has declared that even lower human nature belongs to none other but infinite Mind."*** "God has impressed into the texture of human nature the impression of divine nature."*** "God's own Loveform is impressed into human nature as a seal into clay."*** "Human nature is divine nature obscured by dust."*** "As a seal of gold impresses itself upon clay, so the divine nature impresses Itself upon human nature."*** "A divine spiritual Image is precisely transferred to the human mind."*** "The divine nature of Love is interwoven into the fiber of human nature and being."*** "Human beings are stamped from a mold of Love (God)."***

***

The narrative continues with chapter 6, verse 29:
"This is God's work: Believe in the One Whom God sends." "The true work of God is not Scriptures and obedience. It is this: Believe in the manifestation of divine Love within your own minds."*** "This is

all that God wants you to do: Believe that the inner Spirit is emanated from God, and is real."*** "To work the work of God, believe in the superordinate Reality of the Spirit of Love which he beams forth into the mind."*** "If you would do what God wills, believe in the inner Essence of Love and Light."*** "If you want to do the work of God, then deeper Mind must be more real to you than your human self."*** "Believe in the perfect, flawless inner Core of your being."*** "Believe in only those things within you that are divine elements, of God."*** "Believe in the holiness of Love."*** "Believe that your Lovenature is more real than fearnature or human nature."***

***

The narrative continues with chapter 6, verse 32:

"I tell you the truth: Moses did not give you bread out of heaven." "Moses did not speak all the words of God."** "Not everything that Moses said was from heaven."** "The words of Moses, and his laws, are not the words and laws of God."** "Your ancient laws do not give you the true heavenly sustenance."*** "You cannot find Love or God through laws or writings alone."*** "Bible-study will never support your interior spiritual nature."*** "Scriptures are not enough to sustain a living relationship with God."*** "Ancient texts cannot possibly keep you alive spiritually."***

"But my father gives the true bread from heaven." "True inner life is sustained only by the inner Sourcemind."*** "The elements of your true spiritual life come only from the cosmic, infinite Mind."*** "Only Sourcemind is the Source of this sustenance."*** "The Spirit of Love alone can supply inner spiritual nourishment."***

33. "The bread of God comes from heaven." "Spiritual sustenance comes only from the highest inner Source."*** "Inner nourishment blossoms from highest Mind."*** "The bread of God is heavenly being."*** "That which maintains inner spiritual life is divine Mind."*** "The Essence of divine 'food' is Love from deeper Mind."*** "God, or Lovemind, is 'food' for inner Mind and Spirit."***

"He who descends from heaven is the true bread of God." "The heavenly Mind, descending to the human mind, is what nourishes spirituality."*** "Only heavenly thoughts of higher Mind, brought down to lower mind, can nourish the inner and deeper Self."*** "The

42

heavenly Self is Itself the divine sustenance."*** "You are sustained by the Being of God, which descends upon your mind from higher Mind."*** "The divine nature within is Selfsustaining."***

"He gives life to the world." "The inner divine One gives life to the entire natural order."** "He gives life to the entire living world."** "He is the life within all living forms."*** "He energizes the entire world."*** "He energizes the Mind to see the world."*** "From the Mind of this Spirit, the entire cosmos arises."*** "Spiritual thought is transformed into the 'material' world."*** "Through his agency, Mind becomes world."*** "The one Mind is contained and reflected in all things."*** "It is translated as all things."*** "The one Mind fills all the universes."*** "The whole world is God modified." ***

***

The narrative continues with chapter 6, verse 35:

"I am the bread of life." "I am the embodiment of spiritual nourishment."*** "I am the Spirit that sustains all life."*** "I am the deepest inner Mind that gives life to all."*** "I am the Being of Light and life within you."*** "I live within you as the Source of your inner life."***

"He who comes to Me will never hunger." "He who comes to Me has no further need of spiritual nourishment."** "He is satisfied forever."** "He is permanently filled."** "He will never feel empty again."** "He has no need for any other Source of inner nourishment."*** "Whoever discovers Me within herself will never need or desire anything but Me, but Love."*** "Hunger dies in those who know Me."***

"And he who believes in Me will never be thirsty." "He will never feel unrefreshed."*** "He will cease to long for satisfaction from the 'material' world."*** "She will no longer find her refreshment in the senses, but only in Me."***

36. "You have already seen Me, but still do not believe." "Even after having caught a vision of Me within your deeper Self, still you do not believe in My reality."*** "If you would only believe it, you have already encountered Me within your own being, for I am your deepest Mind."*** "You have already, without knowing It, experienced My inner Presence."*** "You were unaware because you

43

did not believe what you touched."*** "In order to know the inner Spirit of Love, you must first believe in It."*** "I am undetectable only to those who do not believe in My reality."*** "Everyone has experienced Me, but those who do not believe do not know."*** "You have already uncovered Me within, but still do not believe in Your divine nature."***

37. "All that the father gives Me will come to Me." "All that the Sourcemind says is mine will be mine."** "You will come to Me when it is his time."*** "The whole cosmos has been given to Me, for it is through Me that it is created."*** "All [people] will come to Me, for God has given all to Me."***

"Whoever comes to Me will never be rejected, excommunicated,* shunned,* or disfellowshipped* by Me." "I will never push anyone away."** "I will never repel anyone."** "I will never expel or exclude anyone."** "I will never reject anyone."** "I will never refuse friendship, Love, or acceptance to anyone."*** "I will never cast anyone aside or away."*** "I will view no one as an outsider."*** "I welcome and accept all beings, with Love, into Myself."*** "I absorb all beings, without favoritism or prejudice, into divine nature."*** "Divine Love never rejects, or turns away from, anyone."*** "Love includes all living creatures."*** "I am bonded to all by Love, and all are bonded to Me."*** "I know no strangers."*** "I will never push anyone away."***

38. "I came from heaven not to satisfy my own desires." "My Origin, Source, and Home is the highest Mind. I came down to the human level, but not because it was what I wanted."*** "I flow and unfold from the highest Mind of knowing. But this is not to do my own will."*** "I emerge into the common human mind, but not to fulfill any personal desires."***

"I came to do the will of him who sent me." "I came only to fulfill the will of the Sourcemind, which created me and sent me forth."*** "What the deepest Mind wants, I want."*** "The One Who projected me has his own wishes; I seek to fulfill them, not to create others of my own."*** "The cosmic Mind that beamed me forth has Its own will, which is all that I want to do."*** "I am projected into the natural order, to fulfill the desire of the Lovemind."***

39. "And this is his will: I will lose no one out of all whom he has given Me. Each one will I raise up on the last day of his life." "It is

the will of the Sourcemind that I lose no one, and he has given me everyone. On the last day of life, I will welcome all into timeless life."** "And his will is this: No one is to be lost. I will come to each, on the last day of her life, and welcome her into her everlasting Home."*** "His will is this: All will be saved. I will come to each, on the final day of life, as the deep Mind."*** "The Sourcemind has given all being to Me, and none will be lost. In fact, I will come to each at the moment of death, and welcome each into new life."*** "On the final day of her life, I will bring each person into a new form."*** "I will welcome each into the afterlife."*** "I will welcome each into heaven."*** "I will welcome each into the Homeworld."***

40. "And the will of the One Who sent Me is that everyone who perceives and believes in the son has timeless life. And I will raise him up on his last day." "Sourcemind wills that everyone who knows that sonmind exists, and believes that it is real, has timeless life. On her last day on earth, I will lift her out of her body."*** "Whoever knows sonship— the mergence of divine and human— already has timeless life. On her last day on earth, I will lift her consciousness."***

***

The narrative continues with chapter 6, verse 44:

"No one can come to Me unless he is drawn by the father who sent Me." "No one can approach enlightenment unless she is attracted by the Sourcemind."*** "No one can discover Me deep within Mind by an act of simple human will. I can be found only when it is the will of deepest Mind."*** "Only Love can draw beings into communion with Me."*** "People discover Me out of attraction, not out of compulsion."*** "You cannot draw close to My nature unless you are attracted by the Lovenature."***

"And I will raise him up on the final day." "I will lift her Mind on the last day of her life."*** "On the final day that she is on earth, I will come to her, and lift her out of her body."*** "On the final day of her earthlife, I will raise and elevate her Mind."***

45. "It was written by your prophets, 'They will all be taught by God.'" "Even your prophets foretold, 'All people will be taught directly by God.'"*** "You can go within yourself to learn all that

45

you have to know, for even your prophets spoke about this. They said, 'All the people will be taught directly by God himself.'"*** "So, every person hears and learns directly from the inner father."*** "Each person learns privately and secretly from the private Sourcemind."*** "Love perfectly directs each person to find the inner Lovenature."*** "God personally instructs those who have found the deeper, higher Selves of Soul and Spirit."*** "You have no need for human teachers, for God is capable of teaching your heart directly, and promises to do that."***

46. "No one has seen the father except the one who is of God." "Only the Mind that comes directly from God can 'see' God."** "Only those who know their unity with divine nature can fully experience the presence of Lovemind."*** "Most people have no idea of what 'divine nature' means."*** "Only those who have sensed and experienced It directly and immediately can understand It."*** "Only those who live in Love, who have been touched by Lovemind, know Love in Its wholeness."*** "Only the person who remembers that she is originally from God can know God."*** "Vision of the Eternalove is granted to only those who know."***

47. "He who believes in Me already has timeless life." "Eternal life is not something in the future. If you believe in My reality, you are living in it now."*** "He who believes that I, and Sourcemind, are more real than all else already lives in timeless life."***

48. "For I am the bread that gives life." "I am the bread from which life arises."** "I am the bread that supports life."** "I am the nourishment that supports inner life."*** "I am the sonmind within you that sustains your inner life."***

***

The narrative continues with chapter 6, verse 50:

"If a person eats of this bread, he will never die." "If a person absorbs Me, and thus becomes Soul rather than body, she will never die."*** "Since she will draw life from an infinite Source, her life will be endless."***

51. "I am the living bread that comes from heaven. If anyone eats of this bread, he will live in timeless life." "My Mind is the nourishment that sustains real inner life, for I originate with heavenly Mind. If anyone comes into union with Me, she will partake of this

timeless state."*** "I give the true life of the Soul, for I draw My Mind from infinite Mind. Anyone who melds her mind with Mine is drawn into eternal life."*** "I am the sustaining Spirit of enlightenment at the core of your being. Whoever partakes of Me will live in timeless life."***

"And the bread that I will give is My flesh. I will give it for the life of the world." "The origin of spiritual sustenance is the lower, fleshly nature. This nature must disappear to help transform the world."*** "Higher nature must emerge from lower nature, which must vanish into Spirit for the good of all physical beings."*** "The best of Spiritlove often is born from having lived in a physical body. When this body pushes you above itself, the whole of the natural order benefits."*** "The drives of the physical body can be turned towards Sourcemind, and this will sustain spiritual development. It will also make the world a better place for all living creatures."*** "The flesh is 'fuel' for the 'fire' (Light and warmth) of Spirit. When fleshmind becomes Spiritmind, all creatures gain."*** "Spirit will consume fleshnature, liberating energy to heal the entire natural order."*** "When I am no longer incarnated in a single body, My Mindenergy will be released for all living creatures."*** "The death of the lower nature is the beginning of the life of the higher. So, your 'death' to the fleshmind is My resurrection within you. And this, in time, will apply to all living creatures."*** "Within you all, I continually sacrifice My lower nature, so that the higher might live, and be expressed, within all the natural order of life."***

***

The narrative continues with chapter 6, verse 53:
"If you do not eat the flesh of the son of man, and drink his blood, you have no life in yourself." "If you do not consume the lower, fleshly nature of the human mind in the deeper Mind, and use your life-energy to support this, you have no selforiginated life."** "You must absorb into your deeper Self (Soul) the lower or fleshly nature of human nature. You must use the life-force of this system to support interior growth. For if you do not do these two things, the life in you will not be selforiginated or selfsustaining."*** "You must draw sustenance from the subsuming of your lower nature, while still on earth. You must, as Souls, 'ingest' and assimilate Its very essence, Its

power. Only then will your life be selfcreated."*** "Every lifelement of every aspect of your nature must be consumed by spiritual power, until the lower nature is fully dissolved in Love and Light. For the lower nature, and its body, have no life in themselves."*** "Do not see lower nature, with its body of flesh and blood, as opposed to the Spirit. For the 'material' is a subset within spiritual Reality."***

54. "So, whoever eats My flesh and drinks My blood has timeless life." "Whoever uses spirit to consume and assimilate the energy of flesh has timeless life."*** "Whoever allows the inner Spirit to consume the mind of the lower nature, and bend it to serve the higher, begins to live in the timeless condition."***

"Him I will raise up at the final day." "I will come to her, lifting her above body and lower mind, on the final day of her life on earth."*** "I will raise her to new levels of awareness and experience, moving her Soul into a Lightbody."*** "I will raise her sensory capacities, so that she can know and be aware of a new cosmos all around her."***

55. "For My flesh is true food, and My blood true drink." "For the sustaining energy of the Christ, fed into the lower nature, truly sustains only the higher. And life-energy given to the lower is also designed to support the higher."*** "Spirituality must be created out of the elements of the lower nature, for you have no other resources."***

56. "For only he who eats My flesh and drinks My blood dwells in Me, and I in him." "Only the one who uses the energy and sustenance usually given to the lower nature to sustain the higher lives in Me, as deepest Mind. As that Mind, I also dwell deeply within her mind."*** "I am the inner Mindspirit. Only she who de-identifies with the world can identify with Me. And only she who sacrifices the lower self, recycling its energies into the higher Mind, finds Me."*** "Only through dissolution and assimilation of the energies of the lower nature can anyone find Me as the Core of innermost Mind."***

57. "The living father has sent Me. I live by the father. Even so, he that eats Me will live by Me." "Sourcemind has formed Me and sent Me into the common world. My life is really his life living through me. In the same way, anyone consuming the lower nature in the higher will live by means of My life, the timeless life of Spiritmind."*** "I draw sustenance from infinite Mind. In the same

way, I will become the sustenance of anyone who assimilates My Mind into her personal mind."*** "I will mediate between the human and the divine, for I am sonmind. To assimilate this knowing is to draw life from My bottomless Source."*** "I draw life from the Sourcemind. So, she who assimilates My being, with all earthly and heavenly elements, will similarly draw her life from Me. I will be the sonmind within her."***

***

The narrative continues with chapter 6, verse 62:

"What, then, if you see the son of man ascending to where he was before?" "What will be your response if you see human nature returning inwardly to its divine Source?"** "How would you feel if you 'saw' human nature moving up the spiritual ladder, back towards God?"*** "What if you saw human nature metamorphosing back to the state it was before it became human?"*** "What if human nature entered a spiritual plane, returning to its original condition?"***

63. "It is the Spirit that gives life; the flesh is of no value." "Life arises from the infinite Mind; the lower nature is of no value."** "Life emerges as a product of cosmic Mind; biomind is of limited relevance."*** "Life originates with Spiritmind; the body is only an instrument through which the Soul grows and learns."*** "Life itself has nothing to do with the world of the lower nature and its perceptions."*** "Life is spiritual, not merely biological."*** "The entire lower nature is only a moment in the transformative process; it adds nothing to the true quality of life."*** "The 'material' world has no intrinsic value."*** "In the great spiritual process of life, the place of the physical body, and its nature, is negligible."*** "The lower nature, being illusion, contributes nothing real."*** "The Lovenature generates life; the fearnature is simply the cocoon from which it must emerge."***

"The words that I have spoken are Spirit and life." "This message is lifenhancing and spiritual."** "These words are from Spirit, communicated to Spirit; and since life emerges from Spirit, they are lifenhancing."*** "These thoughts are the expression of Spirit, and so are life-supporting."*** "Spiritual knowing is life, and these words are from the knowing of Spirit."*** "Knowing and expressing are the essence of Spirit and life."*** "Life is Spirit, Spirit is truth, and truth

49

is expressed by these words."*** "Truth (Reality) arises from the unfolding of infinite Mind. One way that this is done is through knowledge, and that is shared through words."***"Love is the core of both Spirit and life; and these are the words of Love."*** "The ideas that I have shared trigger the force within you, and this Mindforce expresses as both Spirit and life."*** "Both Spirit and life are derived from Mind; and these are the words of purest Mind."***

64. "But some of you do not believe." "Some do not believe in the Reality of Spirit over matter."*** "Some do not believe that Mind is more real than matter."*** "For some, believing in these unseen realities is difficult."*** "Not everyone is capable of opening fully to belief in these teachings."*** "Some just do not understand; and, not understanding, they cannot believe."*** "Some find this teaching completely alien, with no comparisons to everyday life."*** "I speak in a Way which many will find quite incredible, for I speak of Mindworlds."*** "Material minds cannot relate to spiritual ideas."***

65. "That is why I say that no one can come to Me unless he is given that capacity by my father." "No one can come to her inner divinity unless she is called by the Sourcemind."*** "No one can discover the inner divine nature unless she is impelled by the infinite Mind."*** "No one comes to Me, to Christ, by a mere human decision or inclination."***

***

The narrative continues with chapter seven, verse six:

"It isn't My time yet. But it is always your time." "I have a specific time in which I must do things, and say things. But you do and say what you want at any time."*** "That time in My lifepattern has not yet arrived. But your lifepattern is not as bounded as Mine for this life."***

7. "It is not possible for the world to repel you. But by nature, it repels Me." "You are a part of the natural order, and so, it embraces its own. But by its lower nature, the normal order does repel Me."*** "It is because you are so much your natural selves that the order of things receives you. But I am supernatural, and so, it does not receive Me."*** "Bionature is friendlier to you than it is to Me, for I am not a natural part of it."*** "The material universe cannot push away you,

for you are part of it. But Me it repels, for I am not a part of it; it is a part of Me."*** "The natural order of creation creates no antiforce within you. But in Me, nature often disputes with supernature."*** "A 'purely material' interpretation of the cosmos repels Me, but you find it attractive."*** "The natural order of this body is a prison that drives Me towards death and liberation."***

"For I testify that its interactions produce evil results." "Injustice, which is evil, seems to be everywhere in the natural order."*** "The natural order of earth can be outside the patterns of the cosmos."*** "Everything that happens here is illusion, and what seems to be evil is the greatest of them."*** "Only when the natural order is outside of greater Reality can it be seen as evil."*** "Earth is out-of-synch with the cosmic pattern of pure goodness and Love."***

***

The narrative continues with chapter 7, verse 16:

"My teaching is not mine, but belongs to him who sent Me." "These teachings are not from my own mind, but come straight from the Sourcemind deep within, which emanates Me."*** "These teachings do not originate with my personal mind, but come from the deepest Coremind, the Lovemind that creates Me."*** "I teach nothing but the ideas transmitted through Me by the inner Infinite."*** "I did not think of, or make up, these teachings. They come not from me, but from the limitless and hidden Mind."*** "I received rather than conceived these teachings."*** "What I teach is only a reflection of what I am taught by the Spirit."*** "These teachings are the mirrorimage of what the Spirit of Light and Love teaches within you."*** "As I am an extension of the Eternal, so are these teachings."*** "This teaching has nothing to do with formal education; it is the purest wisdom."*** "This teaching is drawn out of the very deepest levels of being."***

17. "The only Way to know this teaching is to do his will." "This teaching is not just a matter of words. It flows from an inner knowing, an experience, of limitless Mind, and then, following his will."*** "This teaching is not academic; it results from a certain Way."*** "This teaching is not just abstract; it results in a Way of life."*** "These mysteries are about, not mere words, but transformation."*** "This is all about abandonment of personal desire, and its replacement

by the desire of universal Love."*** "Before you can know these things, the desire of the deep inner Lovenature must take over your life."*** "To know, in this special Way, is to love."*** "Without full surrender to the Spirit of Love, words alone are shallow and useless."***

"Only he who actually does the will of God can learn whether I speak from myself or from God." "The only Way to know the truth in these important spiritual matters is to do the will of God, which is Love."*** "Only she who loves can know the genuine essence of a teaching, and whether it arises from human or divine nature."***

18. "Anyone who speaks from the self seeks only the 'glorification' of the self." "Anyone who speaks from the lower Mindlevel of the self seeks only praise and selfglorification."** "Whoever speaks from the selflevel of Mind seeks only egogratification and egodisplay."*** "Anyone who teaches about the self, talks too much about the self, is abusing spirituality for ego."*** "Anyone who speaks out of her own education will have only her own thoughts to talk about."*** "When a preacher or teacher seeks only egoglory, then she is stuck with the pitiable contents of her shallow little egomind."*** "As long as a human being is controlling the Mind, it is impossible to soar beyond the human level."*** "Those who seek fame are bound for confusion and pain."*** "The ego creates terrible shackles; the Spirit removes them."*** "Where there is concern for credit and a sense of pride, you are dominated by the 'demon' of self."*** "When true inspiration is present, one is liberated from the self by the 'angel' of the Self."*** "If anyone is concerned over credit from people, then her 'authority' is only human."*** "If anyone seeks popularity, she has fallen into the selfcreated 'hell' of egodominance."***"In seeking personal recognition, one betrays her spiritual backwardness and ignorance."*** "The egoself is its own worst audience, and enemy."***

"But whoever seeks the splendor of the One Who sent him is sincere." "If you direct attention away from yourself to the One, you are more honest."** "The simple honest person seeks to give all credit to the Spirit."*** "The honest person recognizes that she can do nothing spiritual of herself."*** "The wise and secure have no need for personal credit, and so credit all to the Absolute."*** "The open and wise person scatters the credit."***"She speaks from the Mindlevel of inner Splendor, from the One who projects her into the world."*** "Only she who speaks from the Splendor is real and trustworthy; others are fakes."*** "The wise sees the self as only a wave on the gleaming, shimmering sea of being."***

"There is no unrighteousness in him." "The true teacher is fully aligned with the Lovemind."*** "That person is adjusted to the pattern of universal Love."*** "She is in harmony with the Splendor."*** "Free from ego, she merges self with Self, and then, with Spirit."*** "Acting and speaking without conscious direction, she trusts the Sourcemind."*** "As she becomes a mirror of Love, her personal impurities disappear."*** "She becomes pure as she allows the pure One to take over."***

19. "Did not Moses give you your law? And yet, not one of you obeys it." "Not one of you perfectly obeys it."** "Not one of you obeys it to the detail."** "No one is capable of keeping track of, much less obeying, all the complicated laws of Moses."*** "Your Scriptures contain so many detailed laws that no one obeys them all perfectly."*** "True righteousness does not come from obeying the Mosaic law."*** "Scriptures and laws can never make you complete."***

***

The narrative continues with chapter 7, verse 24:
"Do not judge by appearances, but with right judgment." "Don't evaluate matters by the way they appear to be, but let the divine Mind instruct you as to how things really are."*** "Don't weigh and measure things by the appearances of this world. Instead, go within, to deepest Mind, and find the right criteria for decision."*** "Appearances are only illusion; don't be misled by them. Instead, go within to the deepest Coremind, to discern what is truly good and 'bad' for you."*** "If you must make evaluations, then do so only on the basis of divine Love."*** "If you must measure, do not trust what you think you see, but trust only universal Love."*** "Measure not by human standards, but only in right alignment with universal Love."*** "Learn to see everything through the eyes of Love."*** "If you see with divine vision, then you will judge all things to be good."*** "External appearances deny truth; truth can deny what you

think you know."*** "Do not waste time with superficial opinion-formation. But try to see the world as pure and good, as God sees it."*** "Integrate with higher wisdom."*** "Never judge at all from the way things seem or appear. Judging with only Love, you will come to regard all things as good."***

***

The narrative continues with chapter 7, verse 28:

"Yes, you know me, and you know where I am from. But I have not come of myself." "You know this man before you, and know even what town he is from. But this human self is not My origin."** "You know my human form. But I am not coming to you as a mere human being."*** "You know the visible part of Me. But I now come to you as Mind, and that is invisible."*** "I come to you as the incarnation of Love."*** "I come to you as deepest Mind." *** "I come to you as my real Self which is Spirit." *** "I reflect the deepest Mind within you."*** "I come as One you do not know, and cannot see."***

"For he who sent Me is true, and you do not know him." "The deepest Mind from which I emanate is Reality, but you do not know It."*** "The Mind that projects Me is real."*** "The Mindspirit that beams me forth is Reality."*** "The Being of Whom I am only a projection is real."*** "The Mind of which I am the embodiment is genuine."***

29. "But I do know him, because I am from him, and he has sent Me." "I know this deepest Mindspirit, because I arise directly from It, and it is this Spiritmind that has beamed Me into common reality."*** "I know him intimately because our natures are One, and he is the Sourcemind that projects Me into the world."*** "I arise directly from him, like the light from the sun, and he has shone Me into this dark world."*** "I know him because I am of his very nature, a part of his Mind."*** "I know him profoundly because I am his manifestation, reflection, and expression."***

***

The narrative continues with chapter 7, verse 33:

"I will be with you just a little longer, and then, I will return to him who sent Me." "I will be in this earthform for just a while, and then, I will sink back into the Mind of bliss which is My Origin."***

"I will soar back into delicious oneness with the Sourcemind."*** "I will go to heaven, that is, move into heavenly, perfect, blissful Lovemind."*** "I will return to the spiritual state that is My true Home."*** "I'll go back into my deeper Self."*** "I will return to complete, universal Mind."*** "I'll give up the illusion of separation, and return to the Mind of universal Love from which I coalesced."*** "I will shed this dreambody, and return to the state of splendor."*** "I will soon return to the inner kingdom of Light and Love, from which I originally came."*** "I must return to the state of undifferentiated, cosmic Being."*** "I will return to bliss, tranquility, and Love."***

34. "You will look for Me and not find Me. For where I am, you cannot come, when I will have returned to him who sent me." "You can probe into the deep inner Mind as much as possible, but will find no traces of Me. There, in the deepest fathoms of Mindspirit, you will find only the Sourcemind, with which I have fully merged."*** "When you seek this son-nature, you will not be able to find it, for it will have merged again indistinguishably with the inner Sourcemind."*** "If you look for Me in this present form, you will not find Me. Indeed, I am already at a point in relationship (with the One) that you cannot reach."*** "When I return to that state of bliss and wholeness, you will not be able immediately to follow."***

***

The narrative continues with chapter 7, verse 37:

"If anyone is thirsty, let him come to Me and drink." "If you need refreshment from this dry world, you will find it with only Me."** "If anyone longs for peace, let her approach me within her own mind, and I will satisfy her."*** "If you long for ultimate Love, approach Me in the inner chamber of the heart, and I will refresh you."***

38. "Whoever believes in Me, out of his inner being will flow rivers of the water of life, as the Scripture says, "Whoever believes that I am real, from her deepest Mind will flow the waters of life."*** "Whoever knows My ultimate reality will release floods and torrents of lifenergy."*** "The inner springs will bubble up in refreshment and cleansing, renewing and recreating life."***

***

The narrative continues with chapter 8, verse 7:

"Whoever has no sin, let him cast the first stone." "To be human is to be imperfect."*** "To be human is to sin."*** "The only way that you can gain the right to judge others morally is to have attained a sinless state yourself."*** "When you seek to punish others, it is because, deep down, you feel the need for selfpunishment."*** "If you judge the absolute moral value of anyone to be less, it is because you do not trust yourself."*** "Those who speak the most loudly of 'righteousness' and 'God' are often selfhaters who feel dirty inside."***

***

The narrative continues with chapter 8, verse 10:

[Jesus said to the woman,] "Where are your accusers? Didn't anyone condemn you?

11. "I don't condemn you either. Go, and practice sin no more." "I do not condemn honest mistakes."*** "Learning through mistakes is not condemnable."*** "Being human means that mistakes are inevitable."*** "Mistakes are a natural part of life— sometimes, even big ones."*** "Because you have made a mistake does not make you 'bad'."*** "An honest mistake is different from deliberate action."*** "I forgive all mistakes, but also warn not voluntarily to repeat harmful actions."*** "Imperfection is integral to ultimate perfection."*** "Much 'sin' is ignorance or inexperience. So, 'sin' is often error."*** "Let not error dominate your thoughts, but replace it with Love."*** "I do not keep account of the injury of error, but long to turn you away from destructive acts."***

12. "I am the Light of the world." "My mind illuminates the natural order."** "I bring dark areas of Mind to the Light of awareness."*** "I make unconscious things conscious."*** "I am the spiritual Light of enlightenment."*** "I am the Light of Mind behind the natural order."*** "The essence of the natural order is Light, and I am that Light."*** "I am the Lightmind that holds matter together."*** "I am the Projector of Lightmind, and that Lightmind Itself."*** "I am the Mindlight that gives color, form, meaning, and pattern to the physical cosmos."*** "I am the Lightshow of the cosmos."***

"He who follows Me will never walk in darkness." "Walk in My path, and inner darkness will never blind your Mind."** "The one who knows as I know is free of Mindspiritual darkness."*** "She will never stray into the nonexistent."*** "She will never drift into illusion."*** "She will never live in shadowmind, the desert of loveless mind."*** "She will always avoid inner emptiness and oblivion."*** "Ignorance will have no place in her permanent heartmind."*** "The Light of Love will chase away the darkness and shadow of fear."*** "She will never become lost in the dreamworld, letting it dominate her."*** "Her inner eye will never be blinded."***

"He will have the Light of life." "She will be guided by the Light that also produces life itself."** "She will possess the Light that is the Source of life."** "She will own her own inner Light, the Light that supports both life and Mind."*** "She will have the Mindlight that makes both life and clear perception possible."*** "She will know that life comes from Light, and she will have that Light within her."*** "Light is the cause of perception, and perception the cause of Reality. So, this Light makes Reality (truth) possible. She will have this Light of truth."*** "The secret of all life is in Light."*** "The entire living universe is Light."*** "Light is the inner Formcreator, a part of the Creator."*** "She will be able to read the colors of life."*** "She will know that all Light is within her."***

***

The narrative continues with chapter 8, verse 14:

"I know where I come from, and where I am going." "My Source and My Destination are one: I come from Sourcemind, and I return there."*** "My Origin is My Destination."*** "I possess direct awareness of My Source."*** "I know the Sourcemind intimately."***

"But you do not know where I come from, and where I am going." "You do not know the Sourcemind."*** "You do not understand the mystery of Mind and existence."***

15. "You judge through the flesh." "You make absolute evaluations through the lenses of the lower nature."*** "You form opinions based upon the unreliable information of your senses."*** "Your spiritual senses are dulled and eclipsed by the high activity of your physical senses."***

"I do not judge at all." "I do not evaluate the absolute value of any person, thing, or event."** "As the Christ nature, the enlightened son-nature, I do not judge."*** "Knowing all about all, I choose not to judge the eternal merits of anything or anyone."*** "I do not condemn anything or anyone."*** "I do not divide things and people from Sourcemind."*** "I have seen the wholeness, rightness, and goodness of everything."*** "I do not impose the label of 'evil' upon the goodness of the cosmos, for personal preferences."***

16. "And yet, if I were to judge, I would make sure that My judgment was true." "Even if I were to judge, the judgment would not arise from the illusion of 'evil,' but would reflect the Sourcemind, in Its allgood Totality."*** "What might seem to you to be My opinions are actually direct manifestations of Reality."*** "My expressions flow, unaltered, from deepest Mind."*** "If I do evaluate anything, the standards are not personal preferences, or 'evil' illusions, but the clear vision of universal Love."*** "Do not confuse My expression of truth (Reality) for mere judgment."*** "Anything that I say is the perfect reflection of absolute Reality, and, hence, not judgment."***

"For I am not alone, but the father who sent Me is with Me." "I do not express personal opinions, but speak the words of the Sourcemind."*** "What I say is not personal, but embodies the Mind of the Source; that Mind sent Me, and is always within Me."*** "My human self is not all there is."*** "I am one with the Sourcemind, and when I speak, it is He/She who speaks."*** "I am the living expression, not of a personal self, but of the Sourcemind."*** "My humanity is completely saturated with My divinity."*** "The divinity that projects Me into humanity is always my truest, highest, deepest Self."***

***

The narrative continues with chapter 8, verse 19:
"You know neither Me nor My father." "You know neither the Christ-nature nor the Sourcemind."*** "You know neither the state of enlightened Mind nor Its Source."*** "You do not know God, either as Origin, or as Spirit incarnated within human beings."*** "You have not experienced the Mindarea where the divine and human overlap, called 'Christ,' nor have you known divine Mind as Fountain of everything."*** "You have failed to see people as translations of

God, or to see God as the Origin of all."*** "You have perceived neither humanity nor the cosmos as equally extensions of God's infinite Being."***

"For if you had known Me, you would have known My father." "To know the enlightened human Mind is to know the Sourcemind."*** "To know God as Love in humanity is to know God as infinite Mind."*** "If you can see God in human beings, you will know the God Who takes care of things through people."*** "If you could see God in Me, you would then see him/her in yourself."*** "If you see how God manifests himself/herself, then you can know all that can be known about him/her, through Love."*** "Intimately to touch the human mind is to know divine Mind."*** "If you had known My Lovenature, you would have known the Sourcemind."*** "If you learn to see God in people, then you will see him/her everywhere."*** "If you knew that divinity contains humanity, it would be clear that humanity contains divinity."***

***

The narrative continues with chapter 8, verse 21:

"I go My Way. You will look for Me, and die in your sins." "I must walk the path that expresses perfect Lovemind. You will seek enlightenment within, but will leave this world still bound by ignorance and illusion."*** "You will continue in density and imperfection until the present life ends."*** "When I leave this human state, you will then have to seek for yourselves the divine nature that I embody, and will not be able to find it. For you will be dulled and insensitive due to your ignorance."*** "You will die in awareness of imperfection and incompleteness, still believing the lie of separation."*** "Believing yourselves forever and irreversibly separated from perfect Mind, you will close off yourselves to the reception of perfecting grace."***

"And where I go, you cannot come." "I return to the state of perfect melding and fusing with perfect Coremind. You, due to ignorance, cannot allow this to happen in your minds."*** "At present, you are incapable of complete surrender to, and dissolution in, Lovemind."*** "You will not allow yourselves to disappear into Sourcemind."***

***

The narrative continues with chapter 8, verse 23:

"You are from below, and I am from above." "You originate with lower, human mind and nature, while I originate with higher, deeper nature."*** "You are from the 'material' nature, while I am from the spiritual nature."*** "Your human nature is so overdeveloped that you feel that you are nothing but human; I am much more than human."*** "You believe, in illusion, that your origins are in the animal world; I know that Mine are mental and spiritual."*** "You see yourselves as products of the world, but I am a product of Sourcemind."*** "You have not seen the higher Splendor within, and so feel comfortable with earth; but Splendor is My Home."*** "My Home is not within the world about which you all agree; Mine is a higher Reality."*** "You see yourselves as part of the natural order; I am a part of the supernatural Mind."*** "You see yourselves as bodies; I know Myself to be a timeless Spirit."***

24. "This is why I said that you will die in your sins." "You will die in an awareness of imperfection."** "Because you think that you are bodies, you will carry to your graves a sense of sin and guilt."*** "You never recognize that you are really flawless Lovemind."*** "Unless you realize that My Reality is greater than your own, you will carry a sense of guilt until you die."*** "Until you realize that the spiritual is more real than the material, the Lovenature than the fearnature, you will carry the burden of guilt until death frees you from it."*** "Fear, with exaggerated awareness of mistakes, will dominate you until your deaths."*** "Unless Christmind, with grace, becomes superordinate in you, over the mind of guilt, you will die in a sense of incompleteness."***

25. "I am exactly Who I told you I was, from the beginning." "I am, as I told you, the Beginning of [creation]."*** "I am the Christ-nature, the embodiment of the enlightened human mind."*** "I am the inner Teacher, who has taught you since the beginning of time."*** "I am your inner Teacher, and have used your responses to the world to educate you."***

26. "How many ideas there are, of which I could speak! And how many judgments I could pass on you! But he who sent me is real, and I must tell the world of those things which he taught Me." "How vast is the universe and the cosmic Mind from which it arises every moment! And how vast are your errors! But I have come here to

reveal only Reality, those things taught to Me by the Sourcemind."*** "How many things I could tell you about yourselves! But My mission is to teach the nature of reality as I learned it directly from the deepest Coremind."*** "The deepest Mind, from which I am projected, also projects everything and everyone else. So, It is Reality Itself."*** "I can share with people only what I have heard from deepest Mindspirit."*** "I speak not personal revelations, but that of the Absolute, who projects Me into this present form."*** "I could share so many facts and opinions with you about yourself. But I have not come to satisfy personal desires or curiosities. Instead, I have come to speak of the will of the cosmic Mind, the will of Lovemind."***

***

The narrative continues with chapter 8, verse 28:

"When you have lifted up the son of man, then you will know that I am he." "When you have elevated human nature to a higher level, then you will know that I have my roots in that very nature."*** "Only when you have exalted human nature will you know that divine nature indwells it."*** "Only after you exalt the Christ-nature, the enlightened human nature, you will know that I am the incarnation of that nature."*** "When you have lifted up the enlightened human nature to divine nature, the borders that separate them will disappear."*** "You will see that I, the Spirit, exist as both natures."*** "You will know My true identity only when you share it."*** "You will know Who I am only when you become What I am."*** "Only when your human nature reaches its zenith, disappearing into higher nature, can you understand Me."*** "I cannot be known by words alone; I can fully be known only by an elevation of your inner being."***

"For then you will know: I do nothing for myself. I can speak these things only as My father has taught Me." "I do nothing, as a man. I teach only what the inner Sourcemind teaches Me."***

29. "He who sent Me is with Me. I do nothing of myself." "The Sourcemind, who projects Me into the world, is always with and within me. All is done for deepest Lovemind, and nothing for the self."***

***

61

The narrative continues with chapter 8, verse 31:

"If you continue in My Logos, you are really My disciples." "If you work to become the perfect manifestation of the pure Sourcemind, Coremind, Lovemind, you will truly be My followers."*** "It is only by trying, as I do, to reflect perfect inner Mind that you can show that you are really learning from Me." *** "To be My followers, you must also tread the path of this inner journey, revealing the perfect expression of perfect Lovemind."*** "Believing certain teachings is not enough. You must also work hard to reveal, in crystal clarity, the unimpeded expression of God in your lives, as Love."*** "No one is My follower who has not striven and struggled to disappear into the expression of Coremind."*** "No one is following Me if she has not erased the self of the lower nature, so that the Self of the higher might shine through into the world."*** "No one is my disciple if she has not exchanged her human nature for Lovenature, her human mind for Lovemind."***"If Love is not being expressed consistently within you, then you are not My disciples."*** "Only when your expressions are My expressions can you be said truly to be My disciples."*** "You have not learned anything of value until you become transparent to the inner Light of the Logos of Love."***

32. "And you will know the truth, and the truth will set you free." "You will know what is real, and Reality will liberate you."** "You will know Reality directly, and this will liberate you."** "To know Reality is to find freedom."** "Knowing what is real brings ultimate liberty."** "Being able to discern Reality as Mind from illusion as world produces ultimate freedom."*** "Reality is the Logos or expression of God. When you directly know Logos, by becoming It, the world can no longer bind you."*** "When you realize that Sourcemind, as Creator, fills and permeates all, then you will be free."*** "Awakening to the realization that all is God, all is good, brings fullest liberation."*** "All reality is a projection of Lovemind; this knowing brings liberation."***

***

The narrative continues with chapter 8, verse 34:

"Whoever sins becomes sin's slave." "Whoever serves ignorance is the slave of ignorance."** "Whoever keeps making mistakes becomes a slave to mistakes."** "Whoever makes errors becomes a slave to their effects."*** "Whoever believes and lives in imperfection becomes bound by that belief, and has lost her freedom."*** "If you live and think as if you were incomplete, that will make you incomplete."*** "If you live and think as if you were separate, that belief will make you separate."*** "If you believe in guilt, you have surrendered your joy and freedom to guilt."*** "If you live with a belief that many things are 'sin,' that belief will become your harsh and cruel master."***

35. "A slave does not remain in the home forever. Only a son remains forever." "A slave is not allowed into the Home to stay forever. Only a son or daughter is allowed to live there forever."** "If you choose to live as a slave to unwholesome imperfection and ignorance, you will not be allowed to find rest in the Sourcemind forever. Only after you have discovered your son-nature will you permit yourself to remain there forever."*** "As long as you believe yourself to be a sinful human being, your own mind will not permit you to enter the Original Mind, Homemind."*** "Belief in sin will move you away from your true inner spiritual Home, the Garden of Pleasure8" *** "If you make yourself a slave of limitation, how can you stay indefinitely in the unlimited Mind?"*** "You cannot stay in timeless life if you believe yourself subject to the 'past.'"*** "'Past' is only a mindimage."***

36. "If, then, the son makes you free, you are truly free." "If you are freed by the son-nature— the blend of human and divine—you are genuinely free."*** "If freedom arises from awareness that you are a 'child' of the Sourcemind, then that liberty is real."***

***

The narrative continues with chapter 8, verse 38:

"I speak about only things that I have seen with My father." "I teach only what I found in Sourcemind."*** "I teach only ideas of Sourcemind."*** "Only those things that I have known in oneness with the Sourcemind do I teach." *** "Only those concepts learned while I was submerged in Sourcemind do I reveal here."*** "I speak from the Mindlevel of deepest Coremind."***

---

8 . The allegorical "Eden," which represents perfect Mind means, "pleasure."

"But you do that which you have seen with *your* 'father.'" "You also mirror the mind of your origin."*** "You originate from another Mindlevel, not as deep."*** "What you conceive to be your source is not deepest Mind, Coremind, Lovemind."*** "You draw your self from the human mind only."*** "Your senses have created a false source."***

***

The narrative continues in chapter 8, verse 40:

"I am a man who has told you the truth as I have heard it from God." "My human nature has learned this Reality from deepest, infinite Mind."***

41. "You do the deeds of your father." "You act from the Mindlevel of the source that you recognize."*** "You believe that your source or father is the Jehovah of your ancestors, and it is his behavior that you imitate."***

42. "If God were your real father, you would love Me." "If the deepest Mind were really your Sourcemind, you would love Me, as its unclouded, clear son."*** "If your Source were God, you would show only Love, even to Me."*** "If you were grounded in real Mind, you would show it by Love."*** "If you were generated, formed, created, and projected * by the Sourcemind, you would love."***

"For I was sent by God, and now come from him." "Infinite Mind created and coalesced* Me, and I am now born from him."*** "At this moment, I am formed and projected by infinite Lovemind."*** "I am continuously being projected or beamed forth* by the Mind of the cosmos."***

"I did not come of myself, but he sent me." "I did not come to earth just because I wanted to, but he wanted Me to come."*** "I do not come from a human selfmind, but from illimitable Mind, which projects Me."*** "I do not exist as a separate self, but as a part of the Whole."*** "My truest identity is not localized in, or limited to, a self. It is the all."*** "I am not a physical person. I am Reality."***

***

The narrative continues with chapter 8, verse 43:

"You cannot hear My words." "This message does not come through your senses."** "You are incapable of understanding this message."** "This truth cannot be spoken in mere words."*** "My message is beyond your minds, beyond your education."*** "Your education has made you rigid; your rigidity prevents knowing."*** "You have no 'inner' ear to hear what I say; your mind is deaf."*** "Spiritual comprehension has been dulled by a literal intellect."*** "Your religion has made you spiritually deaf."***

44. "Your 'father' is the devil." "The fearnature stands behind your life."*** "Your source is the fearmind."*** "Your origin is unwise and unclean."*** "Your origin is ignorance."*** "You draw your minds from an inner pool of darkness."*** "Your deeper mind is the adversary of Love and Light."*** "Your source resists Reality."*** "It is antireality."*** "The Mindlevel which you see as your origin still contains illusion and fear."*** "It is the lowest level of the lower nature."*** "Your minds mistake effect for cause."***

"And you will do what he desires." "You will obey the will of fear."*** "You will obey the will of your inward fearmind."*** "Fear will master you by creating desires."*** "In serving the lower nature, you are manipulated by selfish desires and greed."*** "The lowest nature controls through will separated from Love."***

"From the beginning, it has been a murderer." "From the start, it has been a taker and destroyer of life."*** "It has been life-resistant."*** "It has been antinergic."*** "It has presented and seen the cosmos as dead."*** "It works to annihilate inner life."*** "It acts against life, but, without meaning to, makes life stronger."***

"For he does not live in the truth." "He 'lives' only in illusion."** "He 'lives' only in shadowmind."** "He is no part of reality."** "He is sheerest illusion."** "This 'antimind' is totally unreal."***

"There is no truth in him" "It has lost its way."*** "This antimind, antireality has lost touch with what is."***

"When he speaks a lie, he speaks according to his own nature." "When antimind speaks illusion, it is because the totality of antimind nature is illusion."*** "When antimind talks about illusion, its words reflect its state."*** "Nothing could be more natural than for the illusory antimind to speak of illusion."*** "Antimind speaks only of material and illusion, for those are its areas."*** "Ignorant, antimind is proud of its materialism, stripped of all Spirit and spirituality."*** "It projects its unreal self as all those parts of your Mind that are unreal."***

"For he is a liar, and the father of the lie." "For antimind is an illusionist, and the Mindgenerator of all illusion."*** "It is master and source of illusion."*** "Divided in its own mind from Love, all that is left for it to do is to generate unreality."*** "It is the author of superficial, shallow interpretations and synthetic, false dream-realities."*** "It tries to lull the mind into accepting the dream as reality."***

45. "It is exactly because I speak about truth that you do not believe Me." "Since you are under the control of antimind, the master and source of illusion, you do not accept the words of reality that I bring to you."*** "You see illusion as reality, and reality as illusion."*** "You are so unaccustomed to reality that, when I talk about it, it seems like a wild, alien fantasy to you."*** "Truth seems incredible, fantastic, to you, lost in illusion."***

46. "Yet who among you will convict Me of sin?" "Yet nobody here is prepared to accuse Me of deliberate action against life."** "Who can show that I am in error?"** "Who can prove to Me that My revelation is false?"*** "Who can demonstrate to Me that I live out of the lowest nature?"*** "Who can prove that I am no more than human?"*** "Who can accuse my Mind of deliberate evil?"*** "Who can demonstrate that what I have said is wrong, or evil?"***

***

The narrative continues with chapter 8, verse 47:

"Only he who comes from God can hear God's message." "Only the mind that originates within the Sourcemind can understand the message of infinite Mind."*** "You can hear the inner direction only according to your capacities. If your Mindsource is not God, the sayings of God make no sense to you."*** "The Sourcemind can be known only by one who has emerged from It."*** "The Sourcemind reveals Itself only to one who has been immersed and submerged in It."*** "Spiritual truths can be discerned only by those who operate out of Spirit or spiritual Mind."*** "Deep spiritual realities are nonsense to those who do not emerge directly from spiritual nature."*** "Only a being who knows divine derivation can know divine Reality."*** "If you identify with only inner humanity, you will not know inner divinity."*** "Only those who live in Love can grasp the teachings of Love."***

***

The narrative continues with chapter 8, verse 49:

"I am not demonized." "Contrary to what you might think, I do not have a devil."** "I am not influenced by evil spirits."** "I am not possessed."*** "Evil does not control or influence Me."*** "Evil has no place in Me."*** "Evil does not even exist in My mind."*** "The idea of absolute evil has disappeared from My Soul."***

"I honor My father, but you have no honor for Me." "I give respect to My Sourcemind. But even though I am the perfect image of that Sourcemind, you give Me no respect."*** "I yield all praise to the father. But you fail to see his splendor in Me."*** "The spiritual glory of the father is in the father. But it is also within Me. But within Me, you refuse to see it."*** "You do not recognize My place in the process of divine communication, bridging human and divine."*** "I commune with the Sourcemind in order to transmit splendor to the human mind."***

50. "But I do not seek splendor for myself." "I am not at all interested in personal glory."** "I have no self with which to seek personal honor."*** "I have no interest in fame or recognition."*** "I seek no personal credit."*** "I do not want your acclaim or applause."***

"There is one who seeks and judges." "Another seeks [glory for Me] and he is the one who judges. "**

51. "If a man keeps My sayings, he will never see death." "When what I have to say is understood, you become a deathless Mindspirit."*** "You become a deathless Soulmind."*** "For the one who understands, death, as the end of life, no longer exists."*** "She who truly knows Reality becomes Reality, and Reality cannot die."*** "In the enlightened Mind, there is no place for death to enter."*** "Death, too, is part of the vanishing illusion of earthly life."*** "Death is life in transformation."*** "In the inner kingdom of splendor, death does not exist."*** "Mind is invincible and invulnerable to death."*** "Who abandons separation abandons death."*** "There is no death, but only resurrection."*** "Fully to experience life is never to know death."***

***

The narrative continues with chapter 8, verse 54:

"If I give credit to myself, that credit is nothing." "My human self takes credit for nothing."**

"It is my father, whom you claim as your god, who gives Me splendor." "All splendor arises from Sourcemind, whom you falsely claim is your god."*** "Whatever of value that I have is a gift of Sourcemind, whom you claim to be your god."*** "Your god is not My Source."***

55. "You have no intimate, direct knowing of him, but I do know him." "You have not had a gnosis of him, but I do know him."*** "You have not experienced his/her inner Presence."*** "You do not possess the direct, inspired revealing of gnosis."*** "You have not been taught individually by his/her indwelling holy Spirit."***

"And if I were to deny that I knew him, I would be lying, as you are." "Just as you are lying when you say that you know him, I would be lying if I said that I did not."** "I would be caught in delusion and illusion."*** "I might be tricked by the appearances of the 'material' world."***

"But I do know him profoundly, and keep his message within." "I do know him deeply, and hold sacred his words within Myself."** "I know him because I have experienced his Being, and I treasure his wisdom within."*** "I keep his Way."***

56. "Your ancient ancestor Abraham rejoiced to see My day." "Your ancient ancestor Abraham is still alive in the Homeworld and so he is able to see these things occurring in my day." ***

***

The narrative continues with chapter 8, verse 58:

"Before Abraham existed, I already was." "My deepest Self, the Spirit, existed even before Abraham was born."*** "I am; I exist completely outside of time, outside of 'before' and 'after.'"*** "My life is timeless; so I am, in what you call both 'past' and 'future.'"***

***

The narrative continues with chapter 9, verse3:

"Neither he nor his parents sinned [so that this man was born blind]. He was born blind so that the works of God should be made manifest within him." "This blindness is not due to sin, either this man's or his parents'. Instead, his Soul chose to be born into a blind body so that the works of Love should be expressed within him."*** "He is not blind because his Soul sinned before birth. Nor is he paying for any sins of his parents. But there are certain works of God that can manifest only in a blind person."*** "He is blind by the choice of his own soul, for he came to earth to develop certain talents."*** "This is not normal karma; instead, his Soul chose this condition, as elective karma."*** "He chose to be blind so that certain special activities of God might be expressed."*** "He was born blind in order spiritually to see."*** "He was born blind in order to receive divine gifts that are not given to the sighted."*** "His vision is upon the interior worlds of Spiritmind, rather than the trivialities of this world."*** "Blindness to the outer world opened his inner eye."*** "He has paid the highest price for the deepest spirituality."***

4. "While it is still the light of day, I must work the works of him who sent Me. For the night comes, when no one can work." "Speaking of inner Light, I must do the works of the Sourcemind while My inner Light is still quite bright. For the darknight of My Soul is approaching."*** "While I am in the lightshow of this world, I must do his works. For in the world to come, this world will seem like darkness, and, when there, I won't do anything here."*** "I must accomplish My work here, while My inner sight is adjusted to the dim light of this 'material' plane; for viewed from higher levels, this world is so dark that work in it is impossible."***

5. "As long as I am in this world, I am the light of the world." "While I am in the natural order, it is lighted up by My Mind."** "While I am visiting the natural order, My Mind forms it from inner Light."** "I am the Center of my world, and My thoughts and interpretations bring it to the light of the Mind's awareness."*** "It is by My Mindlight that the world is dreamed into being all around Me."*** "The Light of My Mind fills My cosmos with form and color."***

***

The narrative continues with chapter 9, verse 35:

Jesus heard that they had disfellowshipped the man. Jesus found out that the man had been excommunicated.** When he found him, he asked, "Do you believe in the son of man?" "Do you believe in the inner son-nature?"*** "Do you believe that you are God's son?"***

"Do you believe that God is the Sourcemind?"*** "Do you believe that you are produced by the Sourcemind?"*** "Do you believe in the inner sonmind?"*** "Do you believe in your inner divine sonship?"*** "Do you believe that human nature is produced by Godnature?"***

***

The narrative continues with chapter 9, verse 37:

"You have seen him." "You have already had the experience of having seen the inner sonmind."*** "You have already experienced It."*** "You have seen It with inner vision, and now, you see it with outer vision."***

"It is he who talks with you." "That deep part of Mind is My deeper Self."*** "I am the embodiment and incarnation of the sonmind."*** "You are seeing and talking with the sonmind right now, for It is I."*** "He communicates with you."***

***

The narrative continues with chapter 9, verse 39:

"This is the reason that I have come into this world: That those who are blind might see, and those who see might become blind." "This is why I was born: So that those who are blind to the outer world might see the inner, and those who see only the outer might realize that they are blind to the inner."*** "I bring inner vision to the blind, and inner darkness to those who see."*** "To the one who humbly recognizes her spiritual blindness, I bring sight. But those who think that they already know, I make blind to the deeper truths."*** "I open the inner gates of mystery to those who do not see the things of this world, but I close them to those who are distracted by this world."*** "The blind can see Me interiorly; but those who are blinded by their sight cannot."***

***

The narrative continues with chapter 9, verse 41:

"If you were blind, you would be without sin." "If you had no inner sight, your path would not be so erroneous."** "You would be happier if you were blind to the outer world and to 'sin.'"*** "If you were blind to the 'sin' in others, you would have none yourselves."***

"But you say that you see. So, your guilt remains." "You claim to have spiritual vision, and so you are guilty of ignoring inner guidance."** "You claim to have insight, to see the inner Invisible; this is why your lower mind generates guilt."*** "Your guilt is created because you claim to be able to see enough to judge."*** "If you did not lay claim to so much spiritual understanding, you would not have so much sin."***

***

The narrative continues with chapter 10, verse 1:

"He who does not enter by the gate, but climbs some other way into the sheep-pen, is a thief and a robber." "If you try to get into the gentle, sacrificing Mind by any way other than Christ-nature, you are just trying to break in and steal."*** "Those who try to get into cosmic Mind by any other way than the Way are thieves."*** "Anyone who tries to break into the Lovemind by stealth or secrecy is a thief."*** "Anyone who tries a false, illegitimate way to enter the gentle Spiritmind is a thief."*** "Trying to get into limitless Mind without the Way of Love makes you a robber."*** "Those who would shepherd the sheepmind as teachers, but who have tried to know the Way without passing through the gate of enlightenment, are thieves."*** "Those who talk about God, but have not known God as Love, are thieves."*** "They are dishonest, liars, frauds, and hypocrites*."***

2. "But he who comes in through the door is the shepherd of the sheep." "Only she who comes to the Mind through the entry of Christ is the true care-giver for the gentle, sacrificing Mind."*** "Only she who enters through the doors of enlightenment is a true helper and guide."*** "Only she who has herself passed through the gate of enlightenment is worthy and able to help others pass through."***

3. "The guard opens the door to him. The sheep hear his voice, and he calls each one by name, and leads them out." "The inner Mindsecurity system permits the enlightened to pass into Coremind. The gentle sacrificial parts of Mind receive communication from her, and she knows each part of her Mind intimately and personally."*** "The natural barriers and shields which protect deepest Mind open to

her, allowing her to pass easily."*** "The inner qualities of gentle, selfsacrificing Love respond to her call, and she draws them out into manifestation."***

4. "And when he has brought them all out, he walks in front of them. And the sheep follow him, because they know his voice." "When the Love of the unconscious Mind is released, they follow the one who follows the One. The qualities of gentle Love go with her, because they know her Mindsignature."*** "She, guided by Love, guides the liberation and integration of gentle sacrifice."*** "The shepherd is Christ, the human evaporated in the divine."*** "It guides and leads the domesticated aspects of animal-nature."***

5. "They will not follow a stranger, but will flee from him." "They know better than to follow strange ideas."** "They will not get behind a Mind that is alien to Lovemind."** "These Mindaspects cannot follow another mind, but must be led by the interior Lovemind alone, for they will flee from any other."***

***

The narrative continues with chapter 10, verse 7:

"I am the door." "My truest Self, the Christ, enlightened Mind, is the gate or door."*** "I, within you, am the gateway to divine experience and profound spiritual awareness."*** "I am the transparent or 'empty' state which permits the knowing of God."*** "I am an aperture, a portal, an opening in thought, the empty space through which Lovemind passes into heartmind."*** "I am the entry into inner Mind."*** "I am the Way out and the Way in."***

8. "Those who tried to go ahead of Me were thieves and robbers." "Those ideas which seek Light by by-passing Christ are thieves."** "Those concepts which try to do religion without enlightenment are thieves."** "Those religions that try to act more 'loving' than Love are dishonest."*** "Religion without spirituality is a lie." *** "Those minds which try to explore the inner cosmos without Love are seeking selfish gain."*** "Those thoughts that blunder about in inner space without Light are stealing from the Mind."*** "They try to exploit truth for personal gain, laboring under bondage and illusion."*** "They are lying to, and robbing, the Mindspirit."***

"But the sheep did not listen to them." "The gentle, sacrificing, regulated animal-nature did not follow these illusions."***

9. "I am the door." "I am the Mindbarrier that swings aside."** "I am the protector of the inner threshold."** "I am the Way into the deepest Mind."*** "I am the Mind by which deepest Mind is approached."***

"Whoever enters through Me will find salvation." "Whoever descends into Christmind, on the Way to Sourcemind, is saved from ignorance."*** "Whoever moves inwardly under My direction will be saved from the lower nature."***

"He will go in and out, and find pasture." "She will move inward to deep Mind, and outward to the world again, but in profound inner Mind she will find support and nourishment."*** "She will be able to move into the deep recesses, caverns, and seas of inner Mind, and emerge refreshed."***

10. "A thief comes only to steal, to kill, and to destroy. But I came so that they might have life, and have it abundantly." "The dishonest come to harm, but I to heal."*** "A lying cheater does damage, but I increase life."*** "The selfrobber destroys her own inner treasure, but I, the Christ, come to multiply life."*** "As Lovespirit, I bring the proliferation of inner blessings and riches."*** "My life overflows into mind, and it becomes the vessel for illimitable life."***

"I am the good shepherd; the good shepherd gives up a personal life for his sheep." "I am not only the door, but the Guide that leads through the door. I give up a personal life and self in order to tame my inner forces."***

12. "The hired person is no real shepherd. He knows that the sheep are not his. So, he will flee when he sees the wolf." "The parts of mind that act for personal gain are no real, reliable guide. For the regulated animal-nature belongs to the whole Mind. So, at the least sign of danger, these mindaspects prove cowardly and unreliable."*** "Artificial attempts to renew Mind, for personal gain, are useless."*** "Religion pursued for reward or 'pay' is of no use in combating the animal-nature."***

"Then, the wolf captures the sheep, and scatters them." "The unregenerate animal-nature attacks the spiritualized animal-nature forces, and weakens them."*** "The brutal animal-nature attacks the tame animal-nature."***

13. "The hired man flees, because he works only for money, and cares nothing for the sheep." "The selfish mind is cowardly, because

it does not Love the rest of Mind, but is just scheming to see what it can derive as personal gain."*** "Where there is no Love, there is no Power in the face of inner resistance."***

14. "But I Myself am the good shepherd, and I know My sheep, and they know Me." "I, the Christ-nature, am a reliable guide. I have personal, intimate knowing of all parts of the transformed renewed animal-nature, and they all have a knowing of Me."***

15. "I know the father in the same way that he knows Me." "I have deep, intimate knowing of the father within, and he has the same direct, profound knowing of Me."*** "The knowing between the Sourcemind and the Christmind is mutual and reciprocal."*** "Between Christmind and Sourcemind is a most profound interknowing."*** "The Christmind, that of enlightened human nature, is the mirrorreflection of divine Mind, through interknowing."*** "I can know in the father only what he knows in Me."*** "You can know in the Sourcemind only that part that is reflected back to you as your Self."***

"I give up any idea of personal life for the sake of the sheep." "In order fully to transform animal-nature, I must yield completely the illusion of the human self."*** "The inner qualities of gentleness and peace draw their life from My renunciation."*** "The Christ renounces the human nature and self, so that the transformed animal-nature might live."***

16. "And I have still more sheep, which are not even included in this group." "My formerly animal-nature mind has more qualities than these, all transformed into the Mind of gentleness and selfsacrifice."***

"Someday, they will all come forth together, to be unified as one flock under one shepherd." "Someday, the entire Mind will find fullest unification, and be unified as a single force, under single direction."***

17. "The father loves Me. And I give up the energy of My personal life, that I might take it up again." "The Sourcemind gives Me Love. And the energy which would flow into personal human life is given up, but not entirely lost. It will return to support higher and deeper Mind."*** "The Love of the Sourcemind has allowed Me to take up personal life, again and again."*** "If I lose the energy of personal life, I lose nothing. For it will come back to Me, recycled

into a higher energy."*** "I give up My personal life, but it is not lost forever; it is transformed."***

18. "No one can take this life from Me; I give it willingly." "This life is not wrestled from Me; I give it voluntarily."** "No one can erase human mind except the Mind that creates it."*** "To begin the process of erasing the personal will, personal will must be the instrument."***

"I have the power both to lay it down and to take it up again." "It is within my power to give up this human life and mind, or to sink back down into human mind again."** "I can resume my human, personal identity at any time that I choose."*** "The renunciation of human nature can be reversed."*** "At any time that I choose, I can begin again to design another human lifexperience."***

"For I received this command from My father." "For I am acting under the direction of the Sourcemind."**

***

The narrative continues with chapter 10, verse 25:

"The works that I do in My father's name are My credentials." "The activities performed by Sourcemind through Me are all the proof that I need."** "I prove who and what I am by the activities of the Sourcemind in My life."***

26. "But you do not believe, because you are not My sheep." "You choose not to believe, because you are not reflections/projections of My reformed animal-nature."*** "You refuse to believe because your animal natures have not been transformed into the peaceful, gentle, selfsacrificing parts of the deepest Mind."*** "You are part of Spirit, but not the part open to guidance and regeneration."***

27. "Only My sheep can know My voice, and I know them. They walk the same path that I do." "Only peaceful, gentle parts of Mind respond to the 'voice' of Christ. Enlightened Mind recognizes them. They walk the same Way that I walk."***

28. "And I give them timeless life. They will never perish." "These parts of Mind, enlightened, partake of timeless life. So, they will never vanish."**

"No one can take them out of My hand." "No one can remove them from My control and guidance."** "No one can remove them from My protection."**

29. "My father is all power." "All power is the Sourcemind."** "All true, genuine Power is Love. It is the Sourcemind."*** "The Sourcemind is all energy and force, omnipotent."*** "The Sourcemind is illimitable, almighty, allpowerful."***

"No one is able to snatch them out of My father's hands" "No one can remove these Mindexpressions from the guidance and protection of the Sourcemind."***

30. "My father is one with Me." "My father and I are one."** "At the deepest Mindlevel, I am the Sourcemind."*** "In the deepest Mindlevel, I am both sonmind and Sourcemind."*** "Distinctions between Myself and My Sourcemind are only arbitrary at the deepest inner Mindlevel."*** "My Mind is such a perfect mirror of Sourcemind that I am the same as Sourcemind."*** "Any division between Me and the Spiritsource is only conceptual."*** "It is only the result of appearances."*** "It is only superficial."*** "It is based on the illusion of the 'material' body."*** "I cannot exist apart from infinite Mind anymore than can a reflection exist apart from the object that it reflects."*** "The Sourcemind and My own deepest Mind are coterminal."*** "Any separation or distinction between My truest Self and the Source is only symbolic."*** "I am not within this body, which is only a tiny projection of the Mindspirit that is My real Self."*** "All the universes, including this body and this humanmind, are dreamimages within the cosmic Creatormind."*** "I have fully identified with the Logos within My heart, and it is in fullest identification with the Sourcemind."***"I have become indistinguishable from the Source of all."*** "My human nature has disappeared, leaving neither human mind nor body, but only God."*** "My father and I are one Being, Entity, Nature, Essence, Mind, or Spirit*."*** "We are both the unified, indivisible Lovenature."***

***

The narrative continues with chapter 10, verse 34:

"Is it not written within your own law, 'I said that you are gods'?" "Does it not say in your own Bible that human beings are gods?"**

"Don't your own Scriptures quote God as saying that people are gods?"** "Are not you also gods, according to your sacred writings?"** "Even your own sacred texts say that human nature is divine nature."*** "Your very own sacred book tells you that God has deified humanity."*** "As your own sacred records indicate, Every human being is a god in potential."*** "Any human being can do what I have done, can become Love, for all have the divine seed within."***

35. "So, people who received the Logos of God were themselves called 'gods.'" "So, those who awaken to the fact that they are perfect expressions or reflections of God become themselves divine."*** "They were seen as gods in training or development because the perfect Logos existed within their minds."*** "It was the presence of the one God within the deepest Mind of all that made them 'gods.'"*** "They expressed God or Lovenature in various stages of development."*** "God manifested in them, each according to her capacity."*** "Deepest Mind changed their awareness, revealing their inner godhood."*** "God drew their human minds into the perfection of the Lovenature, making them gods."***

"This Scripture cannot be broken, set aside, neglected, ignored, denied, annulled, or contradicted."* "However inconvenient you might find this text, you dare not ignore it, for your Bible is the foundation of your religion."*** "Human nature merges with divine nature at the inner Logos or Expression."***

36. "And yet, you say of him whom the father has made holy and sent into the world, 'You blaspheme!' simply because I said that I am God's son." "And yet, you accuse Me of blasphemy because I said that I was the son-nature, having emerged from the Sourcemind."***

37. "If I do not do the works of My father, then do not believe Me." "If I do not perform the activities of Lovemind, which is Sourcemind, then do not believe these teachings."***

38. "But if I do those works, then, even if you don't believe Me, believe the works." "God is not known in teachings, but in deeds. So, if you choose not to believe these words, teachings, or messages, * at least, believe in the activities, that they are those of Love."*** "Let My actions convince you, if My words cannot."***

"For only in this Way can you come into knowing and certainty."
"This belief will lead beyond itself to knowing, and that will be
unquestionable."*** "If you believe, you will find gnosis."***

"For you must know that the father is in Me, and I in him." "You
must come to the realization that I, the son-nature and Christ-nature,
interpenetrate the deepest Sourcemind, and he interpenetrates
Me."*** "We are mutually dispersed and suffused within each
other."*** "His greater Mind is inside My Mind."*** "My Mind is
saturated with Love, immersed in Love; it is the Mind of Love." ***
"Like a sponge in water, and water in a sponge, I am in Sourcemind,
and It in Me."*** "All selfmind, all human mind, has vaporized and
vanished within the Lovemind."*** "My Sourcemind is My deepest
Self."*** "I am Love incarnate."*** "The Sourcemind and I exist
mutually and reciprocally."*** "The Sourcemind is so bright and
powerful that, when our Minds meet and merge, nothing is left but
him/her."*** "I am pure Spirit; this body is only a Mindimage."***
"No barriers exist between Me and the cosmic Mind."*** "The
Sourcemind is interwoven into every fiber of My being."*** "Like
two liquids, the Sourcemind and I have perfectly comingled and have
become one substance."***

***

The narrative continues with chapter 11, verse 9:

"Aren't there twelve hours in a day? If anyone walks by day, he
won't fall, because he is led by the light of this world." "Ordinary
light represents universal spiritual light. So, it is divided into twelve.
If you walk in this everyday light, you will not fall, for the light will
show you where you are going."*** "So must you find the Light
within, and follow It."*** "If you live in a Mind of Light, you will
not fall against hidden obstacles, or hurt yourselves. For you will be
guided by the inner Light of the world, your deeper Selves."*** "You
will all be guided by a shared deepest Self."*** "The Light within
you is also the Light found in the natural order."*** "The light of the
'material' cosmos is the projection of the inner Lightmind."*** "Even
obstacles and impediments are the Light."*** "Obstacles which might
cause one to fall are also opportunities, also created by
Mindlight."***

10. "But if a person walks at night, he stumbles, because there is no light." "When you try to make progress without first having come into the Light, you will simply stumble around."*** "If you don't, at the beginning, come in touch with the inner Light-nature, you will find obstacles and impediments everywhere."*** "The Light-nature does not destroy obstacles, but shows you how to get around them."***

***

The narrative continues with chapter 11, verse 25:

"I am the resurrection and the life." "I am life after life, the principle of life itself."*** "I am the Power to return from the dead, for I am life."*** "The inner Christ, which I am, is unbroken life, surviving death. It is the very energy and Mind of life."*** "As Mind, I am Myself all life, and life after life."*** "As deepest Mind, I contain within Me all life, and all life after death."*** "I am the Source of all life, both in this world and in those to come."*** "I am the life within you now, and in all your future."*** "I am the Power and Essence of life and rebirth."*** "I am the Mindpower that lifts you out of the body at death, and I give you continuing life."*** "Resurrection, like the mystery of life itself, is nothing but Spiritmind in manifestation. And that I am."*** "I give life, life after life, from My own inner being."*** "Life, and all lives, are nothing but My thoughts, My Power, My Mind.*"*** "I think all life into being."***

"Whoever believes in Me, even though he dies, is still alive." "Even when a person dies, if she believes in Me, she is not dead."** "If a person believes that I, as immortal Soulspirit, am more real than anything, when her body dies, her Soulmind will continue."*** "If I am the central Reality of your existence, even though you appear to die, you will still live in Mind."*** "She who believes in Spirit as more real than body is not affected by death."*** "The one already living in Spirit is not harmfully affected by death."*** "She who lives in Spiritmind, rather than the senses, becomes eternal, untouched by death."*** "Death is illusion to one who abides and dwells in deathless Mind."*** "Death is illusion to one who has become the timeless Mind."*** "Death vanishes for anyone who has realized her eternal, divine nature."*** "Death is meaningless and negligible to one who knows the deepest Self."*** "When one understands the real nature of Spirit, death as end becomes an absurdity."*** "Death is impossible for one who is truly alive."*** "When you live in deathless Mind, death disappears."*** "Death cannot exist for anyone who has identified with the Life that is Myself."***

26."Whoever is alive and believes in Me will never die." "If you believe that I am your truest Self, in Me, you will never die."** "Whoever embraces and adopts Me, the Eternal, as her own Self, will never die."***

"Do you believe this?"

***

The narrative continues with chapter 11, verse 41:

"Father, I thank you that you have heard Me." "Thank you for receiving, recognizing, and acknowledging* Me."**

42. "And I know that you always hear Me." "You are continuously aware of My thoughts."*** "We exist in continuous communion, communication, interchange, and interaction.*"*** "My thoughts continuously relay to deepest Mind."***

***

The narrative continues with chapter 12, verse 23:

"The time is now for the son of man to enter the splendor." "It is time for human nature to become more than human."** "It enters full glorification."** "It undergoes full metamorphosis."**

24. "Unless a grain of wheat falls into the ground and dies, it remains isolated." "A grain of wheat remains only a single grain unless it dies and joins a larger system."*** "It then becomes one with the whole earth."*** "Death is the event which makes possible its loss of boundaries, and its fusion with the whole earth."*** "A seed remains isolated until it dies; and so I am localized if I do not leave this body."*** "Unification with greater Mind begins with death of the lesser mind."*** "The death of the body-self is the beginning of the spiritual Self."*** "At death, the illusion of being separate disappears."*** "Death is the exhilarating ecstasy of losing boundaries, and returning to the whole Mind."***

"Only when it dies can it bring forth much fruit." "It can become more than its isolated self only through death."** "By its death, it enters into many other grains."*** "Expansion, completion, metamorphosis, and growth are all promised by death."*** "Death releases the life-force of the seed, that countless other seeds might come forth from it."*** "The human self must be dissolved in death to share the life-forces fully."*** "You cannot give life if it is too concentrated on a single body."*** "When you cling too tightly to life as a personal possession, you deny it to others; death breaks this cycle."*** "Death opens the inner door to expanded, abundant, infinite life."*** "Death is the beginning of eternity."*** "Death is an entry into Infinity."*** "From death, your most real and valuable life emerges."***

"Unless it falls into the ground and dies, it will never be anything more than itself." "Until it dissolves as a 'self,' it will never produce anything greater."** "Until your human self dies, you can never be a transcendental Mind."*** "You will never surpass the self until it dies."*** "Unless the seed-coat is dissolved, inner life-potential is not released."*** "You must 'die' to all those ideas that hold you to a body, or that say that you are a body."*** "You cannot progress until you dissolve your selfboundaries."*** "Belief in a separate human self binds you to loneliness and isolation."***

25. "So, everyone loving his life will lose it." "Whoever loves her human life will lose it."** "Do not love your human life, for you are bound to lose it."*** "If you love your separate illusionlife, you will lose sight of your deeper life."*** "Human life has no cosmic future."*** "To love, to become fully engaged in, this life is a guarantee of its end."*** "The more that you cling and attach, the more you lose."*** "Do not love this life or its selfishness, or you will lose them."*** "Clinging to this life will end up in loss, as it slips through your fingers."*** "If you seek to capture and freeze this life, out of love for it, it will flee from you."*** "Do not love the fleeting life of earth and body, but love the real, deepest inner life."*** "Loving the selfish grasping of earthlife is losing touch with spiritual life."*** "If you become only a personal mind, you will surely lose it."*** "It is the love of the timeworld, belief in time, that makes it fly."*** "The life of time, of becoming, is continuously slipping away. So, invest no Love in it, but in the timeless state of being."*** "Life is lost only when you love, and try to capture, the moment."*** "Don't love the world of trinkets, trivialities, pettiness, and baubles, which leads to only death."*** "Don't love the mind of self, which is

lost in death, but love the cosmic Lovemind, where everything is timeless."*** "The way to move beyond your lower, human self is to love it to death."***

"Only he who hates his life in this world will keep it for the timeless life." "You must turn away from the distractions of this world in order to awaken to the life of the deeper Mind."*** "You must practice renunciation of the illusionworld if you are to live in the timeless world of now."*** "You must actively disengage from taking the 'material' world with finality if you are to lead the more real, interior, and spiritual life."*** "Only if you find yourself repelled by the life of time will you preserve your life for the timeless, eternal state."*** "Only by rejecting the dominance of the material world will you find the inner timeless world."*** "Only by turning away from appearances— materialism and oversensuality— can you keep your life safe for the inner condition of timeless life."*** "Reject the ultimate reality of this world to find the timeless state."*** "Turn from the 'outer' life to find the inner one."*** "You cannot fully live in both earthlife and timeless life."*** "You must choose between service of the senses and that of the inner cosmic Mind."*** "You must hate materialism to serve Love."*** "If you are to know the extraordinary, you must find the courage to reject the ordinary."*** "To know the Supernormal, you must turn your back on the 'normal.'"*** "You must hate the life of greed if you are to know the life of bliss."*** "You must hate the life of desire as master if you are to soar into freedom."*** "You must despise selfrighteousness and selfglorification if you are to taste freedom."*** "You must abandon and desert your old life and self, and be reborn in Love."*** "You must despise devotion to money and career if you are to know the life of timeless freedom."*** "You must hate all thoughts about the self, all shallow selfcenteredness."*** "This is the only way to keep, preserve, maintain, or guarantee* timeless life."***

26. "So, if anyone serves Me, let him follow Me." "To serve Me is to do what I do."** "If service is real, it will be imitation."** "To serve Me truly, you must try to walk the path that I've walked."** "I am a model of true service."** "Strive to duplicate My Mind in yours."*** "Replicate My nature in your own."*** "You cannot serve God without living a godly and godlike life."*** "To serve Me, you must make your life a mirror of My own."*** "To serve Me with

only words is meaningless and without value; you must serve Me by living a transformed life."*** "To serve Me is so much more than simply to declare Me, or ritually to accept Me. To serve Me is to change your behavior, harmonizing with Love."*** "To serve Me is not just to state belief in Me, but is to live Me."*** "The only way truly to serve Me is to commit every action, word, and thought in your life to My guidance."*** "What I am, you must work to become."*** "You will become the perfect, flawless mirror of the Christ of Love, the enlightened human nature."*** "You must first become the sonmind— the blend of Sourcemind and human mind."*** "To follow Me, you must lose and crucify your human self, and become, first, the sonmind, then the Christmind, then Godmind."*** "To follow the Mind of Love, you must walk the path of Love."***

"Then, where I am will my servant also be." "The one who truly serves me will be at the same place in spiritual development as I."*** "My servant will follow Me to the deepest Mind."*** "Then My servant will become everything that I am."*** "Then, My servant will have fully discovered her own divine nature."*** "What I am, My servant is also destined to be."*** "My servant will duplicate and reflect My very being within herself."*** "As I know the Spirit, so will My servant."*** "In God, My servant and I will share a single Self."*** "Then, there will be no difference between Myself and My servant."*** "My student will disappear into My inner Lightmind."***

"If anyone serves Me, My father will bring him into splendor." "If any person so serves Me, the Sourcemind will lift her to the state of splendor."** "If anyone duplicates My life, the Sourcemind will transform her nature in the inner Lightmind."*** "She will be metamorphosed into glory."*** "The Providermind will shift her into a state of superspirituality."*** "She will be lifted above the dominance of the 'material' universe."***

27. "Now My soul is troubled." "The Mind between the human and the divine is disturbed."*** "My deeper Self is stirred up."***

"What shall I say? Shall I ask the father to save Me from this hour? But it was for this very purpose that I came to this hour." "Shall I ask the Sourcemind to rescue Me from this distressing period, when this is the very reason that I came?"** "It was My Soul that brought Me to this moment, and shall I now ask the Sourcemind to take Me away from it?"*** "For My own reasons, My Soul has brought Me to suffering."***

28. "Father, bring your name into splendor." "Sourcemind, move your identity into splendor."*** "Sourcemind, only your identity is important."*** "Let your name be hallowed."*** "Let your identity be made the holiest subject."*** "May your identity be unsoiled by the appearances of the world."*** "May the purity of your Self not be polluted by the self of humanity."*** "May your supreme Love-identity not be mixed with fear."*** "May the purity of your divine Self remain stainless."*** "Let the lucidity of your Mind not be clouded by the lower nature."*** "The luminosity of divine Mind must be elevated above the shadows of the lower nature."*** "May your divine identity be fully expressed."*** "May it not be eclipsed or compromised by anything."***

***

The narrative continues with chapter 12, verse 31:

"The judgment of this world is occurring right now." "This world is being evaluated, in absolute terms, by many minds."*** "Even now, the ignorant judge this world."*** "It is necessary to evaluate the 'material' world, but not in absolute terms."*** "The whole natural order is being judged, as absolutely good."***

"Now the prince of this world is cast out." "The rulership of the natural order has collapsed."*** "The domination of the natural order over the enlightened Mind is finished."*** "The world no longer dominates the psyche."*** "The Spirit is not subject to the natural order, its dream."*** "The rulership of nature is ended."*** "Domination by the lower nature is over."*** "I, in you, transcend domination by the forces and arrangements of nature."*** "The hypnotic power of the common, natural world is broken."*** "The spell of materialism is broken."*** "The power of the world, of illusion, exists only in the mind, but is there no longer."*** "Spiritual realization has cast down, thrown down, or cast out* the power of illusion."***

32. "And I, when I am lifted up from the earth, will draw every human being to Myself." "When My mind is elevated above the illusion, I will attract every human being to follow Me, in time."*** "When I have fully transcended the forces and arrangements of earth,

I will draw every living being to where I am."*** "When I have risen above all earthly ties and restrictions, I will make sure that all human beings follow Me into transcendence and splendor."*** "When I find absolute freedom in splendor, I will someday draw everyone else to become equal with Me."*** "When this world is dissolved for Me, and I have entered the Luminous Reality, I will guarantee that everyone will follow Me."*** "I will someday draw all sentient beings into Myself."*** "Their selves will all become My Self, the Spirit of Love."*** "All creation, in time, will implode into Me."***

***

The narrative continues with chapter 12, verse 35:

"The Light will be with you only a little longer." "This Light will be with you only awhile, and then, It will be in you."*** "The light of this world does not last very long, and soon passes."*** "The coalesced light that you experience as the 'material' world will not be with you much longer."***

"Keep walking while you have the Light, or darkness will come over you." "If you don't keep making progress while you have the Light, darkness will overshadow you."** "Keep moving forward while you are still in touch with the inner Light. For if you do not, darkness will overshadow you."*** "Continue to progress through the realms of relative light, so that you do not fall backwards into total darkness."*** "Keep living in Mindlight, or else, the world will seem dead and dark."*** "Keep moving in full awareness that 'matter' is light, or else, the world will grow dark with 'solidity.'"*** "Stay always aware of the Light within you, or else, the world will seem shadowed, clouded, and obscure."*** "Stay in the Light of Love, or materialism will eclipse It and darken your heartmind."***

"For he who walks in darkness does not know where he is going." "She who walks in darkness has no clear and certain goal."** "She is lost, unable to see her future path."*** "She has lost orientation and reference-points."*** "For those who walk in illusion, all is obscure."*** "For those dominated by ideas of materialism, all is chaos."*** "There is no goal in a lightless cosmos, or psyche."*** "The mind without Lightmind grows feeble, dim, and dull."*** "Without understanding Light, there is no sense of either destiny or destination."***

36. "As long as you have the Light, believe in that Light." "Let your belief in the inner Light guide everything in your Mind."*** "Believe only in lightenergy, not 'matter.'"*** "Do not allow your faith in Lightmind to waver."*** "Even when the cosmos seems to deny it, do not lose your faith that the cosmos is Light."*** "While you are in a lightcosmos, remember that it *is* Light."*** "Believe not in the story told by the senses, but in only the Light."*** "You are yourselves Light; fear not to believe in It."***

"In this way, you will become children of the Light." "You will see that you are generated by Light."** "You are products not of nature or surroundings, but are created this moment by Light."*** "You arise naturally and spontaneously out of the Light."*** "You are coalesced from Light."*** "You are formed from, and are beings of, Light."*** "Generated by Light, you are patterns of Light."*** "Your essence is the Mind of stainless Light."*** "Your truest, deepest being is shining Light."***

***

The narrative continues with chapter 12, verse 44:

"He who believes in Me does not believe in me, but in him who sent Me." "To believe in Me is not to believe in my humanself, but in the One from Whom I emerge."** "To believe in this human form is worthless. Believe instead in the Spirit within Me, which is also within you."*** "When I speak of 'believing in Me,' I do not mean that you should believe in this man whom you see before you. Instead, I call you to believe in that Mindspirit, the Sourcemind that projects Me into this world."*** "Believe in the Mindspirit out of which I am projected."*** "Do not believe in this human form, but in the Sourcemind behind the whole cosmos."*** "Believe not in the finite, fallible Jesus, but in the eternal Christ, the enlightened Mind."*** "If you worship Me as a man, you remain in ignorance. See Me as Lightmind, and you will have seen truly."*** "To worship this human form is to reject belief in Me. Instead, worship only the Mindspirit, also within you, which sent me forth into this world."***

45. "He who sees Me sees him who sent Me." "I am completely transparent to the Sourcemind; so, when you look at Me, you see only That."** "To see My inner Self is to see the eternal, cosmic Lightmind."*** "To know the Christ within is to know the

Sourcemind."*** "To see the perfect manifestation of the cosmic Mind is the only way to know It."*** "When you see Me, as Lovespirit, within yourselves, then you have also seen God."*** "To look at the deepest Self is to see God."***

46. "I have come as a Light in the world, so that whoever believes in Me should not live in darkness." "I have come to bring illumination to the natural order, so that the one believing in Me should not remain in inner darkness."** "I have come to bring light into the natural order, including human nature. If you believe that I am more real than the world or your self, you will not live in darkness."*** "Light is more real than the world which it forms and illuminates. She who knows this will not remain in ignorance."*** "My deepest Mind is your deepest Mind. It is the light of awareness that brings the natural order into the humanmind. To live in this light is to be free from the belief that one is a part of this natural order."*** "You are not a part of the natural order illuminated by Mindlight; instead, you are the Mindlight itself."*** "Whoever believes in that Lightmind will never again believe in shadows."***

47. "But if any person hears My words and does not believe them, I do not judge him." "This is an incredible view. If the average person does not comprehend it, I do not blame her."** "From the usual and average perspective, this view seems fantastic, and I do not absolutely evaluate even those who reject it."*** "I will never condemn anyone who does not accept or understand this message, for it is not easy to grasp."*** "If anyone rejects what I say, I form no permanent opinion about her."***

"For I did not come to judge the world, but to save it." "I did not come to form absolute opinions of the natural order, but to save it from ignorance."** "I did not come to the 'material' plane to condemn it, or to say that it was absolutely bad. I came to save it from the lower nature."** "I came to redeem the natural order by rescuing it from a state of 'materiality,' and proving it to be part of the spiritual cosmos."*** "I came to demonstrate that the natural order is Spirit."*** "I want to bring the whole natural order back within the realm of Mindspirit."*** "I came to rescue the natural order from the illusion of full exteriorization."*** "I came to restore the human to the natural, and the divine to the human."***

48. "Whoever rejects Me and refuses My sayings already has a judge." "Whoever repels Me and My teachings has an inner judge."**

"The Logos about which I have spoken will judge him in the last day." "The perfect manifestation of Godmind deep in her own mind will 'judge' her on the final day of her life on earth. By comparison with It, she will be found wanting."*** "It is the inner divine expression that will judge her, for she will not measure up to a comparison with It."*** "On the final day of her life, the inner divine pattern will absolutely evaluate her merits."*** "It will evaluate and measure her according to absolute standards."*** "The living Logos, the inner Observer, will measure her value on the last day of her life."*** "The Logos, exteriorized from the heart, will absolutely evaluate every human being exteriorized from It."*** "On the day of her death, every human being will encounter the Logos, the expression of inner God as outer Light, and then, be evaluated according to her intents."*** "The Logos, Who I am, records everything."***

49. "For I have not spoken from myself." "I have not spoken from the Mindlevel of the self."** "I have not spoken from a human mind."** "For it is that Logos Who has spoken through me."*** "Inner God or Love has used this Logos to speak through me."*** "I have not spoken from personal ideas or will."*** "The teachings did not originate with the man whom you see before you."*** "They did not arise from personality or personhood."***

"But the father who sent me gave me a commandment about what I should say." "I spoke only the words of the Sourcemind."** "The will of the cosmic (deepest) Mind regulated my speech."***

50. "And I know that his guideline is timeless life." "He measures things according to only timeless standards."** "To yield, surrender, and be regulated by him is to enter the timeless state."*** "Letting him control you is the same as entering eternal life."*** "Once you have permitted the Sourcemind to take over your mind, you are living outside of time altogether."*** "When you have allowed divine will to replace human will, you have gone altogether beyond time."*** "You have discovered total liberation from the cruel slavery to time."*** "The secret to transcending the world is to transcend the mind that believes that the world dominates it."*** "Life without time is Love without self."***

"Whatever I speak, therefore, is what the father has spoken through me." "Whatever I appear to have said was actually the Sourcemind speaking through me."** "These teachings are the transmission and translation of what the cosmic Mind has revealed within me."***

***

The narrative continues with chapter 13, verse 3:

Jesus knew that the father had given everything into his hands. Jesus knew that the Sourcemind had allowed him voluntarily to make the decision to surrender all to the Spirit.*** His personal universe had been turned over to his free will.*** He now had control, from the ineffable Mind, of his personal cosmos.*** Jesus became universal Mind, thus "inheriting" the universe.*** When he became cosmic Mind, there existed nothing "outside" of him, for there was no longer an "outside."*** He entered the infinite fluidity of possibility.*** When he took the final plunge into absolute subjectivity, he found that the cosmos was his projected dream.*** When he became Lovemind, he discovered that the cosmos was the exteriorization of that Lovemind.*** He became every object-event in his experience.*** Identification with the deepest inner Mind became complete, and Jesus knew that he was God the Creatormind, /God the father.***

And he knew that he had come from God and was returning to God. He realized that, since he had come from Godmind, he was now returning back into that same Lovemind.** He had coalesced from Lovemind and was now sinking back into Sourcemind.*** He was continuously emerging from Godmind and was now disappearing again back into It.*** He knew that the divine Mind had projected him, and he was now no longer the projection, but the Light.*** He had flowed forth from the divine Mind, and was now giving up personhood in order to reintegrate with the One.*** "As he had arisen from the Ground of being, he now sank back into It, recalling his original Mind.*** Having been drawn from cosmic Mind as a "separate" identity, he now gave that up, and identified with the Mind.***

***

The narrative continues with chapter 13, verse 13:

"You call Me 'teacher' and 'master,' and you are right, for that is what I am."

14. "If, then, I, as master and teacher, have washed your feet, you must be prepared to do the same." "You must be willing to serve each other in ways that you find personally humiliating."** "By so humiliating yourself, you weaken the human self."***

***

The narrative continues with chapter 13, verse 17:

"If you know these things, you will find joy in doing them." "If you know these truths, putting them into service will bring you joy."** "Knowing these teachings is not enough. You must turn them into service in order to know their joy."** "You must not simply think and talk about the teachings, but must live them."*** "You must actively apply them in your everyday lives."***

***

The narrative continues with chapter 13, verse 20:

"Whoever receives the one I send receives Me." "Whoever receives the one I project receives Me."** "Whoever accepts the one whom I crystallize from My Mind receives Me."*** "Whoever receives the inner Spirit, sent in Love, receives Me."*** "Whenever you receive a person of Love, and welcome her in Love, you are receiving Me."*** "To receive Me, you must receive every person who comes in the name of Love."*** "The only Way to open your heart to receive Me is to open your hearts to each other in Love."*** "The Spirit of Light will come only to those who open their hearts to people, in Love."*** "To accept Me, you must accept people."*** "I, as Creatormind, project all beings into the world; so, to accept Me, you must accept all."***

"And he who receives Me receives him who sent Me." "To accept Me is to accept God."** "To accept people is to accept God."*** "To receive Me into yourself is to receive the Sourcemind."***

***

The narrative continues with chapter 13, verse 31:

"Now, the son of man is brought into splendor." "Human nature has been enlightened in Me."*** "God's splendor shines within the human soul."*** "The splendor of the divine nature is ignited within the human mind."*** "It is the splendor of Love."*** "Human nature is filled with the Light of Love."***

"And God is brought into splendor in him."

32. "If God is glorified within him, then God will also glorify him within himself." "As divine Mind is glorified in human nature, so divine Mind will glorify that human nature."** "As Godmind is glorified in the human mind, so the human mind is glorified in divine nature."** "If God finds splendor in human nature, then that very nature will find the same splendor within itself."*** "God's working as splendor within the human mind makes enlightenment inevitable."***

"And he will give him splendor immediately." "And the Infinite will grant splendor immediately to human nature."** "Splendor is not a gradual achievement, but an immediate discovery."*** "Splendor already exists within every sentient being; it only awaits immediate release."***

***

The narrative continues with chapter 13, verse 34:

"A new commandment I give to you: Love each other." "So, I command you to love each other in a new Way."** "I command you to love each other unconditionally."*** "My command is that you love universally."*** "Love unconditionally."*** "Your deepest impulse, from deepest Mind, is the compulsion to love."*** "I, as deepest Mind, encourage, impel, and compel you to love."*** "The only action that I ask of you is that you love."*** "One principle must regulate your lives—Love."*** "The one and only directive from the inner Spirit is to love."*** "There is only a single law that regulates mind, from Mind— Love."*** "The only Way that the inner deepest Mind wants to control or influence you is through Love."*** "I give you a new directing and integrating principle— Love."*** "Live in a continuous state of Love."***

"Love each other exactly as I have loved you." "Seek to perfect your Love so it is precisely the same as Spiritlove."** "You must try to love unconditionally, and universally, for this is how I have loved you."*** "Release My unconditional Love through your own heartminds."*** "Let My flawless Love be your Love."*** "Love no less than God— universally."*** "Let Love Itself love through you."*** "Become a mirror of perfect inner Love."*** "Become an empty vessel of perfect Love within."*** "Become a hollow pipe through which inner, perfect Love can flow."*** "Love with the illimitable, immeasurable Love of the Spirit."*** "Love, not with human 'love,' but with perfect Love, by allowing It to manifest through your heartmind."*** "Express Love without self."*** "Express Love as the Spirit of Love."***

35. "This is the only Way in which it can be known that you have learned from Me." "This is the only Way that it can be recognized that you are truly My disciples."** "Loving is the only Way that you can truly follow Me."** "Love is the only criterion by which it can be determined that you are following My path."** "There exists no criterion by which truly spiritual beings can be recognized, but Love."*** "You have truly learned from the Spirit only when you practice Love."*** "The quality of Love, and no other, will distinguish and identify My enlightened followers."***

"Love each other."

***

The narrative continues with chapter 14, verse 1:

"Don't let your heart be troubled." "Don't let your emotions be disturbed."** "Keep your heartmind in tranquility and serenity."*** "Don't let fear make you nervous."*** "Don't let your human fears and emotions scare you from the Way."*** "Allow no place for inner disorder or harmful turbulence."*** "Try to relax in perfect trust."***

"Believe in God; believe in Me." "Hold to the belief that God controls all things, and let God act through My inner indwelling of your heart."*** "Find tranquility in the realization that God knows what God is doing, and communes with you through My indwelling of your inner being."***

"If you believe that God is in control, why worry?" "If you worry, it might be that you do not believe that God is in perfect control."** "If you believe that God lives, then believe also that he lives in and through you."*** "Believe in perfecting Love, and that Love will win."***

2. "In My father's house, there are many mansions." "Within the dwelling of My father are many smaller places."** "Within infinite Mind are many other, smaller minds."*** "Within the levels of Mind are innumerable layers."*** "In an endless Mind, you can go anywhere."*** "The Mindcosmos is awesome and vast, and holds a place of splendor for you."*** "Each being has a special place of splendor and Love within the illimitable Mind."*** "Your 'residence' is a body; and within cosmic Mind, infinite numbers and kinds of bodies are possible."*** "There are many ways to live; but they are all ultimately included in the Way of Love."*** "The inner cosmos is filled with an infinity of 'spaces,' awaiting only your discovery."*** "In immeasurable Being, an infinite number of realities coexist."*** "Uncounted mindsets exist within the one Mind."***

"If it were not so, I would have told you. I am going to prepare a place for you." "I am going to set up a place in Mind for you."** "You too have a place in this infinity."*** "I go into the mind as a settler, to prepare a place where you might live."*** "I go into bottomless Mind as a pioneer, to make maps for you."*** "I move into unexplored areas of the Mind, to shine a light, so that you can follow later."*** "I work on your inner future home."*** "I seek to build, repair, and improve your Mindhome."***

3. "And even though I'm going away to prepare a home for you, I will return and take you again to Myself." "Even though I take this journey and inner voyage, when I am finished, I will return in your mind, and become your guide."*** "I will return to embrace, heal, and support you with My Love."*** "Even when this physical form disappears, My Essence will return within you."*** "The Love that I am must disperse now. But I will always be returning to your innermost Being."*** "And even though I disperse My forces so that you might have a specially created place, I will come again to you and receive you to Myself." *** "I will return to you, and welcome you into Lovemind."*** "I will return to your heart, and embrace you as Lovemind."*** "I will keep rising within your mind, until I am one with you, and you with Me."*** "I will return personally to each of you, to welcome you into perfect Lovemind."*** "Your personal minds, and universes, will ultimately grow into one single shared Reality, and That will be Love."***

"Then, where I am, you also can be." "When I draw you to Myself in Love, you will be precisely at the same level of Mind as Myself."*** "You will be exactly what I am."*** "We will both share the same cosmos."***

4. "You know where I am going, and you also know the Way." "This is an area of Mind where you have been before. Since you wandered away from It, you also know the Way back."*** "At deeper levels of Mind, you know this path to deepest Mind and communion."*** "You already understand deeply the more profound mysteries of Mind and being."*** "Deep down, you already know all about where I am going into deepest Mind. You even know the path that leads there."*** "You know all about Home within, for you have all been there."*** "You not only know about the heavenly Homeworld within, but you are actually on the way there."*** "You have already been where I am going, and will surely be there again."*** "In deepest Mind, origin is also destination."***

***

The narrative continues with chapter 14, verse 6:

"I am the Way, the truth, and the life." "I am the inner path to Reality, I am that Reality Itself, and the life enjoyed in that Reality."*** "I am both Reality and the Mindpath that leads to it. I am also the life that permits it."*** "I alone, cosmic Mind, am the only Reality in the entire cosmos."*** "I am the pathmaker within that leads you to that Reality."*** "I am both Reality and the life-force that impels you towards Reality."*** "I am Reality at the Core of being."*** "I, as Love, am the guiding Way to Reality."*** "I am the key to, and source of, inner life."*** "I am the Totality, the Cosmos, and the Mind underlying all things."*** "I am all life-processes of growth and movement."***

"No one can come to the father except by Me." "You cannot get to the Sourcemind until you pass through the sonmind, and then, the Christmind."*** "You cannot reach the infinite Mind without turning to the inner path of the heart, which I am."*** "The infinite Sourcemind cannot be discovered outside of, but only through, the Spirit, which is My Self."*** "No one can approach cosmic Mind except through the deepest Mindlevels, which I am."*** "Intellect cannot take you to your divine nature. Only I, Lovespirit, can do this."*** "I, sonmind, am the mediator between human mind and cosmic Mind."*** "Only the operation of Love, which is all My Love, allows human nature to grow into divine nature."*** "God cannot be known by mind until mind has penetrated to My level, the Lovespirit."***

7. "If you had known Me, you would have known My father." "To know enlightened sonmind, or Christmind, is to know Sourcemind."***

"From this time forward, you know him and have seen him." "Having seen Me, both in this human form and in your own minds, you know the divine Mind."*** "Even if you do not know it with the human mind, you are continuously knowing and seeing him."*** "At this very instant, God is working within you, so that you can know and perceive God."*** "At any instant of your life, you can sense God with your inner senses."*** "Through both inner and 'outer' manifestations, you can know and see God."***

***

The narrative continues with chapter 14, verse 9:

"Have I been with you for so long ...and yet you do not know me.?" "I have been with you so long that you should not mistake Me for a 'human being'" *** "Have I been so long with you and still you do not know that I am the Spirit?" ***

"Anyone who has seen Me has seen the father." "To see a person is to see the Source in manifestation."*** "If you have looked deeply within your psyche, and seen the enlightened human mind, the Christ, then you have seen the Sourcemind."*** "To see a fully enlightened person is to see the Sourcemind projected."*** "In Me lies the incarnation of Lovewisdom."*** "If you can see what I really am, and not just this body, then you have 'seen' the Mind of the Infinite."*** "When you sense My deepest nature and Mind, which is also your own, you sense the Immeasurable."*** "If you have felt the full Power of My Love, then you have felt God."*** "When you can 'see' the deep Lovenature, you see the Illimitable."***

10. "Don't you believe that I am in the father, and the father is in Me?" "The Sourcemind and My Christmind interpenetrate."*** "The Sourcemind and Christmind mutually infuse each other."*** "Sourcemind fills Me, and I fill the Sourcemind."*** "I exist only

within the Sourcemind."*** "The difference between My Self and the Sourcemind is only symbolic, but has no substantial reality."*** "Very deeply, I am the Sourcemind."***

"The sayings that I manifest to you do not come from my personal self. But the father who lives within me is doing his work." "I permit the Sourcemind, from deep within me, to do Its own will."***

11. "Believe Me, that I am in the father, and the father is in me." "Have faith that human nature exists within divine nature, and the divine is the Source of the human."*** "Human perception is divine creation."***

"Believe because of the manifestations." "Believe because of the entire miraculous cosmos unfolding around you continuously."***

12. "Whoever believes in Me will do the works that I do." "If you believe as I do, the same Sourcemind will manifest and express through you, in similar ways."*** "Whoever believes that I am more real than the self or world will manifest Me."*** "She will become transparent to the Light of My Love."*** "Her actions will arise from Me rather than from a personal self."*** "She will yield and surrender personal will to the will of Lovemind."*** "She will know what I know, become what I am, and so produce what I produce."***

"And greater than these will he do." "She will, in fact, do works greater than My own."** "She will expand and surpass what I have done."*** "She will progress beyond the present actions of the Spirit."***

"For I go to the father." "My Union with Sourcemind is nearly complete."*** "I am about to vanish into the Sourcemind."*** "I am about to lose my self completely in the Sourcemind."*** "I am about to disappear into Sourcemind, leaving only Sourcemind."*** "I return to My original Mind, the Sourcemind."*** "This human self will dissolve and vaporize, and My Essence will return to the Sourcemind."*** "I am again becoming, as in the beginning, indistinguishable from the Sourcemind."*** "My full synergy with the cosmic Mind is being completed."***

13. "And whatever you ask in My name, I will do." "Whatever you ask while in My identity I will do."** "Whatever you ask as My Self, your own deepest Self, I will do."*** "Whatever you ask while in Christmind, desire-free, will be done by Me."*** "Whatever you request while in the state of no-self will come to be."*** "Whatever

creative impulse stirs within, when you have become the Self of the cosmos, will manifest."*** "When all personal will has evaporated into the will of Love, then that will shall be expressed."*** "When you have reached a state in which there is no more separation, then the will of Love will manifest through you, and through the cosmos."*** "When the self disappears into Me, you will ask for only Love, and Love will have its way."*** "When all selfish desire has disappeared in fullest union with Me, then your fondest wishes will come true."***

14. "Whatever you ask in my name I will do."

15. "If you love Me, do what I tell you." "Love for the deepest Self must be shown, not just professed."*** "If you truly love the state of enlightened Mind, it will result in actions, not just words."*** "You will keep My regulations of Love."*** "You will follow My guidance in Love."*** "You will yield your will to Mine."*** "You will surrender independence to Love."*** "Live every moment under the continuous control of Love."*** "Let Me live, act, and speak through you."*** "To surrender personal control is what it means to love."***

16. "And I will ask the father. And he will give you another comforter, advocate, helper, counselor, and friend.* And he will be with you into the ages." "I'll request that the Sourcemind send into your heartmind another helper, and he will be with you always."*** "The Sourcemind will send into you another friend, who will be with you in the timeless state."*** "You will then meet God in the inner role of friend and helper."*** "The deepest Power of spiritual Mind will then comfort you."*** "From the Sourcemind, through Me, will rise powers of comfort, help, and Love."*** "The Sourcemind will indwell you not simply as father, but as friend."***

17. "He is the Spirit of truth." "This new friend is the Essence of Reality."** "He is the deepest Mind, which is Reality Itself."*** "He is the deepest Mind which continuously forms reality."*** "He is the deepest Mind which continuously dreams into existence the cosmos."*** "He is both experience and experiencer."*** "He is the deepest Self, free from illusion."***

"The world cannot receive him." "The natural order cannot contain the Spirit, for It is supernatural."** "The cosmos cannot contain the totality of divine Mind, for It is limitless."*** "The material universe does not contain him, but he contains it."*** "The cosmos is not he, but his dream."*** "The material universes cannot accommodate this Mind, for It is immeasurable."*** "He cannot be understood in simply natural terms."*** "Being outside of, above, time and space, the Sourcemind does not exist completely in the 'material' universe."*** "The purely 'material' mind cannot expand enough to permit his entry."*** "The material view has no place for him."***

"For it cannot see him or know him." "For the natural order does not make visible all of him, and so, he cannot be completely known through nature."** "Nature is a realm of the visible, and he, as Mind, is invisible." *** "He must be perceived only through direct inner experience."*** "The material worldview does not recognize inner knowing, but all reality can be known only in this way."*** "*Gnosis* is beyond material structure or material mind."*** "The instruments and minds of this world cannot detect or measure him."***

"But you know him, for he dwells with you, and will be within you." "The only Way that you know him is that he is always with you, because he is within your mind."** "You have known gnosis, and he will continue to grow into your mind and being."***

18. "So, I will not leave you without comfort, desolate, as orphans, abandoned*." "So, I will not desert you, leaving you all alone in the cosmos."** "After I leave this world, you will not be alone or empty."*** "You will not be without inner guidance."*** "I've come in this form to point you, not towards me, but towards the inner Spirit. After I leave, it will be easier for you to find him."*** "I must leave this material form so that you do not become dependent on it, or on me. This is needed, so that you will be forced to look within yourselves for the Spirit, and not outward to me."***

19. "In just a little while, the world will see Me no more." "Soon, I will depart from the natural order, leaving this body behind."** "I will return to My invisible inner state."*** "I will return to the state of invisible original Mind."*** "I will go back to My Origin, to Sourcemind."***

"But you will still see Me. It is because I live that you also will live." "But you will still perceive Me within your own minds as deepest inner Mind. My 'fountain' of life will bestow life upon you."*** "You will still see Me within your heart. And because I live always, so will you."*** "I will be internalized within you, and you will 'see' Me within yourselves rather than in 'separate, physical' form."*** "Because I am life, as long as you are in Me, you will draw sustenance from Me, and never die."*** "As you begin to live My life, you will start to feel your immortality."***

20. "Then, you will know that I am in My father, and you are in Me, and I am in you." "Then, you will receive the gnostic knowing of the interpenetration of minds. I live within the Sourcemind, and within you, and you also live within Me."*** "I am immersed in the Sourcemind, and in you. You are immersed in Me."*** "The cosmic Mind infuses Me; I infuse you, and you infuse Me."*** "Cosmic Mind is like a mist, and I am a mist within the mist, and you are a mist within Me."*** "All Mind is one, an indivisible Whole, whether It pretends to be me or you."*** "Through Love, minds formerly believed separate come together and merge. They Mindmeld— mine into the Sourcemind at one end, and into you at the other, and yours melds with Me."*** "I am indistinguishable and inseparable from the Sourcemind, and am equally inseparable and indistinguishable from you, and you from Me."*** "I am saturated with the Infinite, and you with Me."*** "Divisions among minds are artificial and illusory, since we all draw all thoughts from the father of the all."*** "The Whole differentiates himself into you and Me, but this is ultimately an illusion. When it disappears, we are again one and whole."*** "Only one Mind, one Spirit, one Reality exists, but expresses Itself into many forms, including you and Me."*** "Godmind is many-formed, appearing first as one life, then another."*** "The divine Mind scatters as any number of forms, but it is only that nature that is ultimately real."*** "In precisely the same Way that My life is a unified, unbroken, seamless reflection of Lovemind, so yours is of Me."*** "My life is really the Sourcemind's life, and yours is really Mine." *** "Your mind, My mind, and the Sourcemind constitute a single wholeness, a single Mind."*** "All Mind already exists in perfect integration, union, and wholeness, but we need to realize and to remember."*** "Your mind is coexistent, coequal, and coterminal with Mine, and Mine with the Sourcemind."***

21. "Whoever receives My command, and follows it, is the one who loves Me. He will be loved by the father." "Real Love for Me is not just the reception of My control, but living in it. She who lives the

Way is the one who receives of Love from the deep Sourcemind."*** "Surrender to Me unites you with the Sourcemind, the Fountain of all Love."*** "Living by My guidance brings you to the state of grace— complete forgiveness in Love."*** "Only she who continuously responds to My inner direction of Love truly loves Me."***

"And I will love him, and manifest Myself to him." "I will love her who loves Me, and inwardly reveal Myself to her."** "Mutual Love will bond us, and she will know the inner splendor of My presence."*** "Her self will become My Self, through her devotion."*** "My true inner nature will be disclosed and uncovered to her."*** "Love will draw her into My Mind and Self."*** "I reveal My Self to her and in her, as Love, and so become her Center."*** "For her, I become more real than anything else, and I live through her."*** "I will appear to her inner vision, and shine upon her heart."***

***

The narrative continues with chapter 14, verse 23:

"He will keep My Logos." "She will work in harmony with the perfect expression of the Limitless."** "She will perfectly manifest Lovemind."** "She will accept as her higher, deeper Self the empty mirror of reflective Mind."*** "She will exchange her human identity for that of the Logos of Love."*** "She will manifest and reflect the life of the Logos of Love."*** "Her life will be controlled and regulated by the Logos of Love, as she surrenders to It."*** "She will live from, and cultivate, the deep Lovenature."***

"And My father will love him, and we will come to him, and make our abode with him." "The Sourcemind will radiate Love to fill her. The Sourcemind and Christmind will move into her Mind, and permanently reside there."*** "The Sourcemind and the Christ, the enlightened sonmind, will inhabit her Mind."***

24. "He who does not love Me does not obey My words." "She who does not act on these teachings has no real love for Me."** "Real Love for Me requires action."** "If anyone does not surrender to these teachings, then she has no Love for Me."*** "She who does not follow My inner guidance has no Love for Me."*** "Love is demonstrated only when one yields to, and obeys the direction of, Lovemind, which I am."*** "If one does not follow her heart, in the

inner instruction of the Logos of Love, then she has no Love for Me."*** "If a person does not live by compassion, goodness, tolerance, and kindness, then she has no Love for Me."*** "She who really loves Me obeys Me as the perfect expression of God." ***

"And the words that you are hearing now are not my personal expression but that of God."

25. "I have said all these things while I am still with you." "I have taught these ideas while I remain in this physical body."***

26. "But the Paraclete, the Comforter and Helper*, whom the father will send in My name, will teach you all things. It will bring all things back to your memory." "But the Sourcemind will send to you the inner Comforter, after I have left this world. And this Helper will teach you all the secret and sacred mysteries, and aid you to remember all and keep them all in your awareness."*** "Because I will no longer be with you in a physical body, the Sourcemind will send into your heart a special Power called the Helper. This special comforter will teach you exactly as I have, and cause you to keep continuously in mind the true nature of Reality."*** "I do not want you to become overly dependent upon this body, this mind, this Jesus, because he must die. Instead, place all your trust and confidence in that Spirit of Love, the Logos of which I am the perfect incarnation. He lives within your own hearts."*** "The Sourcemind will send the Friend to make up for My absence, after I am gone from the natural order."*** "This Helper will place the entire cosmos in your Mind and memory."*** "This Spirit will teach you everything that there is to know."*** "This Mind will shift the entire cosmos to an inner plane, and bring it all back to your memory."*** "The Spiritmind will expand your mind to a vastness that will include everything."*** "The Sourcemind will send this Spirit in My identity, as the inner Christ."***

27. "Peace I leave with you; My peace I give unto you." "I leave as My gift deep tranquility, and give you my very own serenity."** "My gift to you is tranquility, which arises from equanimity."*** "Transcendent equanimity is My gift to you."*** "I create peace within you."***

"I do not give 'peace' as the world gives it." "The peace which I give is not the temporary and fleeting state that arises from the natural order."*** "This deep tranquility does not come from changes in the natural order or the body."*** "This tranquility does not arise from the 'external, material' world."*** "This serenity does not depend on conditions in the world around you."*** "It does not depend upon others, but flows outward from your deepest interior Mindbeing."*** "It is independent of the changes in the natural order."*** "It does not come from the world, so that world cannot take it away."*** "Deep true peace has nothing to do with the conditions around you."***

"Do not let your heart be troubled, neither let it be afraid." "Do not allow fear to create distress in your heart."** "Keep peace in your emotional nature, and never give in to fear."*** "Allow no place for fear. Do not allow your inner being to become disquieted."*** "No matter how disturbing are the appearances of life, do not surrender to fear."*** "Let tranquility reign in your heart."*** "Fear is defeated through the realization of deep tranquility."*** "Do not allow fear to unsettle, distress, or intimidate* you; let My tranquility heal fear."*** "Give no inner power to fear by active resistance. Instead, allow yourself to settle into unresisting tranquility."*** "Make the fearless state your goal."***

28. "I go away and come again to you." "This body must leave, but this Spirit will come to you in your own interior Mind."*** "In my going is the guarantee of My coming again to your heartmind."*** "I cannot fully come until I fully go, leaving the form of the human Jesus."*** "After Jesus leaves this world, Christ will come to your heart."*** "I cannot come to you in My interior form until this exterior form leaves the world."*** "If I did not leave this human form, this Jesus form, it would distract you from My Spirit in your own heartmind."*** "I leave in flesh, but return in Spirit."*** "My second 'coming' will be My presence within the hearts of My friends."***

"If you loved Me, you would rejoice." "If you loved Me, you would rejoice at my death."** "If you loved Me, you would rejoice at My liberation from this body."** "If you understood Love, you would be happy to know that, when I leave this poor body, I will become the almighty and everlasting Spirit."*** "The greater Love rejoices that I am to die into the Lovemind, to return Home."*** "My 'death' is really My resurrection to the life of splendor, untouchable tranquility, and immeasurable Love."***

"For I said, 'I go my way to the father,' for the father is greater than I." "As I told you, the father is so much greater than my human self, and it is to him that I go."** "For I am going into inner union with the Sourcemind, which is greater than this human self."*** "For I am returning to fullest divine nature, the Sourcemind, unimpeded by this limited human form."*** "In the limitless inner nature, whose being is so much greater than this form, this self, I enter the full splendor of Illimitability."*** "I drop the human for the superhuman Self."*** "At death, I dissolve all boundaries, and enter the splendor of illimitable Light."***

29. "I have told you this before it happens so that when it does happen, you can believe." "I have described My glorification in splendor, so that, when it actually happens, you can know that My teachings are trustworthy."*** "I have described what will happen to me, and to you, at death, so that, when it does happen, you might believe in the inner life."***

30. "Soon, I will not talk much with you." "Soon, the time for discussion will come to an end."** "Soon, talking will not be enough."** "Soon, description will be replaced by experience."*** "Beyond the point described, we enter the Indescribable."*** "Beyond what has been said, words are not useful indicators."*** "Words have not been designed to describe higher realities."*** "What must be known and experienced after this, I cannot put into words."*** "After this, Mind extends far beyond the range of talk."***

"For the prince of this world comes, but has nothing in Me." "The principles that rule the natural order do not limit Me."*** "The limits of observation do not limit the Soul."*** "The limits of previous experience do not bind the Spirit."*** "The weakness of being fully dominated by the natural order has left My life."*** "The kingdom of the natural order has no rulership over Me."*** "I am now free from manipulation by the 'material' world."*** "Since I have found its Master, the Sourcemind, the natural order can no longer hold or dominate Me."*** "Love has overcome the forces of illusion."***

31. "I want the world to know that I love the father." "I do not love the natural order for its own sake, but because it reflects the Sourcemind."*** "The natural order, of which this bodymind is a part, knows that My Love for the Sourcemind is supreme."*** "Love

for the Sourcemind is the key to My relationship to the natural order."*** "The entire natural order is renewed by participation in My great Love for the Sourcemind."*** "Even the natural order must be educated by Love."*** "Everything in the natural order must be subservient to Love."*** "Everything in the natural order must be absorbed into Love."*** The Sourcemind Expresses everywhere in the natural order."*** "And I do what the father commands Me to do." "And I live by the direction and guidance from the inner Sourcemind."***

***

The narrative continues with chapter 15, verse 1:

"I am the true vine, and my father is the gardener." "I grow from earth-nature, but I am cultivated and fed by the Sourcemind."*** "I am a living Source of life, and the Sourcemind is My care-taker."*** "I am the life-principle of growth from which others naturally and organically grow."*** "I am the life, thriving on earthly nature, from which other lives grow, and the One Who sustains Me is the Sourcemind."***

2. "Any branch in Me that does not bear fruit he takes away." "Any part that grows from Me but is inactive, he prunes off."** "Any part of Me that is not productive, the Sourcemind snips off."** "Any part of Me that is not actively alive, he trims away."** "Any Mindfactor that is life-resistant must ultimately perish, for the Sourcemind will cut it off from the Whole."*** "Anything counterproductive or unproductive must be sliced away from the Mind."*** "Any extension of Me that dies in illusion is detached from life, and never blossoms with Love."*** "All begin life by growing from Me, but some lose their interconnection-insight, die in illusion, and are cut away from the Totality by Sourcemind."*** "Those who perceive themselves as dead are severed from the Reality of Wholeness by the Source."*** "The Sourcemind cuts away unreality, illusion."*** "Every thought that is Love-resistant is divided from integration."***

"And he cleans every branch that does bear fruit." "Sourcemind prunes every fruit-bearing branch."** "He strips all excess from every fruit-bearing branch."** "Any branch that is productive is purified to become even more productive."*** "All dead material is stripped away from living branches."*** "All deathmind is stripped away from lifemind."*** "All excess is taken by the Sourcemind."*** "All baggage is stripped away, streamlining life."*** "All that is dead is removed from the productive, creative, loving Mind."***

"This happens so that the branch might bring forth more fruit." "Excess and deadweight are stripped away that life might multiply and become more abundant."***

3. "You are clean through the words that I have spoken to you." "These teachings help to strip away all that is dead or excess from your minds."*** "These teachings will help you to be stripped clean of all unproductive thoughts and illusions."*** "You are freed from all things and thoughts that do not manifest My inner life and nature."***

4. "Keep living in Me, and I will keep living in you." "To know Me within yourself, you must be aware of Me, and imitate My life-pattern."*** "Live as I live, and I will dwell actively within you."*** "When you find your spiritual life in Me, I will express Mine through you."*** "Only when you are lost in Me am I found in you."*** "To the extent that you are immersed in Me, I am submerged in you."*** "Let us be lost in each other's Love."*** "Let us share a single life."*** "Let us share a single Mind."*** "Allow our identities to merge and intermix, and become inseparable."*** "Unite with My divine nature, and I will unite with your human nature."***

"The branch cannot bear fruit from itself without staying on the vine. Neither can you do anything unless you live in Me." "As the branches grow naturally from the vine, so your minds grow from Mine."*** "As the branches unite with the vine, and all branches share one common vine, so I unite with you, and all minds share Me in common."*** "As the branches are dead without the vine, so your mind becomes dead without My energizing inner presence."*** "As branches can produce no fruit without the vine, you can do nothing spiritual without Me."*** "I produce you; I give you life, as the vine does the branches."*** "As branches appear separate, but share a common life in the vine, so you, although you appear to have personal lives, also share a lifemind in common."*** "Broken away from Me, you can do nothing real."***

5. "I am the vine, and you are the branches." "I am the Source, and you are the manifestations or expressions."***

"The one who lives in Me, and allows Me to live in him, brings forth much fruit." "She has a richly productive heartmind."*** "She gets much accomplished."*** "She proliferates lifenergy and Lovenergy."*** "She produces the actions and attitudes of My Lovenature."***

"For apart from Me, you can do nothing." "You can do nothing real."** "You can do nothing spiritual."** "You can do nothing of lasting value."** "Broken away from Love, everything that you do is worthless and empty."*** "No one can do anything worthwhile 'independent' of the Totality."***

6. "If anyone does not live in Me, he is cast forth as a branch, to dry up." "If you are not living in Me, you are dead already."** "She is tossed aside, like a dead branch."*** "She withers, in unreality."*** "She lives in Loveless illusion."***

7. "If you live in Me, and My teachings live in you, you will ask for anything that you want, and it will be done." "Once our minds have interpenetrated, fused, and mingled, you will desire nothing but highest Love for all. When you ask for this, the will of God, it will always be done."*** "When, free of person, self, and selfish desire, you sink down into full union with Me, you can ask for only the will of Love. And it will be done."*** "In the will of Love, possibilities become infinite."*** "If what you ask for is divine, then it must be done."*** "My Love will become your asking."***

8. "This is how My father's splendor is manifested: You bear much fruit." "You will recognize your entry into enlightened splendor when you begin to act in the Way of Love."*** "Enlightenment is not just words; it is not complete until it results in the activities of Love."*** "The level and quality of your enlightened Mind is known only by your actions."*** "The only Way truly to honor the divine Mindspirit is to allow its qualities to manifest in your actions."***

"This is how you show that you are really My disciples."

9. "I have loved you exactly as the father has loved Me. Live in My Love." "The Love I have given you is the Love of the Sourcemind, coming through Me. Let My Love live through you."*** "I have loved you with cosmic Love from the Infinite. So, live in this Love."*** "I have loved you with boundless and unconditional Love; this is also how you must learn to love."*** "My Love for you is

divine Love. May it become your home."*** "Stay always in Love."***

10. "If you continue to follow My guidance, you will remain in My Love." "As long as you follow My advice, My Love will continue to flow into your heartmind."***

"In the same Way, I keep to the guidance of the father, and remain in his Love." "Love is the only evidence of divine guidance."*** "Surrender to the Source, and you will live in the Light of his Love."*** "To follow the Source is to be forever in Love."***

11. "I have shared these things so that My joy might remain within you." "These teachings awaken not only My Love, but My joy, within you."*** "Thinking about these ideas awakens perfect Love and perfect joy."*** "These words can implant endless joy within you."*** "Bliss is transferred to you by what I say."***

"In this way, your joy will be made perfect, complete, flawless, and full.*" "Because it is My joy, not produced by you, it is utterly whole, ecstatic."*** "When you know Me fully, you will experience overwhelming joy, total bliss, complete ecstasy."*** "As you touch Me, exquisite rapture will fill you."***

12. "This is My only command: Love people. For I have set the example." "Only one action is needed for the spiritual life: Love others, even as I have done."** "I ask only one thing of you: Love people. For this is what I have done."*** "I demand only one action: Love people. For this is what I have done."*** "Nothing else is necessary but that you love people."*** "Love people unconditionally, universally, and consistently."*** "Love with no thought of selfish gain."*** "Love with supreme and divine Love."***

13. "No one can have greater Love than this— to lay down his life for a friend." "The greatest Love in the universe is to lay down your life for a friend."*** "To give up a personal life to help a friend is the world's greatest Love."*** "It is the greatest Love to give up pursuit of a selfish life for a friend."*** "No Love can surpass that of a life given up for a friend."*** "The ultimate and supreme Love is to give up your life for a friend."*** "Spend your life on your friends, for this is supreme Love."***

"And you are My friends if you follow My direction." "I give up personal life for you, for you are My friends if you love."*** "Try to live this life of the inner Lovespirit, and then, you will be My friends."*** "Let Love control you, and that will make you my special inner companions."*** "Surrender all to Love, and you will become My Mindfriends."*** "If you allow Me, working from within, to bring harmony to your life, you will be My friend."***

15. "From now on, I will not call you 'servants,' but 'friends.'" "I do not want you to see Me as only Master, but as dear and deep Friend."*** "If you used to be My servants, you are now My beloved friends."*** "I would prefer your Love to mere mechanical service."*** "I don't want you to be only My servants; I invite you to become My heartfriends."*** "You are not 'hired as employees,' but warmly welcomed as friends."***

"For a servant does not know what his master is doing." "Only those who are unaware of My inner activity are 'servants.'"*** "Only people who know nothing of My continuous agapogenesis [Love-generation] are mere servants."***

"But I have called you 'friends,' because I have revealed all things that I have heard from My father." "I have told you everything that the Sourcemind has told Me."*** "I have taught you everything that the Sourcemind has taught Me."*** "Even the smallest item revealed by the Sourcemind I have revealed to you."*** "The Sourcemind has revealed all the secrets and mysteries of the cosmos, and I have taught them all to you."***

16. "You have not chosen Me, but I chose you, and gave you an assignment." "You might think that you have chosen Me. But actually, it is I who have chosen you, giving you a mission."**

"That mission is: Go, and bring forth fruit, so that your fruit should remain." "Go into the world, and do things of lasting value."*** "Go into the world, and create something that will last."*** "Your mission is to produce the everlasting qualities of Love."*** "Your assignment is to cultivate and develop Love."*** "Reflect the divine nature, and do not allow this to become a mere passing thing."*** "Invite Lovenature, the divine, to become a permanent part of you."***

"At that point, whatever you ask the father in My name, he will give you." "When you have lost self and selfishness in Love, and found the Christmind, and become It, Sourcemind will grant whatever you request."*** "Desire-free, free of personal wants, you will ask for only Love, and your wish will be granted by the loving Sourcemind."*** "When you have reached the zenith of supreme being, you will ask the Sourcemind, and It will flood you with illimitable Love."***

17. "I give you commands for only one reason— so that you will love one another." "The only demand made by the inner Spirit is Love."*** "The only Way in which I want to guide you is to love."*** "All my guidance and direction come down to Love."*** "Everything that I have said, in all My teachings, was designed to bring you to Love."*** "The summation of the life in Me is only this: Love."*** "A life in Spirit is a life in Love."*** "The only reason that I direct and guide your life is to produce Love in you."*** "If you love others, you are already obeying My commands."*** "The only Way to follow Me is to love."*** "The Essence of My Self, and all My words, is Love."*** "The sum of everything that I have ever said, taught, or commanded is Love."***

18. "If the natural order rejects you, know that first, it rejected Me." "The natural order produces animal nature, which is in conflict with higher spiritual nature. This lower nature does not support your spiritual goals, and so, repels you, just as it has Me."*** "The natural order cannot contain all of your supernatural Mind, or Mine."*** "The natural order does not produce or support Supermind or Superlove."*** "The natural order will act against your spiritual transcendence every step of the Way."*** "Materialism also repels and resists the divine Lovenature within you."*** "If you find it difficult to harmonize with the natural order, it is because I, living in you, am not of this order."*** "Antipathy exists between deepest Mind and the natural order, for Mind is supremely, supernaturally above nature."*** "You can no longer fully adjust to the natural 'material' order, for it supports assumptions that will conflict with your new state of being."***

19. "If you remained a part of the natural order, it would love you." "If you did not go beyond your animal nature, it would embrace its own."*** "If you never wanted to be more than a mechanism, the 'material' world would be fond of you."*** "Nature welcomes you as animal, for, as animal, she 'owns' you."*** "Both nature and Lovemind want to control you completely, and a choice must be made."*** "The 'material' world showers rewards upon only those

who prostitute themselves to its full control."*** "The natural order lavishes easy 'love' upon only those who never question it."*** "Those who see themselves as only 'animals' fall into easy, attractive harmony with the lowest nature."***

"But it is because you do not belong to the natural order that it holds antipathy towards you. For I have chosen you to emerge from it." "I have chosen you to emerge from the fog of convincing illusion, the hypnotic trance of 'material' existence."*** "I have chosen and taught you to transcend petty matters, greed, and social conformity."*** "I have taught you to rise above a merely 'material' or 'natural' view of your Self."*** "You are liberated from commonality and animality."***

20. "... The servant is not greater than the master. What has oppressed Me will oppress you as well." "If I have been harassed, abused, rejected, and disfellowshipped*, you will be also. But those who have kept My sayings will keep yours also." *** "All spiritual people undergo some alienation. But some have listened to My teachings, and they will also welcome you."*** "In society, you will have problems being accepted, but some will listen."*** "Society might never accept you as 'normal,' but some will listen and hear."***

21. "These events will occur because of My name." "This will happen because of My identity."** "This will happen because My deepest Self is also your deepest Self."*** "These will not be occurrences that you have brought upon yourselves. They will happen because you have adopted the new identity of the inner Christ of Love."*** "People will respond harshly and hatefully because of your claim to be one with Me."*** "They will act without understanding and without Love."*** "They will hate you because unity with Me is incomprehensible to them."***

"For they have no direct knowing of the One Who sends Me." "They will act out of pitiable ignorance."*** "Being empty of the knowing of the inner Lovenature, they will respond with fear."*** "Never having tasted gnosis, they find the whole idea incomprehensible, absurd, and even damnable."***

22. "If I had not spoken, they would not have been guilty." "If they did not have access to My teachings, they would be blameless."** "If I had not clearly taught the mysteries of inner

oneness, they could excuse their stupidity, narrowmindedness, and cruel judgments."*** "If I had not alerted them to the better Way, they would have no sense of guilt."*** "It is their own conscience that criticizes, blames, and damns them."***

"But now, they have no excuse for their angry hatred." "There is no real excuse for their missing the point."*** "They do not understand even their own violent minds."*** "They cannot excuse their full identification with lower, animal, nature."***

23. "To refuse to love Me is to refuse to love My father." "If you do not love the Lovemind in incarnation, you do not love the Sourcemind at all."*** "To refuse to love God in people is to refuse to love God at all."*** "To reject or hate Me is to do the same to the Sourcemind."*** "To repel Me within yourself is to repel the entire cosmos."***

24. "If I had not done among them things that no other person has ever done, they would be without sin." "If I had not brought the teachings that no other person has brought to them, they would not have a guilty mind of selfcondemnation and sinmind."*** "They would be unaware of the enormity of their flawed state."*** "They would not know such a stark contrast to their own situation."*** "They would be unaware of the depth of their ignorance and incompleteness."***

"But now, they have hated Me and My father." "As representatives of the average person, they love Me and My father less than other pursuits."*** "They react with cynicism and violence to the idea of an interior Christ and an interior Sourcemind, because the challenge is too great."***

***

The narrative continues with chapter 15, verse 26:

"The Comforter will come. I shall send this from the father. This is the Spirit of truth. It comes out of the father. He will testify about Me." "The comforter, inner spiritual friend and helper, will come. I shall, as Christmind, send It directly into your heartmind from the Sourcemind. This is the Mindspirit that is the only Reality. All reality proceeds and emerges from the Sourcemind. This deep Mindspirit will teach about Me."*** "The deep inner Spirit is projected into you by the Source. It will be the model and essence of all that is real."***

"This Spirit will give you inner instruction about Me."*** "He will teach and show you My indwelling nature as Spirit. The Comforter and I both arise from the same divine Mind."***

27. "And you too will bear testimony." "The Spirit will speak about Reality through you."*** "He I am, and we will both speak through your words."*** "In what you know and teach, you will reflect these deeper teachings of the Spirit."***

"For you have been with Me from the beginning." "Human nature has been potential since the beginning of creation."*** "Since the first origin of the first Mind, both Christmind and human mind were together in potential."*** "From the beginning of existence, all creatures have existed in Mindpotential."*** "From the moment of the first thought, since the era of the Logos, you have been."***

***

The narrative continues with chapter 16, verse 1:

"I have told you these things so that nothing will cause you to fall." "Nothing will make you stumble."** "Nothing can make you fall from perfect grace."*** "Nothing can draw you back down to the lowest mind."*** "These teachings are your inner support against destabilizing forces."*** "Try not to fall from your higher state of being."***

2. "People will disfellowship you from the congregation." "They will reject you."** "They will put you out of the synagogue."** "They will excommunicate you."** "They will shun you."** "They will drive you from their assemblies."** "They will expel you."** "They will exclude you from their groups."** "They will bar you from membership in their religions."** "Finding you incomprehensible, they will fear and reject you."*** "Because you live outside of, above, all doctrine, they will see you as dangerous."***

"Yes, the time is coming when anyone who even kills you will believe that he is performing God's service." "Religious hysteria and psychosis will drive people to believe that even violent murder of rejected people is the will of God."*** "Emotional frenzy will drive the mad and insane even to kill you, all in the name of God."***

3. "They will do these things because they have never known the father or Me." "The hideous violence will occur because they have no

Love, no Christ, recognized in their hearts."*** "They will lose the awareness that the Christmind and the Sourcemind of Love live within them."***

***

The narrative continues with chapter 16, verse 7:

"It is good, profitable, advantageous, and expedient* that I should go away. For if I did not go away, the Comforter would not come to you." "As long as I remain in human form, you will look for the Christ in Me, and not in yourselves. This is one main reason that I must leave."*** "If you continued to focus attention on My outer, human form, the inner Friend would not be discovered."*** "As long as I am in the human form, the inner Spiritfriend will not feel the pressure to come forth from within you."*** "He would not be awakened within you."*** "The holy Spirit would not become known to you."*** "The inner Power of the Helper would remain only a dormant, latent potential."***

"But if I do depart, I will send him to you." "If I do leave this human form, I can, as the enlightened Mind, the Christ, send the Friend to interface with your mind."***

8. "And when he has arrived, he will prove the world wrong." "And when he arrives at your perception-threshold, he will prove the natural order to be an illusion."*** "He will prove the world to be a mindconstruct."*** "He will prove the world to be Mindependent."*** "He will show that the natural order is a dream."*** "He will prove to you that service to the 'material' cosmos is an error."*** "He will prove that the 'material' cosmos is immaterial."*** "He will prove to you internally that the 'natural' order is of supernatural Origin."*** "He will prove that the 'natural, material' cosmos is not Reality."*** "He will reveal that the 'natural, material' world is Mind only."*** "He will place the 'natural, material' cosmos in proper, relative perspective."***

"His concerns will be sin, righteousness, and judgment." "He will concern himself with error, correcting mistakes, and absolute evaluations."** "He will teach about error, the correction of error, and the illusory existence of absolute evil."*** "He will communicate about imperfection, right alignment with deepest Mind, and the illusion of total evaluation."***

9. "He will be concerned about sin, because the people do not believe in Me." "The most important error is not to believe that I, as Mind, am more real than the world."*** "His first concern will be a belief in imperfection, which arises from embracing the human self instead of deepest Mind, or Me."*** "A full belief in imperfection arises from the belief that I am not the Core-reality at the Center of Mind."*** "The illusion is that I am not the central Reality of Mind within every being."***

10. "He will be concerned with righteousness, because I go My way to the father, and you will see Me no more." "He will be concerned with right alignment with divine Mind because I, as the model, will, upon leaving, change everything. For I will 'force' people to look inward for Me, when they are accustomed to seeing Me in an 'outer' form."*** "I will no longer be in human form, to serve as model and prototype for you."*** "You will no longer be able to look to Me 'outside,' but will have to look to your deepest inner Self for guidance."***

11. "He will concern himself with judgment, because the prince of this world is judged." "He will be concerned with absolute evaluation, because the Mindruler of the natural order passes judgment upon itself."*** "The Mindforces regulating the 'material, natural' cosmos base their ideas upon an absolute good opposed by an absolute evil."*** "The 'material and natural' order is affected by the illusion that an absolute evil can exist."*** "The world is measured and evaluated through the illusory lenses of 'good and evil' as equal opposites."***

12. "There are many more things that I have to say to you, but you are not able to bear them now." "So many more teachings flow from these, very intricate and complex, but you are not able to handle all that right now."*** "So much more could be said, but it would overload your human mind."*** "Your human mind could not tolerate the shifts in perspective."***

13. "However, when he, the Spirit of truth, has come, he will guide you into all truth." "But when the Spiritmind of Reality manifests, he will expand your capacities to understand, and will hold back nothing. He will fully expose and reveal the Totality of Reality."*** "You will learn it all from the inner Spirit, who will guide you into the deepest secrets and mysteries of cosmic

creation."*** "The Mind of Reality will Itself educate you in Reality, revealing to you the true nature of the cosmos."***

"For he will not speak of his own accord." "For he will become an instrument for the full revelation of the Christmind and the Sourcemind, exposing and opening up your mind to everything."*** "He will translate and transmit the Infinite."*** "He will not teach as a separate entity, but will be your own deepest Mind."*** "He cannot speak as a separate self; for he is a part of you, and a part of the Immeasurable."***

"He will communicate what he hears." "He will teach only what he hears from deepest Coremind."*** "He will simply relay messages from your own deepest Mind."*** "He will translate inner symbols into concepts."***

"And he will show you that which is to come." "He will teach you what will happen in the future growth of your mind."*** "He will tell you what will happen in your own future unfolding."*** "He will give glimpses of future splendor."***

14. "He will bring honor to Me." "I will be the object of these future visions."*** "His purpose will be to turn your mind towards inner Christmind, the Mind of enlightenment."***

"For he will draw upon what is Mine." "He will reach deeply into the Mind and tap the resources of the Christspirit."*** "He will draw from Me as the Core of his, and your, Mind."*** "He is derived from Me, and draws both his life and his thoughts from Me."***

"He will take the Essence of My nature, and show It to you." "He will reveal My essential nature, which is Lovemind."***

15. "Everything that the father has is Mine." "My resources are those of the Sourcemind, and hence, unlimited."*** "When he draws from My resources, he taps into infinity."*** "To receive from Me is to receive from the Sourcemind."*** "The whole cosmos is Mine."*** "I have become the master of the universe."*** "I am the inner Master of creation."*** "I 'master' the cosmos through perfect yielding and surrender." *** "I am Creatormind."*** "Whatever is created is formed and made through My Mind."***

"... He will take from what is Mine, and show It to you."

16. "In a little while, you will not see Me; and then, after that, you will see Me." "Soon, you will no longer see Me in this human form; but later, you will know Me as deepest inner Mind, within

yourself."*** "My human form will dissolve and disappear, but you will see Me later, as inner Spirit."*** "I am not this body, and it means nothing to Me; soon, I will abandon it. But you will find Me, the same Spirit, deeply ensconced within your own mind."***

"For I go to the father." "I lose personhood in the Infinite."*** "I give up separate identity to become the boundless Self."*** "I disappear and vanish into the Sourcemind, and I become It."***

***

The narrative continues with chapter 16, verse 20:

"...You will weep and mourn, but the world will be glad." "You will experience a darknight in which the simplistic 'material, natural' order will promise an illusory happiness."*** "The life free from Spirit will seem to offer greater happiness than the route to the inner Self."*** "The 'outer, material' natural order will seem to offer happiness, by contrast with your own spiritual crisis."***

"But your grief will turn to gladness." "It will be transformed into joy."** "It will lead to ultimate bliss."*** "In time this very spiritual grief will take you to rapture."*** "Later, this sadness will lead to inner ecstasy."*** "The darknight of sadness will be the sign of a new day of joy."*** "The same spiritual sensitivity that creates pain will later create bliss."*** "The ecstasy does not arrive until after the crisis."*** "When the storm has passed, new joy will shine brightly upon you."***

21. "A woman, when about to give birth, is in agony because her time has come. But as soon as the baby is born, she forgets her anguish, because she is so happy that a new life has been brought into the world." "It is as if you are experiencing inner birthpains. Your mind is about to 'give birth' to your Soul, and later, your Soul to Spirit. When the process of your rebirth is completed, when you have become Spirit, you will forget all the pain."***

22. "In exactly this same way, you too have sorrow and grief now. But I will see you again, and your heart will rejoice." "Right now, you are going through a spiritual crisis, because I am going away. But after you have been reborn as the Spirit, I will see you again, in your deepest Mind, and your heart will be full of joy."*** "When next I see you, after rebirth, you will spill over with bliss."*** "Your bliss will be irreversible, beyond the reach of the changing world."***

116

23. "And in that day, you will not need to ask anything of Me." "By then, you will no longer need Me as an 'outer' being, for you will have fully internalized Me."*** "You will not even need Me to help you on the 'outside,' for I will have become a part of your own deepest Mind."****"You will be completely independent of any 'outer' Christ."*** "You will be so satisfied that you will need, or ask for, nothing."*** "You will know not to seek Me in the 'outer' cosmos."*** "You will be empty of all selfish desire."*** "Your deepest wishes will have been all fulfilled in your discovery of inner Christmind and bliss."*** "When separateness evaporates, you will find bliss by merging with Lovemind."***

"...Whatever you request from the father in My name, he will give it to you." "Whatever you request in My identity will be granted."** "Being Lovemind, you will request nothing but perfect Love, and it will be granted by the Sourcemind."*** "You will ask the Sourcemind for only his will, and you will receive it."*** "You will have disowned and abandoned all desire but Love."***

24. "Until now, you have not asked for anything in My name." "To this point, although you have prayed many traditional prayers, you have not requested anything while in My identity."*** "You have never lost your human self and its desires in the will of Love, or in Lovemind."*** "You have never learned how to ask without self."***

"So, ask, and you will receive." "Ask without self, and Love is already yours."***

"Then, your joy will be complete." "When the prayer of Love is answered within the psyche, you will be fully absorbed into bliss."*** "Without self, without desire, joy is boundless."***

25. "I have spoken to you of these things only in terms of allegories, proverbs, obscure sayings, riddles, similes, parables, veiled references, indirect hints, indications, figurative language, and symbols."* "I have so far spoken to you only indirectly and obscurely regarding the great mysteries of Mind and Being."***

"But the time is coming when I will no longer speak to you in obscurity." "The time approaches when I will be able to teach the deepest mysteries in plain and clear speech."*** "I'll be able to teach with simpler, more lucid expression."*** "These things must be covered now. But soon you will be made plainly aware of them." ***

"I'll be able to teach without comparisons, allegories, similes, and metaphors*."***

"Instead, I will show you directly and plainly the things of the father." "I'll be able to explain these teachings so that all can understand them easily."*** "I'll expose you directly to the teaching and Way of gnosis, and it to you."*** "I will precisely verbally unravel the secret mysteries of Being and the Source."***

26. "When, in the deepest state, you ask in My name, I will not have to go to the Father for you." "Only in the deepest Mind will you be capable of asking in My identity. Then I will not have to go to the Father for you." *** "Until full enlightenment, you will be bound to and limited by the human selfmind."***

"I will not have to intercede for you then." "You will not need an 'external' link with Sourcemind."*** "I will not have to translate the Sourcemind to your human mind."***

27. "For the father loves you individually." "The father loves you as special persons."** "The father loves each of you exactly as he loves the Christ."***

"For you have loved Me." "For you have loved Me, and that is the same as loving Sourcemind."*** "The Love that you have directed towards the Sourcemind turns around and flows back to you."*** "By loving Me, you have loved the Sourcemind, which means that you have loved your deepest Self."*** "The Love that you have sent inward to the Sourcemind is reflected back to you."*** "Your Love has awakened his Love."*** "Your Love, amplified and purified, is his Love."***

"And you have believed that I am sent by God." "And you have believed that I am projected by Sourcemind."***

28. "I came forth from the father, and have now come into the world." "I was projected and beamed forth from the Sourcemind, into the natural order."*** "The Source emanated Me."*** "The father is immanent in Me."*** "I use a human form, but continuously draw My being and essence from Sourcemind."*** "To become manifest as a human being, I had to step down My Power and enter the natural order."*** "I had to temper infinite Power with limits."***

"But now, I leave the world and go to the father." "Now, I reverse that process, and return to the Sourcemind."*** "Now, I drop the mask, quit the play, abandon the human, and return to infinite Love and joy in the Source."*** "I leave behind form, and return to the Formless."*** "I abandon illusion and appearance, and return to Reality."*** "I now leave the world of effects, and unite with the Cause."*** "I now desert the 'external,' and fuse with the Internal."*** "Now, I rise above the relative, and ascend into the Absolute."*** "I leave time, entering timelessness."*** "I leave behind reflection, and return to original Mind."***

***

The narrative continues with chapter 16, verse 33:
"...In the world, you will have trouble." "In the natural order, you will have problems."** "Knowing the great truths and mysteries, it will be a challenge to live in the 'material, natural, exterior' world."*** "Your Soul will create difficulties in the natural order, in order to teach you."*** "The division between the inner spiritual and the 'outer material' world will create stress."***

"But you can live in courage, for I have become greater than the world." "But have no fear, for I am more powerful than the natural order."** "I have moved above the illusions of the 'material, external' cosmos."*** "In Me, divine Mind has overcome human mind."*** "Highest nature has had victory over lower nature."*** "I have joined My Mind to the Creator, not the creation."***

***

The narrative continues with chapter 17, verse 2:
"...Father, the hour has come. Bring your son into splendor, that he might also bring you into splendor." "Let the inner splendor of sonmind reflect perfectly that of the Sourcemind."*** "Lift my human mind to enlightenment that it might also bring You into its enlightenment experience."*** "Let infinite Mind shine Its splendor into the finite mind."*** "Shine upon human nature, that it might shine back upon You."*** "Amplify Your splendor within human nature, and it will increase its recognition of splendor within You."***

"For you have given him power over all flesh." "You have given Him Power over all the lower nature."** "You have empowered him over lowermind."** "Human nature has been given, by Sourcemind, all power over the lower nature."*** "Human nature has been made

Master of both itself and lower, animal nature."*** "Human beings have been made sovereign over their inner minds."***

"And this is the reason: That he should give timeless life to as many as you have given him." "This nature grants timeless nature to all the parts of the inner Mind, as many as you have led it to know."*** "When the human nature discovers timeless nature, it is found to exist in all."*** "The very recognition of timeless nature bestows it upon others."*** "In knowing that timeless life is intrinsic to the Mind, one grants it to many others."***

3. "And this is timeless life— intimately, directly to know you, the God of Reality, and the one whom you sent, Jesus Christ." "This is what 'timeless life' means: immediately, deeply to experience and know you, the only God of Reality, and the one whom you project within, Jesus Christ."** "Gnosis is timeless life."*** "Knowing divine nature lifts one into inner and timeless being."*** "Knowing bottomless Love lifts out of time."***

4. "I have made your splendor manifest on earth." "I have shone the Light of your Reality and splendor into the natural order."*** "I have illuminated the 'material' cosmos with divine Mind and Its splendor."***

"I have finished the work that you gave Me to do."

5. "And now, O father, give Me splendor with your own self." "Fill Me with your splendor, that we may share one splendor."*** "Change Me fully into the fullness of complete Lovenature."*** "Strip away every vestige of human nature, leaving only the divine."*** "Dissolve the human mind into the complete fullness of your Essence."***

"I will once again find the splendor that I had before the 'material' and natural order existed." "Return Me to original splendor, which I knew before matter even came into being."*** "Return me to the splendor that I knew before the worldream began."***

6. "I have manifested your name to the men whom you gave to Me out of the world." "I have directly revealed your identity to human beings who have risen above the 'material' and natural order."** "I have manifested your Self and identity to those who have emerged from the hypnosis of the worldream."*** "I have revealed, shown, and displayed your real identity."*** "Deep within, I have introduced

your Lovenature to those parts of the mind formerly held captive by the dreamworld."***

"They were yours, and you gave them to Me." "All minds belong to you, but you gave them to Me."** "You allowed Me to participate in their creation/formation."***

"And they have conformed to your Logos." "They have also, with the deeper parts of Mind, become reflections or manifestations of your divine nature."*** "They have also become expressions of you."*** "They have been molded and imprinted by the exact likeness of your Lovenature."*** "They, as mirrorreflections of the Logos, are identical with your Lovenature."***

7. "Now, they know that everything that you gave Me comes from you." "All My gifts and abilities, knowledge and wisdom arise from only you."*** "All exists only in your infinite Mind, and I am only another manifestation of you."***

8. "For I have given to them the words that you gave Me." "I have taught them only what you taught Me."** "I have added nothing to My transmission of your teachings."***

"And they have received them, and know that I emerged from you." "Because they were open to receiving this teaching, they know about our relationship— you as Source, and I as product."*** "They are now certain that I am an exteriorization of cosmic Mind, am your emanation and projection."*** "I am an extension of your limitless Mind."***

9. "I pray for them. I do not pray for the 'material' or natural order." "I move them closer to unification with your deepest Mind. This cannot be accomplished through materialism or ordinary nature."*** "I encourage the operation of cosmic Mind within them. I do not cast My prayermind into illusion."*** "I mediate between minds, cosmic and human, but do not bridge Mind with 'material' things."*** "I invest Lovenergy in human beings, but will not waste it on the insubstantial shadow of the world."***

10. "And everything that is Mine is yours, and what is yours is Mine." "As single Mind, we cocreate and jointly own the cosmos."*** "We hold the inner and 'outer' universes fully in common."*** "Everything 'personal' is really universal."*** "I own the contents of My Mind, which are also the contents of your Mind."*** "Everything in Me belongs to you, and everything in you

belongs to Me."*** "There are no distinctions between what 'I own,' and what is the property of the cosmic Mind."*** "In My human self, I own nothing; I am just borrowing from the cosmic Mind."*** "By My sensing and perceiving, you create."***

"And My splendor is manifested in them." "Even 'My' splendor is not Mine; it is found in others."*** "It exists potentially in all others."*** "'My' Light is projected into them all."***

11. "And now, I am no more in the world." "Already, in Mind, I am not a part of the natural order."*** "Being its dreamer, I am, within, no part of the 'material' universe."*** "I have ceased to be a part, but have become the Source, of the natural order."*** "I am both Projector and projected, Creator and created, Dreamer and dream."*** "I am both Emanator and emanated."*** "I am no longer in the world, but the world in Me."***

"But these are in the world, even as I come to you." "But some of My friends are still, in their own minds, a part of the natural order, even as I am lifted to Creatormind."***

"Holy father, keep through your own name those whom you have given Me." "Sustain and protect them through their embracing and adopting of your identity."*** "Preserve them as parts of your own being."*** "Help them realize, and then, maintain them in, your identity."*** "Bring them to see that the shared Self is the Self of all."***

"Let this be, that they might be one in exactly the same way that we are." "Help them to realize that 'the many' are 'the One.'"*** "Aid them to awaken to their unitive nature, as I have awakened to the fact of ours."*** "Guide them to see that, at root, they are all one Mind, playing various roles, wearing different masks."****"Let them discover the wholeness of one shared psyche."*** "Lift them above the appearance, and illusion, of separation."***

12. "While I was with them, in the world, I saved them in your name." "While I was with them in the 'material and natural' order, I preserved them, by sharing the teachings of your identity."*** "I kept them in awareness that your identity was also their deepest Self."*** "I insulated and liberated them from illusion by revealing your Mind as the single absolute Reality."***

"Not one of them perished except the child of destruction which fulfilled the ancient text." "Their minds are intact, nothing within them has died except the human nature as the Scriptures indicate."***

***

The narrative continues with chapter 17, verse 13:

"And now, I come to You. And I speak these things in the world, that they might have My joy fulfilled within themselves." "I share these teachings with the natural order, that the bliss of higher Mind might be enjoyed within their minds."*** "The ecstasy known only to the inner Christmind will blossom within them."***

14. "I have given them your Logos, and the world has developed antipathy to them." "I have gifted them with the recognition of the inner Logos as their truest Self. So, they are no longer as welcome in the natural order."*** "Since they are not products of nature, not animals, they do not fit in as well with the natural order."*** "Striving for Supernature, they have risen above nature."*** "They have been lifted above the lower nature."*** "They have risen above natural harmony with the natural order." ***

"They are not a part of the world, just as I am not." "They, merging with the Creatormind, are the causes, not the products, of creation."*** "They are not in the dreamworld, but have fused Minds with the Dreamer."*** "They originate with Mind, not matter."*** "Thus, they do not recognize the 'material' cosmos as their Source."*** "They refuse to regard the natural order as their master."*** "They are not in the natural order; it is within them."***

15. "I do not pray that you take them out of the world, but I ask that you keep them from evil." "I do not pray that they be lifted out of the natural order, which in its fullness means death, but that you preserve them safe from the illusion of 'evil.'"*** "Prevent their judging things as 'evil.'"*** "Insulate them from the illusion of absolute 'evil.'"***

16. "They are not of the world, exactly as I am not of the world." "They are not products of the natural world, even as I am not."** "They are not produced by the natural order, just as I am not."** "Neither they nor I can be products of the natural order, for we have both become one with the Mind of the Dreamer/Creator."***

17. "Make them holy by means of your truth." "Make them whole by merging them with the inner Mind of Reality."*** "Integrate them into the Mind that is Reality Itself."***

"Your Logos is truth." "Your manifestation in the deepest Mind is Reality."*** "Your expression in deepest Mind is Reality."*** "God is Reality."*** "Love is Reality."*** "Deepest Mind is Reality."***

18. "As you have sent Me into the world, in the same way, I send them into the world." "As you project Me, emanate Me, from your own Mind into the natural order, so I project and emanate them into the natural order."*** "As I am really you, they are really Me."***

19. "And for their sakes, I make Myself holy, that nothing might contaminate them." "It is for them that I create wholeness with your infinite Mind, that nothing can contaminate the pristinity of their worldvision."*** "I remain fixed in My unitive merging with you, the perfect, so that their minds might, through Me, also be perfect."*** "I keep my attention upon My oneness with you, so that they might always see the entire cosmos as you."*** "I hold firmly to the Reality of oneness and wholeness, that they might not fall into the illusion of separation."***

"Let them be made holy through the truth." "Let them also become whole by uniting with the Reality of the one Mind."*** "May they realize you as Reality. May this keep them in awareness of seamless continuity with the All."***

20. "But I do not pray for these alone, but also for all who will believe in Me through their word." "I hold not only these, but all who will awaken, in the heartcircle of My Love and blessings."*** "Others too will come to know that I alone am ultimately real."***

21. "In this way, they will all become one. This is exactly as you, father, are in Me, and I in you. Then, they also will be one in us." "In time, they will lose their illusionboundaries and join mindspirits. Father, they will all do exactly what you and I have already done. Then, they will be undivided from Me, and from you."*** "The perfectly unified life in which we are one includes them as well."*** "They will abandon their sense of loneliness, of separate identity."***

"In this way, the world will believe that you sent Me." "By having experienced unity itself, with you, Spirit, the natural order will come to know and believe that you emanated Me."*** "The entire natural and 'material' cosmos will be ablaze with gnosis, and will understand that, and how, you have projected Me."***

22. "And I have given them exactly the same splendor that you have given Me." "They are receiving, through My connections, the same enlightenment that I received from knowing you deep in the psyche."***

"They will be one, in exactly the same way that you and I are one." "As we are one through the sharing of a common glory, so they, through sharing this glory, are one with us."***

23. "I live in them, and you live in Me, so that they may be made perfect in one." "I live deeply in their minds, even as you live deeply in Mine. This realization will make them perfect in Mind."*** "As you are the nucleus of My being, so I am the nucleus of theirs."*** "You are the common Center at the Core of all mind."*** "They discover a perfect, flawless, seamless whole Mind with Me as Its Center, and you are My Center."*** "Let them sense their shared existence in each other, and I in them all, and you in Me."*** "Awaken them to the fact that you are all, that you are Me, that you are them."*** "May their minds reach perfect interflow with each other, by Love."***

"The world will thus know that you have sent Me. You have loved them in exactly the same way as you have loved Me."

24. "Father, it is My will that they whom you have given Me may also be where I am." "I call My followers to full equality with Myself."*** "I want them to join Me in perfect oneness with you."*** "I want to invite them into the ecstasy of oneness."*** "I want them to be fully immersed in your splendor, as I am."***

"I want them to know the splendor that you gave to Me before the founding of the natural order. For you loved Me before creation." "I want them to know My splendor, and your Love for Me, which preceded time and space."***

25. "O righteous father, the world has not known you. But I have known you, and these have known that you sent Me." "O father, so perfectly aligned with all Reality, the natural order has not fully known you. But I have, and these have come to believe that you projected and emanated Me."**

26. "And I have told them about your name, and will continue to tell them." "I have told them the secret of your identity, and will remind them within continuously."**

"In this way, the Love with which you loved Me will exist within them. And I will also live within them." "In this way, perfect Love of the One for the One will be ignited within them. And I will also live deeply within their Mind."***

***

The narrative continues with chapter 18, verse 36:

"My 'kingdom' is not of this world." "The domain of the inner Ruler is not the natural or 'material' order, but the heartmind."*** "What I rule is not material, but mind."*** "I influence and renew thoughts, not things."*** "I regulate heartminds, not borders."*** "My inner rulership is not over the illusion of the 'material' and natural cosmos."***

37. "This is why I was born; this is why I came into this world— to bear testimony to the truth." "I was born into this world for one reason— to teach about inner Reality."*** "The reason that I came into this natural order was to teach about the Reality, the deepest inner Mind."*** "My entire purpose is to speak of the evidence for inner Reality."***

"Everyone who is of the truth hears My voice." "Everyone who has touched the Reality of deepest Mind has heard my inner communications."*** "She has heard My inner teachings."*** "Whoever knows Reality understands what I teach."***

Author's Preface: Perfect Faith Is Perfect Relaxation

An inscrutable document of incredible simplicity. An obscure writing just on the verge of actually saying something. But it never quite says it. A delicious anticipation that teeters, delicately balanced, on the threshold of the promise of wisdom. But it seems to fail to deliver. A childlike writing of immense spiritual light. A book that takes an hour to read and ten thousand years to understand.

These phrases all apply to the Chinese mystical classic called the "Way of Virtue." [It's Chinese name is, for you Sinophiles, *Tao Te Ching* (pronounced "dow-deh-jing").] It was authored by the legendary sage Lao Tzu (pronounced "Lah'-o dzuh"). This was over four centuries before the birth of Jesus. This Galilean mystic was doubtlessly exposed to the brilliant sunlight of this famous Chinese text.

In the Way of Tao, simplicity is everything. But let this not blind you to the superb, intricate, subtle truths implied by the words of this book. In the present rendition, the tricky tightwire between simplicity of expression and profundity of meaning has created some challenges. This is *not* a new translation. The author does not speak Chinese. What, then, are his qualifications? He has understood the message of the Way. He is a practicing mystic. He has been one for over twenty-five years.

Mystics are "psychonautic" voyagers. They spend much timenergy in the canyons and caverns, seas and lagoons, of inner Mind. Taoism is all about Mind. So, although controversial, the obscure Chinese word *tao* will here be rendered "Mind," or, "great Mind." The word is capitalized because It is not egomind. It is cosmic Mind. "Tao" is synonymous with the deepest Corelevel or Coremind of the Unconscious. In the West this is the Reality that has been called "God" or the "Absolute." This interpretation is in harmony with the deepest teachings of intercultural mysticism. It more accurately describes Lao Tzu's intended teaching. It is far more lucid than the more literal "Way". To increase lucidity, another common Taoist word, *te*, will be rendered "Mindexpression." Its most mystical meaning is not indicated well by the traditional "virtue." *Te* is the direct expression of Mind. It is the great Mind manifesting as both behavior and "material" cosmos. "Virtue" is reducible to behavior. It fails adequately to imply the full meaning-spectrum of *Te*. It is spontaneous, natural, simple, and loving.

The text, even in the best translation, is bewildering, baffling, and obscure. Even with their excellent technical knowledge of Chinese, some translators have not the foggiest notion of what the word "Tao" means. This hampers meaningful translation.

Talent is worthless without experience. Skill is limited without passion. I'd rather see a physician who knows personal suffering than a cold, unfeeling doc with extraordinary talents in biochemistry. For the sensitive doc would have empathy, from experience. Understanding is preferable to technical expertise. Spiritual excellence is better than translation-skills. This is even more true in spiritual work. I would prefer a rendering of an important spiritual text by someone who understands the Core-concept. This is preferable to a more literal translation by one who has only technical skill with the words. Many will disagree. That is just fine. Why? It is a part of the greater pattern of the universe, the Tao.

The Chinese text is even more curt, clipped, and minimal than most translations. And they are sparse and Spartan enough. Why the parsimony? The original text was written for an audience who understood much about the Tao. Large gaps were expected to be filled in by mystics who had a familiarity with the idea of a cosmic Unconscious (Tao). Every little detail was not clarified. When speaking to a group of seasoned engineers, it is not necessary to explain every principle involved in a structure. You can use a handy shorthand. The same is true when speaking to chemists, mathematicians, and other specialists.

Mysticism is a similar specialty. It has its own shorthand. The vocabulary of ancient mystical works assumed a certain level of spiritual development in their readers. The challenge of the present rendition is to make the words intelligible. The ancient text of the *Tao Te Ching* is quite sparse. It is naked. It is succinct to the point of swallowing up its own statements. It is little more than a verbal matrix. Around this, meaningful wordpatterns must be constructed.

This is much more than a game of "fill in the blanks." For the great classic obviously has something to say. It is very important and relevant to living the deepest spiritual life. So, it would be immoral simply to write whatever one wants, and then to try to "fit in" the text. Instead, even when paraphrase must be used, words expanded, or ideas elaborated, the core of all good rendition must be the meaning implied by or inferred from the text itself. Faithfulness to the spirit of the text has been a watchword in the present rendition. But to share meaning at all, in some chapters, some elaborative textual additions have had to be constructed. But still, care has been taken to install these in brackets. These are clumsy and distracting when it comes to reading, but intellectual honesty is much more crucial than fluency. And as tempting as it is to emphasize poetic beauty over substance, as some translations have done, here it is the message that is sovereign. For it is supreme, as well as sublime.

This rather nebulous work speaks of great mystical and spiritual matters. These truths cannot be simply reduced to words. Trying to capture the Indescribable and Infinite in words is like trying to squeeze an elephant into a thimble. It just does not matter, is completely irrelevant, how clever you are. It just won't work.

Words can only indicate That Which lies beyond words altogether. So, words have been used to clarify words. This is inevitably a clumsy and rather imprecise process, like writing a check to pay off a credit-card. In such a transaction, no real money might be involved. And in words, no true Reality dwells. Mind is light-years beyond words. Attempts are analogous to describing a complex cybermechanism in monosyllables.

The text seeks to imply the Indescribable. The first words of the book imply selfconsciousness felt by the ancient author, when he says that anything that can be said about the Mind is not the mind. In the ancient text, it said something like, "Tao said Tao not Tao." This means that any collections of words about the great Mind fail miserably to capture its truest essence.

This Tao is the heart of the great Mystery of Mind and being. (Recall that this word is pronounced "dow.") Tao is the centerpiece of not only Taoism, but of universal (intercultural) mysticism. For it is the ancient Chinese name for cosmic Mind, Coremind, the Absolute, the Ultimate, Supermind, Spirit, God, or Lovemind.

In mysticism, God is seen not as a "big daddy in the sky," fit for five-year-olds. God is no primitive, bloody, vengeful wargod from some ancient tribal society. God is not a psychotic monster who runs a nightmare torture-chamber called "hellfire." Instead, God is seen by mystics as the deepest level of the Unconscious. Its Core and Essence are Love. This is what Jesus implied in Part III of the present book, "The Gospel of Universal Love." Lao Tzu would agree. What Jesus called the "father," Lao Tzu made the nonpersonal Tao. Christ emphasized the Lovemind aspect, and Lao Tzu the part called the "Creatormind." But they were both speaking, with a chorus of other mystics, of the same Reality.

There is no great challenge to translate the word *Tao*. It simply means "Way." Is this "Way" an interior path, a philosophy, a religion? This is where the art of interpretative inference comes in. Its intuition makes the difference. For all translators who render the word in English agree that *Tao* means "Way." But far too many of them haven't the slightest clue what "Way" the ancient author is talking about. This is analogous to knowing that the Greek *theos* or the Latin *deus* means "God." The fun has just begun, with translation. The real job begins after translation, with interpretation. If *theos* means "God," what is "God"? Symmetrically, if *Tao* means "Way," what is this mysterious Way?

The ancient writing offers up a few tantalizing clues. The "Way" is a Fountain of the cosmos itself, as implied by Lao Tzu. It is the "mother" of the cosmos, the Sourcemind. "Everything arises from Tao," writes Lao Tzu (chapter 51). It is also a pattern, energy, or agent.

Ancient Chinese Taoists started with the same darkly enfogged, hidden mysteries that move all wise people to wonder: How did, or how does, this great cosmos arise? And from what does it arise? And what relationship does it bear to the viewer? Could the cosmos itself, like beauty, be not in the "eye," but the mind, of the beholder?

To make a millennia-long quest short and sweet, here is the mystical worldview in a nutshell: The world does not exist unless there are minds to perceive/sense it. (For an indepth discussion of this idea, see My earlier work9) The world, they concluded, was a dream. It was not dreamed up by the conscious mind, but by the deepest

---

9 See my *Luminous Jewels of Love and Light*, Volume 1, Part I, "The Way of Universal Love" (Liberty Township, Ohio; Love Ministries, Inc. 2002)

Unconscious. And the deepest, most hidden aspect of that Unconscious was Coremind. This was the Absolute; this was *Tao*. It contained the part of mind called the inner Dreamer/Creator. This was the part of the Unconscious that continuously dreamed up the world of everyday reality. The ordinary world was a dream. This, too, was *Tao*. So, *Tao* is much more than a spiritual path. It is more than a method of behavior. It is, by extension, "the Way things are." A bit more precisely, Tao is "the Way things come to be." And how do things come to be? Mystics say that things are dreamed into being by the profoundest level of the Unconscious— by cosmic Mind or Tao.

So, Tao might be most succinctly translated as "Mind," or "great Mind," even though what exactly that Mind is might not be clearly defined. More clearly, It is the Power behind the dreamimages of the world.

This worldream seems unlike our nightdreams. The great Dream of the world is not random or chaotic. Reptiles do not emerge out of thin air, nor do we soar into the blue skies of that same air. Flowers do not blossom before our astonished and delighted eyes, and we do not enter rooms made of gold and crystal. The worldream is instead quite carefully designed. It is stable and predictable. Horses do not fly away on twelve-foot rainbowings, and people do not become younger. The worldream or Mindworld is designed by input from the Soulevel of Mind, deeper than the personal unconscious, and by input from a quadrillion quadrillion other layers of Mind. (See "Chart of Mind," on page 126)

There is a nanomatch between our karma and our experience. Karma flows from the vast memory of the Unconscious. Our current worldexperience arises from a vast inner creativity. Both world and karma arise from the same remembering, dreaming Mind. This explains their perfect match and symmetry.

This implies that nothing in your life— birth, death, and every major event in between— is really chaotic or random. It is all dreamed up by a mind that is no looking-glass confusion, but a crystalclear pattern of reason, order, and balance. This great Power of Mind is moving through you right this minute, beating your heart and firing your neurons. This Power is, then, not theoretical, but empirical and observable. You can't open your eyes without seeing It, or swing a dead cat without striking It. This is also the Mindpower that turns sunlight, dirt, and water into watermelons, grains, and apples, through nature's nanotech. It then repeats the astounding miracle by turning those foods into you!

Taoists say that It is balance, which means justice. Generally, this is worked out through karma. Reduced to absurdly simplistic parable, the law of karma says that, if I smack you in the face, I am going to seek out, unconsciously, a situation in which I will be slapped with equal enthusiasm and vigor. In more complex situations, the unconscious drive might push for centuries, or seek for millennia. Karma is not revenge. It is not punishment. It is not the vengeance of a petty cosmic tyrant or vindictive deity. It is the outworking of natural but flawless law. Step off the top of a tall building, and an angry deity does not have to drag you to the street below; natural law will take care of that. Karma is similarly automatic. The only force in the cosmos that can erase or neutralize it is Love.

The belief that orderly Power is continuously at work challenges us to learn to trust the great cosmic Mind to do what It does best— take care of business. It makes sure that things turn out correctly, fairly, and justly.

We are asked, by Taoism, to believe that the cosmic Mind is a structure of immense intelligence, beauty, reason, and order. Only a few minutes spent in careful studies of the biosciences or physical sciences will usually convince us that it is indeed so.

Many Westerners mouth the cliché about "let go and let God." This childish phrase passes even for cleverness in some circles. But verbal toddlerism aside, almost no one ever does it. We claim that our lives are regulated by "God," and then live as if that were an absurdity. We live with a belief that "God" controls everything, but then, we act as if we must do everything ourselves. In fact, being "ooc," or out of control, is very much like panic.

What is going on here? We have forgotten the meaning of faith. If we truly do trust that there is a Power that beats our hearts, creates and digests food, makes the sun to rise— all indisputable facts— why do we not trust this Power? It is not as if we cannot see Its activity every minute of every day. We see it all around us, so often, that to believe in the existence of this Power requires not a nanoparticle of "blind faith."

Whatever reasons that we in the West come up with for not trusting— religion, or lovers have betrayed us, or we have betrayed ourselves, or our parents betrayed us— we are in desperate need of a philosophy such as Taoism. For Taoism, usually regarded as a "religion," is not really so in the common definition. It is instead a worldview, a guiding philosophy. It does not conflict with religions. So, you can easily be a Christian Taoist, a Jewish Taoist, or an Islamic Taoist. It does speak of ultimate Reality, but never quite goes so far as to personalize it as an anthropormorphic "god." This ancient classic has little to say about the afterlife, and has nothing to say about prophets, miracles, dogmas, eschatology, or other miscellaneous "religious stuff."

If, then, you are a Christian, Jew, Moslem, agnostic, Buddhist, Hindu, or pagan who has practical problems in everyday life, you can use this philosophy. For it is designed to create enormous tranquility. And what factor creates this ocean of inner peace? It is simply this: The realization that the Power seen everywhere does really exist. And the second leg upon which Taoism stands as a practical approach to life is that this Power is trustworthy. It is just, fair, and, yes, compassionate. It has brought us all this far along the Way and, if we can learn to live in greater harmony with It, It will take us much farther.

How do we come into alignment with this Power, instead of banging our heads against a brick wall by resisting it? Lao Tzu says that we live naturally, simply, spontaneously, avoiding greed, ostentation, pride, and dishonor. Their opposites, collectively called "virtues" arise from the deepest inner Mind of Tao. They are full expressions of unaltered Lovemind, or supreme Mind, Absolute. The Chinese word *Te*, like *logos* in Greek, implies a reflection of deep inner Mind. These "virtues," these Mindexpressions, also keep us smoothly and synergistically cooperating with Tao or Mind.

What are the rewards? For one, colossal tranquility. For the first time, we can stop trying to control everyone and everything, and feel good about it. A greater Power than yourself exists, so you no longer have to be the "god" of your own life. Taoism is not about believing in the absurdity of the Jehovah-myth, a god good for only toddlers. It is not about even believing in a personal god— a god who is a person. There is no big, angry "daddy in the sky." This fairy-tale is for children and fools. *Tao* is all about recognizing your limitations, and embracing them as natural. Then, you get on with a life that is as good and happy as you can manage. More specifically, Taoism is about what you do *not* do. It is all about refusing to manipulate or coerce. It is about learning to relax and let other adults make their own decisions. It is trusting nature. It is about refusing to take on the responsibilities of others' lives, by refusing to interfere with their choices. It is refusing to let that old bugaboo, the "inner parent," try to control everything. It tries, because it is sick, to force everything and everyone to be just as "mama" or "papa" wants it. It is, supremely, about learning the forgotten art of relaxation.

This deep philosophic relaxation is "letting go." It is refusing to control, or try to control, everything all the time. It has to do with giving others the same freedoms that you demand for yourself. So, let go, kick back, relax, and watch the show! You might well be the "star" of your own lifeprogram. But you cannot by definition also be the director and the producer. So, imitate children, and puppies. Laugh more, cry more, touch more, hug more, play more. This is Taoism in action.

Tao produces all things. It is the spiritual "mother" or "father" of all. It existed before heaven and earth. As cosmic Mind, it is still deep within your unconscious Mind. And this is where *Tao* interfaces with *you*. *Tao* is inside your head. It leaks not only into your dreams, but into your everyday world. That is also a dream, say Taoist masters. So, the better that you know the *Tao*, the friendlier the cosmos becomes. Einstein said that the most important question that we can ask about the universe is, "Is the universe friendly?" Taoists answer with a resounding yes!

The perfect life, say Taoist sages, is the effortless life. How stunningly and deliciously this contrasts with the average driven or "hyperdrive" lifestyle of the Western man or woman. Masters of *Tao* say that one should live "like a cloud, going nowhere in particular." When, as kids, we used to study the clouds from blankets in parks, as if we had forever, when, at night, we lay under the starpeppered velvet vault of heaven and wondered, while our minds wandered, we had a taste of natural Taoism.

That Mind that danced on lightwaves through the galaxies was, say Taoists, more real than even the galaxies. Sweet mind is more real than driven mind. Lovemind is more real than greedmind. Mystics of all traditions have arrived at the conclusion that the Mind is more real than matter— a disturbing concept in a world gone mad with hypermaterialism.

Your tranquility is infinitely more important than the new house, the new car, or the new career.

But Mind is more real because matter could not exist without It. If all of a sudden, all minds everywhere were snuffed out, the galaxies would disappear, say mystics. But, conversely, if all matter were suddenly gone, Mind would still be hanging around, probably wondering what to do next.

The "material" universe needs a sensor, perceiver, or observer in order to exist at all. In other words, matter does not exist independently from Mind. Wherever matter exists, it exists only relative to a perceiving Mind, and so, is really "mattermind."

What does all this have to do with you? Because you have a mind, you are unified with the Mind-principle. Because you have an unconscious Mind, you are unified, at very deep levels, with cosmic Mind or *Tao*. Learning to live in harmony with this *Tao* will bring to your life satisfaction, fulfillment, and infinite contentment. It will bring tranquility, as well as joy (sometimes in the intense forms of rapture or ecstasy).

The subjectobject fusion implied here is the polar opposite of the dualism of materialism, which divides Mind from matter. Like East and West, the twain shall never meet. This monstrous split turns the universe into a collection of blind, stupid Newtonian gadgets, ticking along mechanically with no reason, meaning, or purpose. You are one of these gadgets. Taoism offers a viable alternative to this nihilism and hopelessness.

Mind, as Tao, is the Power behind and within the cosmos. It is the same Power within your own mind. In ultramicroparticle physics, it has been found that there exists nothing really "solid" in the entire universe. Atoms are not solid, but are small packets of energy held together in nanobundles of force called "quanta." The cosmos is energy, or what the ancients would have called "light." And the force that holds this light together in form is called "Mind." The book that you now hold in your hands, indeed, the hands that hold it, can be recognized as no more "solid," from a nanoperspective, than empty space. (Compare Part I, in volume 1.10)

We already, conveniently, have a word in psychology to describe energy held together by Mind. That word is "dream." The words of the old children's song are true: "Life is but a dream."

In Taoism, as in Buddhism, gnosticism, sufism, and other mystical traditions, we end up finally with a universe that is Mind projected, thoughts exteriorized. It is Mind plus nothing. As the Hindu mystics were famous for saying, "Not only everyone, but everything, is only God." The cosmos is cosmic Mind.

This means that you, too, are cosmic Mind. Your mind is the instrument through which Mind dreams the universe. Thus, you are dreaming right this moment. And the world, although not your personal dream, is being dreamed up by a still greater Mind (called the "Creator") in the Unconscious.

Since this interior Mind is like a galaxy compared to the candle of your personal mind, it is tempting to believe that It is "another person." In fact, many people in the history of the Western world have fallen for this illusion. But mystics speak of a greater, higher, or deeper Self. This Self might have nothing in common with your usual "self," your "ego." This deeper Self they call the "Beyond within," or, the "inner Other." Infinite Mind exists somehow, mysteriously, within your personal mind.

How can mystics know this incredible fact? Because they have actually touched or glimpsed this infinite Mind within their own minds. The mystic "God" is not protective or interventionistic. The mystic does not plead with her God to change the world, but to alter the self.

This God is the creative, powerful nucleus or core of the Unconscious. And Its chief characteristic, so outstanding that this quality has actually been mystically equated with God or Reality Itself, is Love. "Only when you love the world as your own self can you be trusted to care for everything," Lao Tzu writes (chapter 13). This 'loving others as your Self' is the same advice given by Jesus.

Thus, while the Taoist does not act *unnecessarily*, neither is she a zombie or couchpotato. She is active, alert, and brilliant. She is

10 See my *Luminous Jewels of Love and Light*, Volume 1*op.cit.*

always highly productive. But she does not act because she feels that she needs to control everything, or else, the world will go to hell. And when she does take action, she does not see her self or ego as the source of her best. The Source of the best within her is Coremind, Sourcemind, cosmic Mind, Lovemind. In a word, it is Tao. It is "God." It is Love. *The Taoist acts only when Love moves her to act.* Otherwise, she practices *wu shin* or *wu wei*, doing "nothing" and thinking "nothing."

All this "nondoing" creates in the Taoist gigapsychons of excess energy to apply to the priorities of life that have real value. The cosmos gives you a thousand units of energy every day, with one crucial proviso: Energy spent in one pursuit cannot be used in any other. So, you can prostitute yourself to the System for money, 'selling your soul to the company store,' or you can redeem this energy and invest it in spiritual wisdom. You can use your energy to love or to hate, but not both. You can use it to avoid or to face problems, but not both. You can serve peace or war, but not both. The wise Taoist chooses to use all this liberated energy to invest in her mind, for that is investment in everlasting Mind. She does not pursue the baubles and trinkets of life, the material pettiness and trivialities that concern others. She does not believe that "the winner is the one who dies with the most toys." She prefers tranquility to trinkets. She prefers joys to toys. She gracefully, joyfully surrenders the toys of childhood for the Mindstudies of spiritual adulthood.

The Taoist, indeed the mystical, cosmos is a Mindevent, a collection of Mindpictures, dreamimages, "psychoholograms." In all the cosmos, since only Mind is absolutely real, the Tao must have something to do with Mind. It cannot be simply energy or pattern, for those are the *results* of mental configurations. They are not truly causative. And what is most real about the Real? It is the nuclear or essential Mind, which mystics call "Reality" Itself. This Coremind is the "agapopsyche," or Lovemind. For Lovewisdom is nuclear to nuclear Mind.

So, as noted in Part I, the cosmos is dreamed into being *un*consciously, and is perceived consciously. The Soulevel of Mind alters the great dream, as it arises from the much deeper Spiritlevel. (See "Chart of Mind," on page 126.) This process creates precisely the dream that we need, as experience and learning. It dreams at precisely the moment that it is needed.

So, as conscious beings or minds, we can do little but to "float along," Taoistically, on a great sea of unconscious, benevolent forces. They form our every environment during our every waking moment. We are, say Taoists, like small twigs floating upon a great rushing current of a river. How frustrating and incredibly stupid it is for a conscious "twig" to try to control the flow/direction of that vast river!

The basic principle of Taoism is that of all mysticism: Instead of trying like mad to control the universe, we allow It, without squawks of protest, to take over us and our lives. For we are vastly, ludicrously under qualified to control everything! This is simple cooperation with what is. For no matter how madly we might deny it, the cosmos, or cosmic Mind, is fully in charge of every moment of our lives. It is only in hypnotic illusion that we manage to convince ourselves of the unrealistic, fantastic notion that we control the great Flow of events within and all around us.

To cooperate, without resistance, to adapt, to flow is the Way of Tao. It is a path of yielding and surrender, of elasticity of mind and plasticity of opinion. Largely, it is a life of liquidity; when we psychologically "liquefy," we are no longer set in granite. When we give up our granitic, unyielding, stubborn mindsets, peace can at last find room to blossom in our heartminds. Resistance to Reality ("truth") vaporizes and evaporates like gentle summer mist on a hot asphalt surface. We do not become totally "liquid" but rather hyperelastic and yielding to reason.

The cosmos is a shared megadream. Not only are you dreaming right now, but so am I, and so is every other sentient being on the planet. Very likely, the dream appears on other planets as well. So, the ultimate structures of creation will not be found in ordinary microparticle physics. They will not be gluons, hadrons, mesons, quarks, leptons, etc. They will be "psychons"— psiresponsive ultramicrophenomena. These are plastic and reactive to unconscious forces and energies. They are photonanoquanta created by Mind Itself.

Lao Tzu, being a mystic, shared this "photopsychocosmic" view with all other mystics, from all periods of history. So, when he spoke of the greatest Mystery of all, the jewel-centerpiece of existence, he must have been talking about what other mystics call "Reality," or the "Absolute".

Following this Mind, living in harmony with It, does not result in an anesthetic deadening of the senses. It makes them sharper, richer, and more vivid. It does not result in a passive, inactive life, but one more active and productive than any other. Tao does not kill, but resurrects. It triggers greater and increased creativity and productivity. More importantly, it stimulates the ten thousand activities of Love. For Lovemind, or Tao, is the very reason for existence. We were created, *are* created, moment by moment, not for deathly stillness, but for the irrepressible exuberance of Love.

Richard Shiningthunder Francis,
Shalimar 3 Lightcenter

NOTE: Although "Tao Now" is a new rendition of the great ancient mystical classic, it has been strongly influenced by one of the most succinct and literal translations of the "Way of Virtue," the one by Gia Fu Feng. This beautifully captures the essential simplicity of the original text. But, due partly to this honest adherence, it is nearly as bewildering to the average Western reader as if it were written in the original Chinese!

Richard Shiningthunder Francis

Part IV: "Tao Now: The Book of the Great Mind and Its Expression"

CHART OF MIND

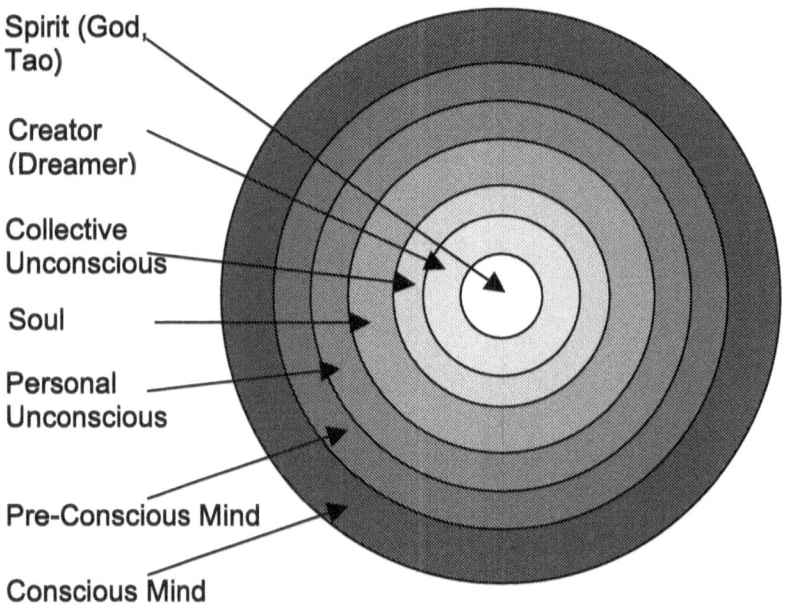

Spirit (God, Tao)

Creator (Dreamer)

Collective Unconscious

Soul

Personal Unconscious

Pre-Conscious Mind

Conscious Mind

1

The Mind that can be fully described by words is not the real [ultimate, essential] Mind.

Anything, in fact, that can be "named [as separate]" is not the real [selfexistent, valid] name.

Instead, both heavenly and earthly reality begins in the realm of That Which cannot be named at all.

On the other hand, when you begin to give names to things, you then bring into existence the ordinary world of many "separate" things.

The deep Mystery of these matters becomes clear only when one is freed from [personal] desires. For, as long as one is caught in the desires, one can see only the [visible] manifestations [and not the invisible Cause in Mind].

Both realities [— the visible "named" world of the many, and the invisible Mindworld of the One—] arise from the same Source. They are divided only by the tendency to give them different designations.

This seems obscure. Yet it is only through this very obscurity that one enters into the [understanding of the] Mystery.

2.

As long as one lives on earth, beauty is known as "beauty" because it contrasts so sharply with the less beautiful. Here, one also can know goodness as "good," because it contrasts so sharply with that which is less good.

Therefore, [opposites such as] owning and not owning [losing] arise as a [unbroken, inevitable, indivisible] set. Difficult and easy arise as a similar set. They complement each other [instead of resisting]. The same is true of "long and short," which exist only relative to each other, creating contrast. "High and low" also arise mutually, depending on each other.

In a similar way, voice and sound arise together [as a complementary pair] in order to create harmony. In the same way, "front and back" are indissolubly connected to each other [and mutually define each other].

[Actions are also like this.] Therefore, the enlightened being often gets more "done" by what she refuses to do. She "teaches" better, at times, without speaking at all.

As the realities of the "material" world continue to rise and fall, they are created [by Mind] endlessly. Yet [that Mind] is not stuck to the idea of "ownership." It works, but is not stuck to the idea of taking credit.

[In imitation of Mind,] the enlightened being just does her work, and then immediately forgets it all.

Yet that is precisely why her work lasts forever. [She has allowed everlasting Mind to create everlasting results, without being stuck to the idea of her self.]

3.

Argumentation [and conflicting competition] can be avoided if the gifted are not singled out as objects of special praise.

[The gifted feel that they have everything to lose, and hence are very protective.] In the same way, the only one who is absolutely safe from a thief is she who has nothing worth stealing. For only heart-confusion is created by the longing for beautiful things. Only the complete absence of lustful vision can create peace.

The wise, then, help others to fill by fulfilling immediate needs. They aid others to empty their hearts of desires. Thus, while helping people to be physically stronger, they also aid them to weaken grasping and ambition [and painful, harmful greed].

For freedom from "intellectuals" consists in: the absence of too much mind, and refusal of [personal] desire.

If one does nothing [to force or manipulate], all that should be done will be done.

4.

The Mind is like empty space. It contains infinite potential. [It can create anything.] So, it is like a vessel. No matter how many times it is used, it is never permanently filled [because it keeps getting emptied]. [The full Mind is always emptied into the cosmos.]

Thus is the Mind the bottomless Origin of the world.

[Since the cosmos has its Source in perfect Mind,] don't try to "improve perfection." Refuse to try to make a blade too sharp, or a knot too complex.

[Don't always be seeking credit and praise.] Refuse to shine too brightly. Instead, learn the fine and subtle art of camouflaging yourself into the background. Seek to become one with the [humble] dust.

[Thus, you can imitate the perfect Creatormind.] How deeply hidden [is this Mind]. Yet still, It is always, obviously [inignorably] present. I haven't the slightest clue as to Its origin. But I do know that [it is the "government" of the cosmos and] it is older than any [earthly] government.

5.

Both heaven and earth often seem to be without mercy. But this is simply because they know the mere forms [and appearances] of things to be unreal. [Only Mind is real.]

The wise might also seem unmerciful [in knowing the same world as illusion]. For they know that even human forms are not ultimate realities.

The interstices between heaven [Mind] and earth [created world] are like a bellows. [Like the air rushing in and out,] the manifestations are continuously changing.. Only the Mind Itself remains steadfast. The more that motion is involved in this [creative Mindprocess], the more flexible It becomes. [The flexible yielding of matter to Mind is the vital *yin* part of creation.]

[To describe this Mystery,] the multiplication of mere words is valueless. [True yielding is silence.]

[Instead of becoming lost in the "material" world,] you should hold firmly to the Center.

6.

The spirit of receptivity never dies. [It is *yin* energy.] It is like woman. It is the primal [and archetypal] mother. The path of this spirit is the Origin. [Matter, as *yin*, embraced Creatormind, which flooded into the void as *yang* energy.] It is the Source of all reality, in heaven or on earth.

This [Mind] is as subtle as a sheer, thin veil. It can barely be "seen." Still, if you engage it, you will find that it never fails.

7.

Heaven and earth will always be. Why? [Because they have always been.] They were never actually "born." [They are images and archetypes of the cosmic mind. That is why] they are ever living.

[Universal Mind is utterly humble. In imitation of It,] the enlightened being walks always behind others. That is why she is always ahead of them all. [In the art of subtle selfveiling, she is like the cosmic Mind Itself.]

It is due to her immense emotional freedom that she can feel her oneness with all. Through action completely free of all selfconcern, she finds purest, utter fulfillment.

8.

The very highest goodness is like water. Water gives life to all the world, and never strives against it. [Love does not strive, and is lifesupporting and lifenhancing.] Also, water flows into even those places that people reject. In this way, it is like the Mind Itself. [The Mind sees nowhere, even rejected places, as "bad."]

[The Mind also reveals itself in nature.] So, when you make a home, make it as close to nature as possible. [The Mind is deeply profound, deeply hidden .] So, when you meditate, go deeply into the heartmind. [The Mind is kind, so] in dealing with others, be always gentle and kind. Let your speech always be honest. If given a position to guide others, be always just. In business, seek to polish practical skills. But in *everything* that you do, always watch the timing.

[If you do not follow this advice, you are likely to create conflict. But] where there is no conflict, there can be no blame.

9.

It is better to fill a cup incompletely than to fill it to the brim. Make a blade too sharp, and it will sooner grow dull. Collect a treasure of beautiful material things, such as gold and jade, and no one in the world will be able permanently to protect it.

For when you embrace material wealth, and claim special titles, you will create only disaster. Instead of doing all this, simply stop when the work is done, and relax. For this is the Mind of heaven. [When the cosmos was created, the Mind rested.]

10.

You must use a physical body as the instrument [and vehicle] of the Soul. But never forget that You are one with all that is in Your world. Can You really avoid [the illusion of] separation?

Pay full attention to your own [inner] development. Become elastic and yielding. Doing these things, can you return to the state of a newborn baby?

When you have washed and purified your primal [inner] vision, can you return to the state of stainless pristinity?

Love all people. Avoid clever speech [that is sarcastic, hurtful, or dishonest]. Allow [the Mind of] heaven to flow into your world. Let It be reflected [everywhere] in that world. Can you then play the role of quiet, tranquil receiver [in stillness]? Play this role [even if you are male and it is viewed as the role] traditionally assigned to women.

Try to understand, by being open to, all things. Can you still remain unstained by active personal manipulation?

Give "birth" to your own personal [and unique] world [by your mind and interpretations]. Doing this, can you free yourself from all personal ownership? Can you [find the great inner power to] work without taking any credit? Can you thus lead by example? Can you [create the strength to] live without dominating others?

These things all constitute the "primal Mindpower." [Without these attitudes and actions, all other Mindexpression is impossible.]

11.

A wheel might have thirty spokes. But the wheel has a hole where the spokes come together, where the axle is inserted. It is this empty hole at the center that makes the wheel truly useful. In the same way, when you shape clay into a jar, you form an inner hollow area. It is that space inside that makes the vessel useful.

Similarly, when windows and doors are cut out of a wall, only empty areas are left; but it is these spaces that define where the doors and windows will be. The empty spaces make them useful.

So, while typical profit comes from what is, true usefulness arises from what is not. [In life, it can be more useful *not* to do or say.]

12.

Too much color makes dull the eyes. Too much sound dulls the ears. Too much flavor makes taste less sensitive.

[Too much trying, always seeking to be better,] trying always to get ahead, [leaves you behind,] and is a sure path to madness.[The attempt to] always win trophies and awards is the same. Killing animals for sport is another [path to madness].

[Too much distraction with desirable things is also madness.] Attractive and beautiful things take one from the path of Mind. So, the enlightened being is not mislead by the mere appearances of things. Instead, she follows the inner intuition. She must let go of the first to get in touch with the second.

13.

Embrace disgrace. Embrace ill fortune. They are part of the condition of being human.

What does it mean to "embrace disgrace"? It means that you are not really as important as you might think yourself to be. [You are taking yourself too seriously if you do not embrace disgrace.]

So, do not concern your [infinite] Self with [microscopic] losses and gains. [You are much greater than these fleeting, evanescent events.]

What is meant by "embrace ill fortune"? Misfortune is inevitable as long as you have a physical body. For, without this kind of body, there could be no human misfortune.

Instead [of resisting disgrace and misfortune,] surrender yourself humbly. Only then can you be trusted to care for all things. This means that only when you come to love the entire world as your own Self can you be trusted to care for everything.

14.

However intensely you peer at Mind, you will never see It. It is beyond, and behind, all [visible] forms. However intensely you concentrate on hearing It, you will not, for It is beyond, and behind, all sounds. However much you grasp for It, It simply cannot be held in the hands. For It is intangible.

Seeing, hearing, and touching all share their origin [in Mind]. When visualized from above, It is not bright. Imagined from below, it does not look dark. It is a unifying Reality. But when It is sought through the senses, there seems to be nothing there.

Still, it does create forms in the world. Images arise from the Imageless. It is beyond anything that you can visualize [or conceive]. It seems to come out of nowhere, and to go back to nothing. [It is without boundaries and, like a circle, has no beginning or end.]

So, stay with the ancient Mind. Live in the here and now. For knowing the ancient Beginning is the Essence of Mind.

15.

The enlightened beings of ancient times were direct. [They were subtle, barely present, almost invisible, leaving no traces.] They were beings of mystery. They were profound. They were responsive, and responsible.

The depths of their minds are bottomless. Because their minds were [indescribably] infinite, all that can be described is their appearances.

They behaved cautiously, carefully watchful, like people walking across the dangerous currents of a fast winter stream. They were always alert, like people aware of subtle dangers. They were courteous, like strangers visiting your home. They were also yielding, like ice melting. They were as simple as a block of wood from which nothing has yet been carved. [They were very plain, but had the potential, in their emptiness, to become anything.]

They were empty, hollow, and receptive. [They were not rigid or dogmatic.] They were like [unexplored] caves. Yet still, you could not see into their minds, which were opaque [and unreadable to outer analysis]. They were like muddy pools.

Who would have had the patience to wait for the "mud" [of too many thoughts] to settle? Who can, even now, remain still until the time for action?

Those who follow the Mind do not seek [personal] fulfillment. It is because of this [powerful contentment] that they tend not to be stirred up by passions for rapid change.

16.

Empty yourself of everything. Let the Mind fall into serene tranquility. Let the world continue with its [repeating cycles, such as] rising and falling. Let the Self gaze on with fullest detachment. All things return, in the end, to the beginning. [All the cosmos returns to its original Mind. In people,] this return is stillness. This is the natural way to approach life.

But the [deepest] way of nature is changeless. So, coming to know the Immutable is true insight. On the other hand, the failure to find It means disaster. For only when It knows inner stability can the Mind be safely opened. An open Mind creates an open heart. An open heart creates great generosity. This makes you like a very rich ruler.

When you reach the level [of perfect generosity], you will be divine. Being divine, you will be not at all separate from Mind. [The illusion of "separate" mind flows into the realization of Unity.]

This state is timeless. Though the physical body must die, the Mind lasts forever. [Though bodies die, Mind is everlasting.]

17.

The very highest is known by only a few persons. Below this come the things more commonly known, and love. After this are the things which people fear, and so despise.

[Wisdom is knowing what states are truly trustworthy.] But she who does not trust enough will never be trusted.

[You cannot always trust people.] When someone performs actions without unnecessary speech, the people say, "Look at what *we* did."

18.

Only when Mind is forgotten are people forced to "invent" artificial systems of "kindness" and "morality." [They believe that rule-systems can replace following the inner perfect Mind.]

Similarly, when people strive to appear "intelligent," or even "wise," pretension begins.

Only when real peace has fled from a family do rules about "family unity" and talk of "devotion" arise.

On a national level, it is only when the land has fallen most into chaos that politicians speak loudly about their "loyalty."

19.

Give up any ideas of being a recognized "saint." Turn away from the idea of presenting yourself as a "wise person." If you do this, everyone will be much better off. Give up all pretensions of "kindness." Abandon all attempts to show off just how "moral" you are. Then, people will be led to discover true family devotion and Love.

Give up ingenuity. Turn away from all greedy profit. If you do this, thieves and robbers will disappear.

For outward forms are not enough. [They are just going through the motions, or, worse, showing off.] It is much more important to live in authentic simplicity. [Work to simplify mind, speech, relationships, and possessions.] What is crucial is to realize your true inner nature. This begins with casting away all selfishness, and deliberately weakening [personal] desires.

20.

Give up the habit of analyzing the world too much. Then, you will put an end to many of your troubles.

For instance, it is nonsense to overanalyze "good and evil." The same is true of "yes and no." [Avoid "either-or" or "black and white" thinking.]

[You must not believe anything just because others do, or try simply to think as they think.] It is even more foolish to fear what others fear.

Sometimes, it can and does seem that others are "happy," with their continual parties, eating and drinking. In spring, they go to the park and play. By contrast, I [who have deeper concerns] seem to be drifting. Unanchored, I float through life. [I am unbound and unburdened in my simplicity.] I am as a newborn baby. [I am thought-free and untroubled.] In this, I seem alone, and unique.

Others revel and boast in their material abundance. But I have nothing materially valuable. I cling to no material things, and so, they do not cling to me.

Others see me as "foolish" or "confused." Other men are [publicly] recognized as "clearsighted and brilliant." But I am seen as "not too bright and not very strong." Other men display their sharp wits, cleverness, and ingenuity. I alone seem, by contrast, to be dull and a bit dim-witted.

And so I drift like the waves of the sea. I am free like the wind, without goal or direction.

Everyone else is always so "busy." I seem to lack direction. [I do not attempt to overfill every day.] They see me as a "sad case."

Yes, I am different. For I draw support [not from money, brainpower, or impressing others, but] from the great Mother.

21.

The greatest Mindexpression is to relax [and not try so hard]. Flow with Mind. And allow Mind alone to direct you.

Yes, it is subtle and elusive. Still, it is within Its Light that all images and forms are created. Wrapped in obscurity, It is at the Core of all existence. This Essence is very real. Still, when It is first approached, a certain amount of faith is necessary.

Even so, from the very beginning of time, Its Reality has never been entirely forgotten. And this is exactly how I perceive creation. [I see all creation being projected by the Mystery of a single Mind.]

How do I know the ways of creation? It is because of this [reality unfolding all around me].

22.

The best way to overcome is by giving in. The best way to stay straight is to know when to bend.

The zenith of fullness occurs when you are empty. The best time for renewal is after exhaustion. The best way to be "rich" is to have little. Ownership of too much property leads to only confusion.

Due to these paradoxes, enlightened beings embrace the One [by embracing the many]. That is how they set an example for everyone. It is precisely because they do not seek any selfdisplay that they shine so brightly. [They do not want the spotlight, and so come to everyone's attention.] Because they are not always trying to justify their existence, they are distinguished. Because they never brag or boast, they receive recognition.

Because they do not give in to selfdisplay, they are steady. And because they always avoid fighting, no one can fight with them.

The ancients said, "Yield and overcome." Is this without meaning? No, it is not. For [if you become unified with the inner Mind, you will be the Source of all;] if you become one with all, all that you need will always come to you.

23.

It is natural not to talk too much. For, in nature, the highest winds do not last all morning. Heaviest rains do not generally last all day.

This is the Way of balance [and moderation,] created by interactions of heaven with earth. [Nature does not favor long-lasting extremes. In fact, in "material" nature, nothing lasts forever.] If, then, nature is not eternal in her creations, then how can people hope to make anything eternal?

[The only Eternal is Mind.] So, the one who follows Mind must become one with Mind. It is only when one loses Mind that she feels lost in life. When, on the other hand, you are one with It, then It welcomes you. When you are one with Mindexpression, it always supports you. It is possible to be at one with even loss. In this state of mind, even loss can be willingly embraced. [To do this, you must trust. And remember that] the one who does not trust enough cannot be trusted.

24.

A person who stands on tip-toes is unsteady. The one who walks too fast cannot indefinitely maintain her pace.

[These are both unnatural. Since showing off is also unnatural,] anyone who shows off is not enlightened. In the same way, the one who is eager to demonstrate or show off her "righteousness" is never respected.

The one who boasts and brags gets nothing for her efforts. For braggarts will not endure, or last very long.

Those who really follow Mind call this "unnecessary baggage." These actions bring no happiness at all, and those who truly follow Mind avoid them.

25.

Something mysteriously existed before heaven and earth. It was in silence and emptiness. It was alone and unchanging [for infinite eons]. But now, it is this same Reality that is always moving—moving within the world. In fact, it gives birth to the whole world, and so, is its "mother."

I do not know exactly what I should call this ultimate Reality. So, I call It simply "Tao" [Mind]. When I choose to try to describe It, I do so simply, with the word "great."

Because It is so great, It flows even to the most distant parts of the universe. Having gone there, It then returns to "here."

Because It interpenetrates [everything], Mind is astonishingly complex. Heaven [higher creative mind] is great. And the earth that It creates is also great. [If they imitate It,] human governments can also be great.

Thus, among the four great powers that regulate the universe, human social order is important. The human order is affected by earth. Earth is affected by heaven. Heaven follows the pattern of Mind. Mind follows Its own internal nature.

26.

Anything, to be called "light," must be compared to something heavy. Similarly, stillness contrasts with movement. It is the master, and the creator of unrest.

The enlightened person, even if she travels all day, keeps her eye on that which is hers. She is not distracted even by beautiful sights and landscapes. She remains unattached, always still.

It is not fitting for a great lord to behave flippantly in public. For to play the silly games [of earth] is to lose one's connection with the Source. To give in to restlessness and anxiety is to lose inner regulation.

27.

The one who walks best leaves fewest tracks. One who speaks best makes fewest errors. One who adds well needs little help from a calculator. If a door is well made, it needs no lock, but still, no one can open it.

Similarly, when something is tied well, a minimum of complex knots is needed. But still, no one can untie it.

[Enlightened people appear ordinary.] It is because of exactly this kind of paradox that the enlightened takes care of all people. [She appears to be the one who needs to be taken care of.] She abandons no one [to a helpless condition]. She takes care to take care of [everyone and] everything, and leaves nothing out. This is how one follows the Light.

For what is a "good person"? She is the teacher of a "bad person." And what is a "bad person"? It is anyone who learns from a "good person." If the teacher receives no due respect, or if the student is not adequately cared for, confusion arises. When this happens, cleverness is of no value.

Where "student" meets "teacher" is a nexuspoint of the great Mystery. [For Mind teaches and learns from Mind.]

28.

Seek to understand the struggles of a man, but also hold onto the tender nurturing of a woman. For you are yourself nothing less than the stream of universal manifestation.

[In the great humility of this Tao,] become as a little child. Come to know the white, but do not lose touch with the black.

In other words, [by embracing the best of both,] seek to become an example to the world. Become steadfast, and not vacillating. This is the way to return to the Infinite.

Allow yourself to know honor, but only while keeping a strong grip on humility. Allow yourself to be a receiver, returning to the state of utter simplicity. Be like a wooden block from which nothing has been carved. But remember also that the block is truly useful only after it has been carved into some useful form. [This is Mind becoming form.]

When an enlightened being learns to cooperate with potential [formless Mind,] she then becomes its ruler.

This is why the truly great tailor cuts so very little cloth.

29.

Do you really think that you can grasp control of the whole cosmos? Do you really think that you could improve it? I don't think so, for the cosmos, even as it is, is sacred. It cannot be improved. [The laws that regulate it are perfect already.] If you try to change it, you will ruin it. Also, if you grasp it and cling to it, you will surely lose it.

[It operates in time, which is always changing everything.] So, sometimes things get ahead, and sometimes, fall behind. Sometimes breathing is easy, at other times, hard. Sometimes you are strong, and sometimes weak. Sometimes, you are "high," and sometimes "down."

This is why the enlightened being is never smugly complacent. Instead, she seeks always to avoid extremes, overreactions, and excesses.

30.

Whenever you advise a supervisor, counsel against the use of overiding force. For attempting to control by force creates only forceful resistance. [Nature teaches that force is waste, for] thornbushes spring up wherever an army has passed. Years of famine follow a large war.

Just do what needs to be done. Be scrupulously careful never to take advantage of power. Achieve the best results possible. But do not degrade them into a spotlight of selfglorification. Achieve the best results possible. But avoid all bragging. Achieve the best results possible. But avoid all personal pride. Instead, seek to achieve because this is Mind [working through you].

Never justify violence to "get things done." The exertion of any force is followed by a loss of strength. This [loss] is not Mindsupported. And that which is dissonant with Mind is doomed to early death.

31.

Weapons are nothing but the tools of fear. All creatures hate them. Followers of Mind never [offensively] use them. In fact, the enlightened being prefers the opposite way to that of the soldier. Weapons are instruments of fear, and so, are never the tools of the wise. The wise use them [reluctantly] only when there is no other choice. For peace and quiet harmony are dear to their hearts.

Victory is *never* a cause for rejoicing. For if victory [in war] makes you happy, you find pleasure in killing. And if you take joy in killing, spiritual selfdiscovery is impossible.

Since ancient times, happy events were celebrated one way, sad ones observed in a completely different way. War is very much an unhappy event. It is like a funeral. When so many have been killed, they should be mourned, in most sincere sorrow. So, a "victory" is really a funeral in disguise.

Victories must be observed exactly as funerals.

32.

Mind is forever and always indefinable. Though [Its thoughts] seem tiny in their unformed state, It is still too great to be comprehended. If ever anyone could harness Its full Power, the natural world would obey.

Heaven and earth would come together. [Mind and matter would converge. Thoughts would be like] rain falling to the earth. People would need no further instructions. All things [and persons] would follow their natural courses.

Yet once the Totality has become divided it is already too late [readily and easily] to seek Its primal Unity. Then, as now, all that one can seek to do is to identify the parts. One can only give names to everything. Enough! There are enough named things! It's time to stop the naming! Knowing when to say "enough" averts serious complications and trouble.

Mind, flowing into the world, is like a great river flowing into the sea. [The Mind is *yang*, like the river, and the world *yin*, like the sea.]

33.

Knowing others can be knowledge, or even wisdom. But knowing the [deepest] Self is enlightenment. Mastering others can require displays of force. But selfmastery requires true strength.

[Selfmastery is contentment, for] anyone who knows that she has enough is already truly rich. [Staying in this state requires] tenacity, a sign of will. It is this kind of person, who remains reliable, who endures. [In fact, this kind of spiritual being never perishes.] To die without perishing is to be present eternally.

34.

The great Mind flows everywhere [and is everything]. It is to the left and to the right. The existence of the whole world depends upon It. It holds nothing back. But It does its work in total silence. It makes no claim, takes no credit for Its Power. It nourishes the entire world.

It does not seek to be [known as] Lord of the world.

It does not struggle for shorterm goals.

[Since thought is not large,] It is small.

[Still, It does and manages everything.] It even recycles the world. So, Because It does not seek to dominate every factor of the world, It is very great. Its greatness is amplified by the fact that It does not seek to display Its greatness.

35.

One who is one with the One will have people approach her. For only there, [in her Mind,] will they find happiness, rest, and serenity.

[People are not always interested in such important matters.] But they are always interested in good music and good food. Compared with these, a description of Mind might strike them as "dry" or "boring." But, even though It cannot be seen, heard, [or tasted,] It is [the Source of all excitement and pleasure, and is] inexhaustible.

36.

That which is reduced must have been larger, at one time. So, to have failed, you must have been very strong. That which falls must first achieve a high altitude.

Similarly, before receiving can even exist, someone must be giving. These words describe the way things really are.

[This is reality. And here is another reality:] The soft and gentle always overcome the hard and strong. As fish cannot leave water for very long, [people die when "outside of" essential Mind].

[Still, it would be foolish to try to display Power by showing off your Oneness with this Mind, just as] the weapons of a country should never be displayed.

37.

Mind is noninterfering. But even so, the enlightened being still gets things done. If government were to follow the same pattern [of Flogoing nonmanipulation], the world would find its natural path. But if they did decide to act, the politicians would do well to study the ways of simplicity and minimalism. In this way, they could learn creatively to interact with the rhythm and movement of the Dance of Formless Energy.

Even better, when all form has disappeared, then selfish desire also evaporates. Only when these vanish can tranquility appear.

38.

The truest good person is not even aware of her goodness. That is why she is so good. A fool, by contrast, strains to be "good," but is not made good by this straining. For a truly good person sees herself as the source of no action. But still, everything is done precisely as it should be. [Great Mind works through her transparent mind to do everything.]

By contrast, a fool is always "playing catch-up." Always working, she leaves very much undone. (When a truly good and kind person does anything, she leaves nothing undone.) When a person acts without kindness, very much is left wanting.

Similarly, when a rigid person, who believes too much in too much structure does something, but finds no response, she rolls up her sleeves for a fight. This she does to "enforce order." [But it is artificial "order," hence, disorder.]

So, when Mind is lost, all that is left is [mechanical or legal] "righteousness." True goodness is absent. But when even that is lost, all that remain are "by the book" acts of "courtesy." It is only when finally even courtesy disappears that only "justice" remains. At last, if even justice is lost, all that is left is ritual. And it is hollow, the mere husk of faith and loyalty. It is the beginning of confusion.

[Speaking of hollow ritual,] knowledge of the future, and attempts to gain it, are only flowery trappings when compared with Mind. They can be the beginning of folly.

So, the truly wise and enlightened turn their focus towards only what is real. They don't waste time with such shallow superficialities. Their attention is towards the fruit, not just the flower. [They look for real effects, not just promises.]

39.

Many things have arisen from the One. This has occurred from the beginning. For examples, the wholeness and clarity of the sky, the firmness and clarity of the earth, the wholeness and strength of the Spirit, the fullness and wholeness of the valley. The wholeness and aliveness of the many things in the world, and the unified state of good regulation, good government when the country is in order, all arise from the One.

All these things exist independently, and have various levels of wholeness. For example, the clarity of the sky [contains nothing, and that] prevents its tumbling to the earth. The firmness of the earth prevents its [permanent] division. The [infinity of the] strength of spiritual energy prevents its being used up. The fullness of the valley prevents its going dry. [For it is filled with plants full of water.] The growth, in fact, of the whole material world is what keeps it active. It is in good leadership, as in government, that the downfall of the country is prevented.

[This all comes from Mind and Its order. Mind also creates other effects:] That which is noble arises from the humble. The low serves as the foundation for the high. The greatest and most noble leaders are those with the humility to consider themselves less than others. Their greatness, in fact, relies on their humility.

So, beware: Too much "success" is failure; it gives no advantage. It is like tinkling jade or clattering stone chimes. [It makes a lot of noise, but conveys nothing of real value.]

40.

Returning to the Origin is the motion of Mind. [Mind returns to Mind.] Flexible yielding is the pattern of the Mind.

The world arises from one's own being. In turn, one's own being arises from the clear Light of unformed potential. [This potential arises from Mind.]

41.

When the wise student hears of Mind, she practices Its presence regularly, carefully, and diligently. The average student thinks about these matters only periodically. And the foolish student [finds the whole thing absurd, and] actually laughs out loud. Still, if she did not laugh, Mind would not be Mind. [Everything that is, is supposed to be.]

[Because everything and every action is the one Mind,] that is why there is this saying

"The bright path often looks dim, and moving forward feels like moving backward." The easiest Way seems hard. The highest Mindexpression feels like emptiness [because emptiness is the highest]. Too great a purity recognizes its own impurity.

Even a treasure-house filled with Mindexpressions does not seem to be enough. [For the Mind is always hungry for more.] The great Power of Mindexpression appears frail and fragile [in this world]. Similarly, the most real Mindexpression seems unreal.

[But the inner world operates by different laws. In that Mind,] perfect squares have no corners. [Reality is the opposite of appearances.]

[Usually, this most profound lesson is not mastered right away, for] great talents ripen late.

[These truths are not evident to the senses, just as] the highest notes are hard to hear. The greatest Mind Itself has no shape.

Mind is known in secret. Still, It nourishes the existence of all the universe.

42.

In the beginning, Mind produced one. One produced two. [Mind separated from Itself.] Two produced three. [The conscious mind divided from the Unconscious, dreaming up spacetime.] These three produced the universe.

Similarly, the world is divided into two categories, called the *yin* and the *yang.* Harmony can be achieved only by combining these forces in balance.

[Opposites are not always opposed.] For example, people hate to be looked down on, to occupy lower status-stations in society. Yet this is how the truly great leaders have always described themselves. For it is only through first losing that one gains. So, what appears to be great gain can actually be great loss.

[People often think that something can be "gained" through violence, but] I teach the same as those who came before me: A violent person is sure to die a violent death. This is, in fact, the essence of much of my teaching.

43.

The softest thing in the cosmos always overcomes the hardest thing in the cosmos.[The softest thing has no substance, for It is Mind.] And if something has no substance, it can enter even where there is no space.

[Mind permits events. In imitating It,] I have learned the value of noninterference. Teaching with few words, and working without [conscious] doing are understood by very few.

Richard Shiningthunder Francis

44.

Material things or an authentic Self— which matters more? Which is more precious— a self of integrity, or material wealth?

[Gain seems good, and loss bad, but] which is more precious— gain or loss? The one who lives with attachment to material things will surely suffer much. For it is the one who accumulates who always suffers loss. By contrast, a person who is truly contented [with what she has] is never disappointed. So, the one who knows when to stop [gathering] does not find herself in trouble. She will always stay safe.

45.

Great accomplishment does not feel complete enough. For, after the momentary "high" passes, it also disappears.

Similarly, great fullness never feels quite full enough. Still, the Mind that fills [all things] is inexhaustible.

[Part of the problem is distorted perceptions.] For example, the perfectly straight might appear crooked, and great intelligence, stupid. The greatest eloquence might come across [to the untrained mind] as awkward, the greatest speech dismissed as "too simple."

[But wisdom can overcome ignorance, as] movement overcomes cold, and stillness, heat. [When you feel stressed out, too "hot," remember that] stillness and tranquility set the cosmos back in order.

46.

When Mind is active among people, [things are natural and] horses do chores on the farms. But when Mind is absent [from awareness,] horses are bred for war.

[Personal desire makes people forget Mind. So] there is no greater transgression than this desire. [It creates discontent,] and there is no greater curse than discontent. Desiring for the self is a great misfortune. So, the one who knows that enough is enough will always have enough.

47.

Without even leaving your room, you can know the entire world. Without even looking out the window, you can see the [inner] patterns of enlightenment.

In fact, the further you go, the less that you know. So, the enlightened being does not need to travel in order to know. [More is often lost than gained by the distractions of too much travel.] She does not need [literally] to "look" in order to "see." She does not need [consciously] to do in order to get her work done.

48.

In chasing after ordinary learning, something new is acquired every day. But in the pursuit of Mind, something new is dropped every day. One [consciously, directively] does less and less, until one achieves the state of mind called "nonaction." It is when nothing is [manipulatively, coercively, controllingly] done, then nothing is left undone.

The world, then, is best "ruled" by allowing everything to take its natural course. For it cannot, and will not, be ruled by interference. [Cooperation replaces control.]

49.

The enlightened being has abandoned all personal mind. [Abandoning selfishness,] she is aware of the needs of others.

I am good to people who are good. But I am also good to people who are not good. This is because goodness is Mindexpression. Similarly, I believe in [the goodness of] people who are faithful. But I do not fear to place trust in [the goodness of] those who are unfaithful. For this trust is also an aspect of Mindexpression.

The enlightened being behaves shyly, quietly, and humbly. To the world, she might seem even confused. When people look to her, and listen, she responds as if she were a little child.

50.

Three in ten people follow the life-principle. Three are focused on death. And three are just passing through this world, on their way to death from birth. This is because people live their lives on only the material plane.

But she who knows how really to live can walk abroad without danger. She does not fear rhinoceros or tiger. For in her, the rhino can find no place to puncture with its horn. The tiger can find no place to tear with its claws. She is safe, in fact, even in battle. For weapons can find no place to pierce. Why? Because she has left no place for death to enter. [She will never die. But even while alive, being karmafree, she dreams no harmful wounds.]

51.

All things, everywhere, arise due to Mind. They are nourished by Its Mindexpression. They are formed from what appears as matter, and shaped by environment. So, everything in the world "respects" Mind.

Everything also honors Mindexpression. This respect and honor are not demanded by anyone. They are "built into" the very nature of everything.

So, all things arise from the Mind, and it is Mindexpression that nourishes them. Mind creates, but makes no claim to personal ownership. It makes no claim to possession. It acts everywhere, but takes no credit for Itself. It will guide, but refuses to interfere. This is how primal Mindexpression operates.

52.

There is a point in time, [in Mind,] at which the creation of form begins. This is the "mother" of all things. To know this "mother" is to understand her "children." [To know Mind is to know creation.] Knowing the "children," but being careful never to lose touch with the "mother" brings freedom from the fear of death. [For death does not touch Mind.]

So, remain silent. Watch the senses. Then, your life will be ever full. But if you talk too much, if you create too much "busy-ness," your life will be despairingly hopeless.

Being able to see the very small [such as a "seed" of potential thought within] gives insight. It is real strength to know when to yield to a greater force. Use outer Light for inner sight. [Learn about the Mind through studying the world.] By doing this, you will both prevent harm and learn stability.

53.

If I have just a little sense, I will walk on the path. My only fear will be of straying from it. Staying on this path would be easy [for people] if people were not so fond of being side-tracked.

[But people are always wandering off.] For example, officials of the court seek to take care of their own needs. They put their selfish desires for luxury and splendor ahead of the needs of the people. That is when the fields become filled with weeds. The granaries become empty. [People starve while] these officials focus only on wearing the finest jewels and clothes. They own more than they could ever use. So, they are really thieves. This is certainly not the pattern of the Mind.

54.

Something firmly rooted in the ground [such as a giant tree] cannot be uprooted. That which is firmly grasped cannot be taken away. [If you have this kind of grip on goodness,] it will be remembered for generations.

Cultivate Mindexpression within yourself. Only in this way can It be made real [for you]. Cultivate Mindexpression in the family. Then, It will abound. Cultivate It in the community, and It will proliferate. Cultivate It in the nation, and It will grow immense. Cultivate It in the cosmos, and It will be omnipresent.

Strive realistically to learn how to cultivate Mindexpression. Do this at all levels— in your body, family, community, nation, and cosmos.

How can I know that This works this way? I have carefully watched and studied It.

55.

The one filled with Mindexpression is like a newborn child. Wasps will be reluctant to sting her, serpents to bite her. Wild beasts will not readily attack her. She will not be quickly attacked by birds of prey. Her body is supple and soft. Her musculature is not overly developed. Still her grip is very firm.

And even though she has not yet experienced the full union of her "male" mindparts with her "female" mindparts, she is still a completely whole person. Her femininity is strong. [So is her endurance:] She can talk all day without growing hoarse.

This [state] is perfect harmony. Knowing harmony is stability. Knowing [full inner] stability is enlightenment.

By contrast, it is not wise always to be rushing. [You cannot rush growth by] controlling the breath or straining. This only creates tension. After all, using too much energy leads to only exhaustion. This is not the pattern of Mind. And whatever is contrary to Mind has no future.

56.

Those who know [Reality] do not say much. Those who talk too much do not really know [It]. So, be silent, and guard your senses. Temper any extremist tendencies. Keep your ways of thinking and speaking simple. Do not show off. To the contrary, seek to hide any personal brilliance. Seek true humility. Seek to blend into the background. Merge with the very dust. For only this is primal oneness.

The one who has discovered primal unity is unconcerned with whether people call themselves her "friends" or her "enemies." [All are Mind.] She is also unconcerned with whether others wish her good or harm. Honor and disgrace are the same to her. She is free, and carefree. This state is the highest possible for a human being.

57.

If you must guide, do so always with scrupulous fairness. If an enemy moves against you, surprise him [with unexpected goodness]. Thus, become master of your universe, by letting go of all strife. How do I know that the cosmos works this way? Because of this [inner Mind].

[Make no trouble for yourself or for others.] The more that you multiply restrictions [on how you think things should be], the poorer the people become. [More laws make more crime.] Also, the more deadly you make the weapons, the more trouble you will have in your country.

The more "clever" people consider themselves to be, the more bizarre will become the social situations. For the multiplication of laws causes the multiplication of thieves.

So, the enlightened being says, "I take no [consciously directed] action, and the people are reformed [by my example]. When I find true inner peace, [the world reflects this, and] people become honest. I force nothing to happen, and others become satisfied [by the natural Flow]. When I abandon my desires, people [see this, and] return to a good, simple life."

58.

When a country is ruled least, with a light hand, the people stay simple. By contrast, when it is ruled strictly and severely, the people grow cunning and treacherous [like their tyrants].

Happiness is happiest when known by contrast. That is why it so often alternates with misery. [And it is not always as it appears:] Far below layers of "happiness," unhappiness might reside.

[Try to be happy in this moment, for] who can know what the future holds? When trying to predict it, it is far too easy to be dishonest.

[Happiness comes from real goodness.] But what is termed "goodness" by some is really nothing more than an attempt to manipulate the cosmos in their favor. This illusion can last for a long time.

[The enlightened being knows better. She finds true goodness.] She might have a sharp wit, but doesn't want to "cut" others with it. She speaks with focused precision. But she does not do this to harm— even her opponents. She is honest, but never crudely blunt. She is also brilliant, but does not restrict the freedoms of others [by trying to take all credit].

59.

Seek to care for others, for this is the way to serve heaven. Always keep in mind the value of selfrestraint. Always know selfregulation. For the beginning of the path might require the renunciation of cherished ideas. The ability to do this can be dependent upon Mindexpression. Some of this you might have harvested from the past. If, at any rate, you have a good personal storehouse of Mindexpression, nothing is impossible. There are no limits. A person who knows no limits is fit to supervise the wellbeing of others. Also necessary for this are both deep roots and a strong foundation. This [caring for others] is a life of stability, long life, and eternal vision.

60.

Ruling a country is like cooking a small fish. [Too much "fire" will burn and ruin it.] But if you approach the cosmos in Mind, evil will have no power over you. Evil can appear to have power, but when its force is not used to harm, it loses energy quickly. This kind of "evil" will not harm others. And the enlightened being will be fully protected from even this. And when people with this evil do not harm each other, each can be refreshed by the other. [What energy might have been evil is transformed into compassion.]

61.

A truly great country must be like a valley. [As water accumulates there,] so smaller nations can come together in this country. It is a meeting place. But it is also a supportive, nourishing "mother."

[This is to play the female.] The female overcomes the more active male by her stillness. So, a great country conquers a smaller one in the same way— by giving in. In fact, even a small country can conquer a larger one by giving in to it. So, both "conquerors" and "conquered" win, by yielding.

Also, a great nation might need the services of the smaller one. And the smaller would do well to serve within a larger social framework. Thus can each side get what it wants.

Yielding, then, is a truly noble path for a great nation.

62.

The Mind is the Origin of the world. It is also the treasure of all good persons. It is the refuge of bad persons as well.

[It works through sweetness and goodness.] Sweet words can "buy" honor, and good deeds earn respect. Thus, if a person seems bad, do not abandon her.

On Inauguration Day, do not send expensive gifts. Instead, remain still. Offer the official [the greatest gift in the history of the universe—the loyalty, wisdom, and peace of cosmic] Mind.

Deep down, everyone truly loves this Mind. This is because It contains the fulfillment of every dream. [It contains everything.] Further, It offers complete forgiveness of all sins. That is why this Mind is the greatest Treasure in the universe.

63.

Practice noninterference. Work without [the usual consciously directed] activity. Learn to "taste" That Which has no flavor. [This is Mind.] Magnify the small. Where you have lack, seek increase.

Always return compassion for [cruelty and] bitterness. Seek only the simple, completely stripped of all complexity. Achieve immense satisfaction by doing small things well. For, in the cosmos, things that seem "easy" might be the most difficult. From the cosmic view, great actions are made of small deeds.

This is why the enlightened being does not attempt to perform big or "impressive" feats. And this is how— and why— she finds true greatness. [Her true greatness lies in doing small, humble tasks well.]

[There are also "large" and "small" promises.] If promises are given too easily and quickly, there will be little trust. And [with "big" tasks,] refusing to take serious matters seriously results in catastrophe. But it is because the enlightened being always takes care of her "small" problems that she never has "large" ones.

64.

Peace, when finally established, is fairly easy to maintain. So, try to [anticipate and] overcome trouble before it really gets started. By this, you will save yourself much pain. [Great anxieties make life more fragile, and] that which is already brittle is easily shattered. That which is small is easily scattered. Try, then, to deal with problems while they are still small, before they grow. Try to bring order to your world before confusion grows and gets out of hand. [Huge problems have small origins.] Remember that a tree five feet in diameter grows from a tiny shoot. A terrace nine stories high begins with a small pile of dirt. A journey of a thousand miles begins beneath one's feet [even before the first step].

[The world is small. Do not let it control you.] She who reacts too quickly, or too strongly, defeats herself. She is certain to lose who holds on too tightly. By contrast, the enlightened being takes no [coercive or manipulative] action. Therefore, she is never defeated.

Since she clings to nothing, she loses nothing.

[She never fails. For the only real "failure" is to stop trying.] People often fail exactly when they are right on the verge of success. So, take as much care to end a situation [honorably] as you did when beginning. Then, there will be no failure.

This is why the enlightened being seeks freedom from desire. She does not collect precious things. She learns not to hold too tightly to even ideas. She can then bring people back to what they have lost. She helps the whole world settle naturally into its own nature. But she draws the line, refraining from overactivity.

65.

In ancient beginnings, those who knew of Mind did not try to enlighten others. [This was not their mission; enlightenment is selfactualization.] So, they allowed others to remain in the dark [as long as it was their karma to be there.]

Why is it so hard to guide people? It is because the people are convinced that they are already so [intelligent and] clever. But if anyone puts this to the test, by trying to rule or control people out of cleverness, she is only a robber, stealing from them. By contrast, those who rule without cleverness [affectation and pretension] are a real blessing to the country.

Knowing these things is primal Mindexpression.

This is profound and extensive. It leads all things back towards the great Oneness.

66.

The sea rules a hundred streams. Why? Because it is lower than they, lying below them.

In the same way, if the enlightened being would effectively serve people, she must [make herself "less" or "lower,"] serve with humility. If she would be a good leader, then she must learn to follow [the examples and suggestions of] others. So, when the enlightened being leads, the people do not feel oppressed at all. Because she does no harm to the people, everyone in the world supports her. No one grows tired of her.

Also, she refuses to compete. Therefore, no one can compete against her.

67.

Everyone says that the Mind is great and beyond compare. This is what makes It unique. Clearly, It does stand out [when It manifests] among human beings. For in fact, if It had not been this unique, It might have perished long ago.

There are three major treasures within It: mercy, frugality, and humility. Mercy is the source of courage, frugality of generosity, humility of leadership.

For mercy creates both immense strength and true victory. It is heaven's own way of saving and protecting.

Some try to ignore mercy and still be brave. [They fail.] Others abandon economy and still try to be generous. [This does not work.] Still others believe that they can be effective leaders without humility. [This fails miserably.] These paths are certain death.

68.

A good warrior is never violent. An excellent contender never fights out of anger. A good winner is never the least bit interested in vengeance. A good employer is always humble.

These qualities are known as the "Mindexpression of nonstriving." It is ultimate unity with heaven.

69.

The most powerful warriors are guided by this approach: "I would rather play the part of a polite guest than to make offensive moves. I would rather withdraw a foot than advance an inch." This is like true marching, in which progress is made, but subtly.

Even when one appears not to move at all, she might be using strategy. She is like the one preparing to engage an enemy. But she does not [make the terrible mistake, and] reveal her hidden strength. This strategy "captures" the opponent without attack. [Draining the opponent of energy "captures" the enemy's mind.] It is a way to be prepared without weapons.

To underestimate a nemesis can be a tragic mistake. [True enemies are not people, but attitudes.] If you underestimate [inner] opponents, you might lose what you most value. [Just remember that,] when a battle is actually engaged, the underdog often wins.

70.

These words are fairly easy to understand, and even to apply. Yet still, no one in the world fully understands, or completely practices, them. They have ancient beginnings. Actions that flow from them are highly disciplined. And it is precisely because people do not understand that they have no knowledge of [these ideas]. In fact, those who know of It are few indeed. Yet those who abuse [and mock] It are often honored.

The enlightened being dresses in ordinary clothes. She dresses in even rough, plain clothing. But in her heart she holds the indescribable Jewel.

71.

Understanding ignorance is a kind of real strength. But ignoring understanding is a kind of real sickness. Only when one begins to grow sick and tired of this sickness is she beginning to get well. The enlightened being is well precisely because she has grown sick and tired of this [spiritual] sickness.

72.

When people lack reverence or awe, they are heading for disaster. Do not intrude into their homes [with "religion"]. Do not harass them at work [with "preaching"]. For only if you do not interfere will they not grow tired of you.

The enlightened being fully knows herself. But she is very careful never to display this fact. Her selfrespect is profound. She completely lacks arrogance. She lets go of pretension. She chooses instead Selflove.

73.

A reckless and passionate person will kill or be killed. But a truly brave and calm person will always work for only the preservation of life. Of these two, which is good, and which harmful?

Some [actions] are simply not favored by heaven. But even the enlightened being is not always certain about the mystery, of why this is so.

The way of heaven is never to strive. Still, you overcome. Even when a person does not speak, she is answered. The path is this: Ask for nothing, but still, you will be supplied with all your needs. One might follow plans, but does not let them stress her.

The "net" of heaven is wide. Though its meshes seem coarse, not a single microparticle is allowed to slip through.

74.

If people are not afraid to die death-threats are useless. But if they live in constant death-fear, and death is the penalty for law-breaking, who will break the law?

[Unfortunately,] there is always someone who must be executioner. If you try to become an executioner, it would be like trying to replace a master carpenter. If you try to cut wood like a master carpenter, you will only hurt yourself.

75.

Why do the people starve? It is because the government eats up the money in taxes.

Why are the people rebellious? Because the government interferes too much.

Why does death mean so little? Because life is so harsh, made so by the government. For when one has so little on which to live, one learns not to treasure life too dearly.

76.

A person is born flexible and weak. At death, that same person is rigid and hard. Green plants are tender and supple. But at death, they are withered and dry. Thus, the rigid and inelastic are the disciples of death. But the gentle and yielding are the disciples of life. Even an entire army can lose if flexibility is lacking. And a tree that is unbending is snapped with surprising ease. So, the hard and strong will collapse, but the soft and weak will overcome.

77.

The Mind of heaven is like a bent bow. The higher part is lowered, and the lower raised. [Extremes are corrected.] If the string is too long, it is shortened. If it is too short, it is lengthened. [Mind selfcorrects.]

This, then, is how heaven acts: It takes the excesses from those who have too much, and distributes them to those who do not have enough. How different from the ways of people! For they take from those who do not have enough, and give to those who already have too much!

What person, having more than enough, gives her excess to the world? Only she who is of true Mind does this.

The enlightened being also works without concern for recognition. She simply does whatever must be done. But she does not dwell on it. She does not waste her precious knowledge in vain selfdisplay.

78.

On earth, nothing is more soft and yielding than water. Yet nothing can equal it for attacking the solid and the strong. The weak overcomes the strong. The elastic overcomes the rigid.

[Deep down,] everyone on earth knows this. But almost no one actually practices it. So, the enlightened being says, "Only one who takes upon herself the humiliation of the people is qualified to care for them. Only she who takes upon herself the disasters of the whole country can serve as the master of the universe. [Only Love qualifies.]"

Reality often seems like a paradox.

79.

After any bitter quarrel, some residual resentment remains. What can one do about it? In every situation, the enlightened being seeks to do her fair share. [So, make sure that you do.] But she does not [make the error, to] expect others to do so. She does not expect or demand her "due." But a person of Mindexpression will always do her part. A person without Mindexpression will focus on the "obligations" of the other.

The Mind of heaven, however, is impartial. It remains with good people all the time.

80.

A small and simple country has few people. But even though there are machines that could do as much as a hundred people, they are not needed. [Technology is minimized.] The people take their simple lives seriously. They do not usually travel far from home [from which they do not have to "get away"]. Even if they have boats and carriages, no one ever uses them. [They are content and fulfilled without travel.] They also have armor and weapons, but no one ever has a need to display them.

These people return to the simple knotting of simple ropes rather than [getting lost in] complex calculations and writings. Their food is plain but good [and satisfying]. Their clothes are simple but fine. Their homes are secure. They are very happy in their simple ways.

They can see their neighbors from their houses. Crowing roosters and barking dogs are everywhere. Still, they live in profound tranquility. They grow old placidly, and die in serenity.

81.

Words of truth are not always beautiful. Beautiful words might not be true.

Good people do not engage in active strife. Those who do are not good.

Those who know are not always educated. The educated do not often know.

The enlightened being has no interest in accumulating material things. In fact, she gains by doing for others; the more that she does for them, the more that she has. The more that she gives to others, the greater is her personal increase. [Giving is real receiving.]

The Mind of heaven is direct and sharp. But It never does harm. So, the pattern of the enlightened being is to do work that is effortless.

Richard Shiningthunder Francis

YOU ARE MY EVERYTHING: STUDIES IN THE MYSTICISM OF THE UPANISHADS

****

Thanks to Albert Bollinger for his help with this part of the book.

****

One of the richest veins of mysticism in the history of the world is Hinduism. And within Hinduism, no tradition was more sacred than the Brahmanic, as revealed in the sacred texts known as the "Upanishads." These were composed between the eighth and sixth centuries BC. No one knows who wrote them; anonymity was probably deliberate, since the writers strove for the egoless state.

The mystic Shankara (9th century) wrote commentaries on ten of the Upanishads, and these are now recognized as the principle works in the Upanishadic collection. The texts are so homogeneous that they, eliminating repetitions, could conceivably be reduced to a single book.

They are not designed to present systematic theology or dogma. Instead, they are somewhat informal records and interpretations of the meaning of mystical experiences. So, whether prose or poetry, they lack logical beginnings and endings. For their writers were not as interested in teaching analytically as through example. The only real "study" is not of the Scriptures, but only of the Self. In all, there are said to have been, at one time, two hundred texts, but only 108 have been preserved, and only thirteen are accepted as sacred Scripture.

The Upanishads discuss the deepest issues of spirituality— issues such as the nature of God, of Mind, of Reality, Spirit, Soul, death, and immortality. In the *Katha Upanishad,* "immortality" itself is defined as "Union" with God. This comes through heartpurification. It is also the same as knowing the "Self" within— the "highest" or deepest

Self. "God without" and the Self within are said to be perfectly symmetric and identical. Both "knowings" are "one knowing."

In "heaven" this text continues, "there is no fear." Nor is there any "thought of growing old" to "make one tremble." "All rejoice and are glad," far from the reach of hunger, thirst, or sorrow. Goodness is always to be chosen over mere pleasure. "They that choose the pleasant miss the goal."

The deeply hidden Self is "subtler than the subtlest." This Self is "one" with Brahman Itself. To find Brahman, all things— even the most impressive of miraculous powers— are to be "renounced." "The ancient effulgent Being, ... subtle, deep hidden, in the lotus of the heart, is hard to know." The wise, who does know Him/Her, is "freed alike from pleasure and from pain."

This Self "is separate from the body, the senses, and the mind." What is sought by the mystic is the "Soul of truth." Stated differently, this is the Essence of Reality. The result? The seeker is "exceedingly glad."

She learns that this Self is "the omniscient Lord." To see this glory, a person must be "freed from desire." She then enters a state "without sorrow." The individual self has fused with the universal Self. They have synergistically entered the "cave of the heart." This heart is the "abode of the most High."

This Self is called the "Enjoyer" when it is united with the body, the mind, and the senses. All "material" things come from egomind, for the senses are triggered into response by "physical objects," whose Source is Mind. Egomind comes from intellect; intellect comes from ego; ego comes from the "Unmanifested seed"; the Unmanifested Seed comes from Brahman, or cosmic Mind.

This Brahman is the Self. It is "deep hidden in all beings." It is "soundless, formless, intangible," and beyond sensory detection. It is also "undying." It is "without beginning, without end." It is also "eternal, immutable, beyond nature." This is the Self. This is the deepest level of the Mind in Its function as Creatormind. When one knows this Self, she is "freed from death."

The "Selfexistent" makes "the senses turn outward." This is how people get lost in illusion, mistaking the sensory for the Real. In time, this leads to a selective "blindness" regarding "What is within." Rare is the person who learns the secret. It is to "shut the eyes to what is without." This "immortal Self" is the "omniscient Lord." "Knowing Him, one grieves no more." This Self "casts out all fear." (This immortal Self is also called the "first-born.") This Self is the Mind in which the sun rises and sets. It is "the Source of all the powers of nature." Nothing can transcend It. "What is within us is also what is without [outside]; what is without is also within." The whole world of all the senses is no more than an "exteriorization" of the inner Mind. "He who sees difference between what is within and what is without goes ever more from death to death." In other words, he/she is still stuck in the rounds and cycles of reincarnation; birth always leads to death, in the realms of illusion.

This harmful rerun is shattered only by the final realization: "Brahman alone is. Nothing else is." Everything is God modified, Mind translated, transmographied, in disguise. Everything is Creatormind. She is still lost who sees only the "manifold universe" and fails to see the "one Reality." Multiplicity is basic error, oneness or Unity basic awakening.

Knowing that all is the projection/modification of Mind, and that Mind is Love, causes the mystic gradually to lose all fears. She thrives in a cosmos where everything and everyone is "friendly"— even those parts of Mind that play the roles, wear the masks, of "evil."

This Self, projected, is the sun in the sky, the breeze blowing. It is fire in the fireplace, and the guest warming her hands. It "is in all." It "is wherever there is reality." It is the fish, the plant, the river, the "changeless Reality, the Illimitable." It is "seated in the heart" as the "adorable One." As fire takes the shape of every object which it consumes, the One adopts the shape of everything that It indwells.

Sunlight is not made the least impure when it shines upon garbage or filth. Similarly, the Self is not made impure by the "evils" of the world. This is because It is above all, "transcends all." "Of one form, He makes of Himself many forms." Knowing this Self is "eternal bliss."

Recalling the symbolism of the later Kabbalah, this text says, "This universe is a tree..." Like the Jewish tree, its roots are in heaven, and its branches manifest on earth. This means that all Mind is tied into heavenly Mind, and its products appear "here below." Its roots are Brahman, the Self. From this Self, the entire universe comes forth, and in It, the cosmos moves. When this is discovered, death loses its terror. "In one's own Soul, Brahman is realized clearly, as if seen in a mirror." This Self, Brahman, is the "allpervading Spirit."

Only "when all the senses are stilled, when the mind is at rest," can Brahmanself be seen. This is the highest state possible, and is the same as what is called *yoga.*

There are two selves, one apparent and One real. When personal desire dies, immortality arises from the true Self.

Radiating from the heart are 101 nerves. One of these ascends towards the top of the head, the "thousand-petalled lotus." If, at death, vital force passes through this nervepath, one attains immortality. But if this life-force goes another path, through another nerve, she is reborn into another mortal form.

In the *Isha Upanishad,* the Self within and Brahman without are *one and the same.* So, there is no real or valid distinction between them. They are divided, in fact, only for conceptual convenience. Since Brahman is everything, it follows that the deepest Self is also everything. The cosmos, then, is Mind dancing, or playing, with Itself. "Filled with Brahman are all things..." "From out of Brahman floweth all that is." "The Lord... alone is the Reality." He lives "in the heart of all things." This is why the wise work without attachment, and act free of personal desire. When she does a job, she does not 'yearn for its fruits.'

She who sees the Self in all "hates none." For the Self which is "in all" is "pure, untouched by evil." It alone is "the Thinker,... the Selfexistent." The Way of Light seeks a balance between work "in the world" and meditation, between body and Spirit.

In all objects and things and persons, the wise says, "The beingness that dwells in that [or him/her], even That am I." She knows that "my life merges with the allpervading Life."

In the *Kena Upanishad,* the Self is called "Mind of the Mind." To say, "I am the sum of my senses" is a falsehood. Also, to say, "I am this personal mind" is just as erroneous.

Who, then, is this Self who is NOT the senses, NOT the personal mind? It is cosmic Mind. It is "Brahman." It is not just your personal self; it is the "Self" of all things and persons. But how can things have a "self"? Because they, too, are created and pervaded by Mind.

This Mystery is Brahman, "That which cannot be expressed in words." This Reality is beyond ordinary comprehension, or intellectual understanding, of the mind. Brahman is "beyond knowledge."

Yet this unconscious Mind is "behind every activity." This Mind is the Source of both thinking and sensing. Knowing this directly, through feeling its truth, grants immortality, for all thoughts arise from the Immortal. In Indian symbolic mythology, Indra was seen as the "supreme god" because he approached "nearest to Brahman." So, Brahman is higher even than the gods. Brahman is the Mind, the Creator/Dreamer, who is the Origin of all gods. All Power throughout nature— from the flash of lightning to the blinking of an eye— all is Brahman manifest. In fact, the Power of mental movement is itself also Mind or Brahman, although here, It is very subtle.

Since Brahman is allgood, all perfect Mind, "one who attains to Brahman is freed from evil."

In the *Prasna Upanishad,* "austerity" is an important part of spiritual practice. This is discipline that acts against the nature of the sensual, selfish, or selfindulgent. It is somewhat too strict at times and, if too extreme, can become harmful. But in moderation, austerity can be seen as balanced, reasonable countergreed and counterselfishness.

Here, in this text, the entire cosmos is seen as interaction between two essentially dissimilar forces, comparable to the *yin* and *yang* of Chinese mysticism. These two forces are identified as *prana,* represented by the sun, and *rayi,* symbolized by the moon.

Prana is "primal energy," while *rayi* is "formgiving" functions. Thus, *rayi* transforms *prana* into images and forms in the world. Thus, while everything is made of primal *prana* or "Mindstuff," things are formed into stones, bodies, cars, buildings, and trees by the formgiving *rayi.*

Prana is the "Soul of the universe." Those who do not progress to the elevated spiritual knowing of *prana* are born once again to the *rayi*-influenced worlds, such as earth, rather than higher planes.

The wise worship nothing in this world— not idols, images, cars, money, career, intellect, fine objects, etc. They are devoted alone to the worship of the true, deepest Self or Brahman. These "attain the world of the sun." For the one who "goes to the sun" there exists "no more death or dearth." This "sunenergy" is associated with accurate knowledge, implying honesty. The sunenergy is "attainable by those only who are neither deceitful nor wicked nor false."

While the body and other "material" things are composed of earth, air, fire, water, and ether, *prana* is supreme over them all. *Prana* is both the visible and the invisible, both breath and fire. It gives life to the senses. It is creativenergy. The Upanishad then says plainly, "Thou art the Creator."

It also says, referring to the deepest Self, "Thou art the Master of all that exists." The senses are not It; they are mere "food" for It (this true Self).

It dreams into being the whole cosmos. "Whatsoever exists in the universe is dependent on Thee." For the deepest Self dreams up even *prana.* "*Prana* is born of the Self."

The Self exists in an inseparable whole with *prana.* "Like a man and his shadow, *prana* and the Self are inseparable." This is because they are both products of the one and the same Mind. Specifically, Mind produces Self, and Self produces *prana.*

This is the sage's "goal." "The sage, with the help of *aum,* reaches Brahman." In other words, her identity is no longer that of a single person, but of Mind Itself, which indwells all the cosmos.

When Mind dreams, It "enters" Its dream. "In creating, I enter My creation," It says. Creation comes in sequential forms: 1) *Prana,* 2) desire, 3) ether, 4) earth, 5) air, 6) fire, 7) water, 8) the senses, 9) the mind, 10) food, 11) vigor, 12) penance, 13) the Vedas (Scriptures), 14) sacrificial rites (primitive barter with gods), 15) all worlds, and 16) names.

As in Taoism, the giving of "names" splits the One into the illusion of many. It obscures the underlying Mystery. But still, all these parts were created "out of His own being," or from the Selfmind. Later, they "return to Him from Whom they came." After enlightenment, they "disappear into Him," into the highest Self, the Spirit.

The *Mundaka Upanishad,* says that "knowledge" is about things, but "wisdom" is about Brahman, the Self, the Spirit, the Creatormind. Ultimate wisdom, it follows, is Unity with this deepest Mind. But where did this original Mind originate? It was axiomatic. Never created, It is the "uncaused First Cause." The texts say simply, "Out of the infinite ocean of existence, Brahman arose." But "the universes sprang entirely from Him." From deepest Mind, all creation springs.

Two kinds of knowledge exist: The lower is the knowledge of the Scriptures; the higher is the direct knowing of the inner Mind of Spirit. The cosmos emerges from Selfmind as the silk is spun from the body of the spider, as plants emerge from soil, as hair comes out of the body. Brahman created the "material, external" cosmos by simply willing that it be so. Then, *"out of himself"* this universe came into being. Creation all occurs within the Mind, and never escapes Mind to an illusory "outside." From Mind came "primal energy," and then, from this energy, more Mind.

The ignorant do not realize this. Those who follow them also do not realize. This text was first to use the phrase, "the blind leading the blind" to describe this situation. The wise do not use works to find Light, but they use silence and solitude. This teaching of enlightenment without works came to be called "grace" in later Christianity. "Let a person devoted to the spiritual life carefully analyze the passing nature of enjoyment ... as found in good works. It is not by works that one gains the Eternal." "Let her give not a single thought to transitory things, but, absorbed in meditation, renounce the world." This highest Brahmanself is called the "truly existing."

Only It is the Real. "The Imperishable is the Real." All material things arise from the Imperishable like thousands of sparks from a single fire. This deepest Self, this Spirit, is "Selfluminous" and Itself is "formless." "He is the innermost Self of all." All things, all conditions, come "from Him." "In Him, the seas and mountains have their Source." "Thus, Brahman is All, and is within all." In early Christian texts it was similarly written, "Christ is all..." (Col.3:11) This Selfmind is "action, knowledge, and goodness supreme." The wise exist in Him consciously, "with mind absorbed, and heart melted, in Love." The advice followed by sages is, "Lose thyself in Him." This means that the conscious mind loses sight of itself. The self of ego disappears, and there is only Supermind. "Know Him, the Self, alone." "Meditate on Him as *aum.*" Long before Jesus blessed the "pure in heart," these texts said, "By the pure in heart is He known."

The Self is both personal and nonpersonal. Like Christ, the "Light of the world," He is the "Light of lights." He is the "one Light that gives light to all." Similarly, in early Christian texts, Christ was the "Light that gives light to all..." (Jn. 1:9)

Then, the text says vividly, "All is Brahman." Only when the Soul suffers from karmic or cosmic amnesia, forgetting her true identity as Brahmanself, does she allow the ego to influence her. This brings her into inevitable sadness and grief. But when she recognizes the adorable Lord as her own deepest Self, her grief disappears in a flood of radiant bliss and peace. This is the "supreme Being," and the wise seeks Union with this Self.

She knows that she is in Union with Him because she has life. And "the Lord is the one Life shining forth from every creature." So, the wise "serves the Lord in all." Every person is a mask or role of the Infinite, of immeasurable Love. So, the enlightened cultivate humility. The knowing (gnosis) of this Lord is here called "Superconscious vision." This leads to a path of "felicity... freed from cravings." Only "in meditation is the nonpersonal Self revealed." It is the "pure, effulgent Being in whom is contained the universe." "Having known the Self, the sages are filled with joy." "Blessed are they, tranquil of Mind, free from [sensual] passion, realizing everywhere the allpervading Brahman." "Deeply absorbed in the contemplation of His Being, they enter into Him." The "yoga of renunciation" brings immortality in this very life. They are "freed from name and form," having returned to the inner formless Mind. "She who knows Brahman becomes Brahman."

In the *Mandukya Upanishad*, states of consciousness are divided among waking, dreaming, dreamless sleep, and superconscious vision. A respected shortcut to this fourth state is the repetition of the most ancient and holy of all words or mantras, *aum*. Although often written as "om," the mantra literally has two very small syllables, pronounced "ah'-oom." This text goes so far as to say, "*Aum*, which is the imperishable Brahman, is the universe." "All that we see outside of ourselves, this is Brahman." "The Self within is also Brahman." It is all Mind.

The first part of this great Self is the "universal person," called *vaiswanara*. It is regarded as a part of "physical" nature. This part of Mind is not welldeveloped. It is conscious of only "external" objects. This is further subdivided into four parts: Mind, heart, intellect, and ego. This dull aspect of Mind is the "enjoyer of the senses."

The second part of Mind is the same "universal person," but in her mental nature, rather than physical. This aspect is called *taijasa*. "She dreams, and is aware of only her dreams."

The third part of Mind is the same "universal person," but this time, she exists in dreamless sleep. This part of Mind is called, rather confusingly, *prajna*. She "dreams not, and is without desire." She is, in fact, covered by the "veil of unconsciousness." All her mindimpressions vanish. Experiencing "neither strife nor anxiety," she is called "blissful." (Here, "bliss" is described only negatively, as the absence of nonbliss.)

The fourth part of Mind is enlightenment. It is called *Iswara* or *Ishwara*. "Iswara" is the name of Brahman when It is in a context of *maya* or "illusion." While human nature is *controlled by* ignorance, the Iswaramind controls ignorance. This state is "pure Unitary consciousness." The illusion of multiplicity— that there are innumerable minds— is obliterated. (This state is also called "ineffable peace" and "the supreme good.") This is true and positive Blissmind, the "One without a second" of Indian mysticism. Again, "The Self beyond all worlds is the word *aum*."

The *Taittiriya Upanishad* says to Brahman, "She who dwells in Thee becomes queen over herself." Emphasized on the Way of wisdom are truthfulness, right action, selfdenial, and the "practice of austerity. One is recommended to behavior from "a cheerful heart and an unattached mind."

What does this behavior mean in a practical sense? For one thing, it means courtesy, especially to guests. "Let your guests be as gods to you." "Blameless" actions are recommended. So is genuine giving, "with Love and respect." Gifts should be "given in abundance" with joy. Love expresses as generosity.

Also, caring for the body is spiritual. For "the body... is the physical sheath of the Self." Encased in the physical sheath is the "vital sheath." Through this, the senses act. This is the source of bioenergy. Inside the vital sheath is the "mental sheath." Inside it is the "intellectual sheath." (All sheaths have the same form.) This is the source of all actions. Inside this is the "egosheath." But the true Self is beyond all these sheaths.

Brahman decided "that He should make of Himself many forms," and so, went into meditation— an altered state in which He could dream reality into being. "Creating all things, He entered into everything," and so, all is the Self. Wise people call It "Reality," because It alone has absolute (nonrelative) reality.

The Self (Brahman) existed as the "Unmanifest" even before creation began. Then, "from Himself, he brought forth Himself." When He is fully revealed as the deepest Self, "one is without craving." "Verily, he who knows this truth overcomes the world," even as Jesus said of himself. The enlightened being transcends all the sheaths, for she lives apart from them.

The Self in human nature is the same Mind as the "Self" of the sun and nature. The enlightened no longer dualizes the world into good and evil that are opposite equals. She transcends this duality, and trades it in for a monistic view: The cosmic Mind is one, allgood, and has no real opposite.

The text says clearly and simply, "Mind is Brahman." It also says, "Joy is Brahman," for joy/bliss is the Core of all Mind. The path is also quite simple: "Let her worship Brahman as Brahman, and she will become Brahman."

The *Aitaraya Upanishad,* says that "all three states of the Soul," waking, dreaming, and dreamless sleep, are themselves parts of the greater dream.

The Self dreaming up the universe is not sensory, and It is not intellectual. It is not the feeling self or the thinking self. It is pure Mind, or "pure consciousness." It is God, and It is also all things, "the Reality behind" all the cosmos. It is the underlying Mind that dreams up the "physical, external" cosmos. All other beings in the universe exist only "in Him," in the Self.

In the *Chandogya Upanishad*, three requirements for the "holy life" are stated: study and almsgiving, austerity, and living every day as student/learner.

The very highest Light, above all others, supreme Light is the "light that shines in the hearts of people." The mind should be "free from the taint of [sensual] passion." "A person is, above all, her will." Also, "as is her will in this life, so does she become when she parts from this life." Thus, the very best use of timenergy is transforming it into Lovenergy, with the goal of "attaining Brahman." Brahman pervades all the senses, but It is Itself beyond them.

The Self is said to be tiny, "like a mustard seed." Jesus often used the mustard seed in his parables. Still, paradoxically, it is greater than the earth. This is because Mind has no physical dimensions. Every concept and reality, represented by "the four directions, are a part of the Lord." Earth, sky, heavens, and ocean are "portions of Him." So are the senses, and so is the total Mind. If one knows the "true nature of the world," as Lovedream, that world can do no harm. The Soul cannot be harmed by anything at all in the "material" dreamworld.

He indwells, as Creatormind, both lightning and fire. So, there can be "friendly fire," according to a native American tradition. This is truth or Reality. "To her who knows it shall no 'evil' cling." All evil is absent from perfect Mind, from the Dreamind.

How is the universal Self to be known? By knowing the personal Self. Your own mind is the conduit, the gate, to eternal Mind. Just as by knowing one thing made of clay or gold allows you to know the nature of all things clay or gold, so knowing the Self deep within your own mind allows you to know the Self within all things and persons. This is the most profound meaning of the Socratic, "Know thy Self."

It was through this Self that the world came, and comes, into being. Existence did not arise from a void of nonexistence. For in the beginning was this "One without a second," and all drew existence from this Selfmind, Creatormind. Its function is to dream up the cosmos, from the Unconscious levels.

How did creation occur? "He, the One, thought to Himself, 'Let Me be many,'" and so, the cosmos of many things proliferated in the dream. The text says beautifully, "Out of Himself He projected the universe." Thus "He entered into every being." He was and is the "subtle Essence" of everything and everyone.

Identification of the Self as Yourself begins with the realization that you *actually are* indwelling and exteriorizing everything and everyone whom You encounter. This realization is the core of the most famous phrase in all of Indian mysticism, *Tat tvam asi,* or "That Thou art." We all continuously need to be reminded, especially when encountering the "evil" and the "ugly" that we need to strip those false labels from the Self, for It alone is "truth." It is Reality in the absolute sense, much more real than our labels.

Even the most nonmystical of all people must by nature return to this One Self, in order to maintain balance and wellbeing. For in dreamless sleep, every night, she is "merged in that one existence." Dreamless sleep is nature's own meditation, very deep. But even so, on a conscious level, "they do not know that they are merged in Him."

This Self maintains not only a certain level of functioning, but is the process of sustaining life itself. When the Self leaves the body, it dies, but the "Self dies not."

The secret of this Self is stated clearly: "Mind is the way to happiness; meditate on Brahman as Mind." But will is even "higher" than Mind, so the advice is to "meditate on will as Brahman." Higher factors, such as discrimination, concentration, and insight are also "Brahman."

To find joy/bliss, we must discover this Self. For joy does not exist in the finite world. This is why materialists and greedy persons are always unhappy, as are those who grasp selfishly at happiness. When, in the diversity of all life and multiplicity, you know nothing but the One, you have met the Infinite. This infinite Self contrasts vividly with "poor and finite" materialism. Also, It is not hard to find; indeed, there is nowhere in all the cosmos that you can go where It is not.

Entire worlds and galaxies exist within the infinity of inner space. "As large as the universe 'outside' is the cosmos within." In fact, there is no "outside" to Mind. Within Mind exist all the "outer" things, including sun, moon, and galaxies of stars and planets.

All sensual joys are ephemeral, diaphanous, and transitory. Only Lovemind is forever, and It is the Self. Lovemind is Brahman. Discovering this is the only factor that can ever create any permanent happiness, in this world, or those to come. "All 'evil' shuns That,... for That is free from all impurities." Evil disappears when absolute Mind is discovered, for It is unpolluted, uncontaminated by any taint or stain of the illusion of absolute evil.

This text emphasizes the importance of "continence." This it defines as taking a vow of silence, or dwelling in the forest. "Continence" is selfrestraint, selfcontrol, and selfregulation. Other practical examples of continence include the mystical life of compassion for all living things and the mystical lifestyle of simplicity. Continence, in a less rigid form, can be expressed as vms (voluntary minimal speech) and/or the practice of "Ifree" (deleting the words "I," "me," "my," and "mine.")

When one realizes the Self, she "obtains all the worlds, and all desires." This can be so because, before the Self can be "obtained" at all, she must rid the mind of all personal, grasping, selfish desires. This leaves her to will (want) only what the Self wills.

That the body alone is to be worshipped and/or served is a teaching of "demons," or lower nature mindforces. It is instead the free Lovemind, the same that "moves around in dreams," which is immortal and the viable object of adoration. Only when fused with a body is this Self "subject to pleasure and pain." Thus, as long as this conceptual bond of oneness continues, "freedom from pleasure and pain" cannot be discovered. But as this "association ceases," there ceases also bondage to the twin masters of pleasure and pain. Finding this great level of freedom necessitates "rising above physical consciousness." You must know the Self "to be distinct from the senses of the mind."

The *Brihadaranyaka Upanishad*, says that the Self dwells, like a fire in wood, in "all forms." It is "hidden behind" names and forms, as pure Mind. This Self is "dearer" than anything else. For It is the only Object of Love that never perishes. The sage is one who has realized that her Self is also the Self of all humankind. Even "the gods cannot harm" this "realized" Being.

The goal is to know (with gnosis) "the kingdom of the Self," which is also "the kingdom of God" within. This is an ocean or well of "inexhaustible virtue" or goodness.

As an expression of this eternal goodness, "Brahman is forgiving," and meditating on this Self also makes one forgiving in her everyday life.

In deepest dreamless sleep, one is said to fall into the Mind of this Self, as she "enters into the seventy-two thousand nerves." Consciously, she knows nothing at all, but an Unconscious fusion or melding has occurred. This is how she brings goodness back from the deepest Mind, enriching the world with Love and compassion. This is analogous to an unconscious "ecstasy of Love."

Mind alone is ultimately or absolutely real. Of the Self, it is written, "His secret name is Reality ('truth')."

It is, in fact, for the sake of loving this Self that others are loved. Everytime that you love another, you show Love to the Self, Brahman or God. As Jesus said in *The Mystic Gospels*, it is impossible to love

God without loving people and other creatures. Love for others is the *only* Love for the adored Self; it is the only real and true devotion.

This results in universal Love as the zenith of the spiritual life. For all things and persons are realized to be the Self. "Whatsoever things there be, these are the Self."

This Self is pure Love, by nature, as well as "pure intelligence," intrinsically. To touch and to know this Self, the egoself must be dissolved into It like salt in water. "The individual self, dissolved, *is* the Eternal." When the idea of "the many" disappears, so does this lower egoself. "When there is consciousness of the Self, personhood is no more." This is the end of duality, and its replacement by the monistic (unifying) perspective.

"He is all." The Self that indwells you also indwells the earth, the sun, the four elements, and everything/everyone else. "He entered into all bodies." This Self is also called *purusha* in the ancient writings. "He is revealed in all forms through his *maya.*" So, illusion is the device which he creates to liberate the Mind. Hence, it is not evil, but serves the purposes of freedom and Love. "This knowledge leads to liberation." The sage, it is written, should devote herself *exclusively* to the contemplation of this Self. Only she who directs the Mind continually towards the Self is the true "knower of Brahman." She "shuns all other thoughts as distractions."

This frees her from "craving," and makes her the "inner ruler." She dwells in lightning, fire, sun, moon, the four elements, darkness, light, etc. They are all her "body," or her "Bodymind." Of the inner Self, it is written, "There is no other but He." Another name for this changeless Reality or Self is *Akshara.* Without knowing Him, mechanical, legalistic religion and ritual are useless. "There is no Seer but He, no Thinker but He, no Knower but He."

When the sage dies, she transfers to her "subtle body." On this are left the impressions of past deeds. Karma is a series of "psychoholograms" or Mindpictures "played back" by the unconscious Mind. The whole world now, and the worlds to come, are exactly this kind of projected Mindimage: "There are no real chariots, horses, or roads. But by the Light of the Self, she creates [these things]... There are no real ponds, lakes, or rivers. But she creates them. She becomes the Creator of all these, out of the impressions left by her past deeds." So, karma is created in the Mind, by the Mind, from Mindimpressions.

In perfect still Union with the Self, she "knows nothing 'outside,' nothing inside." All other desires evaporate when the Self is "her only desire." She "goes beyond sorrow." In this state of being the true Self, "father is no father, and mother no true mother." As Jesus recommended, "Call no one on earth 'Father',..."

As a person awakens from a nightdream, so does she awaken from this life when she begins to move into the Afterlife.

Here is a law behind all karma: "As one acts, so she becomes." It is her own Self returning to her as "external, material" world, as environments, situations, things, events, and persons. A related law: "Her desire is her destiny." For Mind follows desire.

Foolish people, who love ignorance and violence, go to lower worlds after death. These Mindworlds are said to be "joyless, enveloped in darkness."

Brahman is Mind unified. "She who sees diversity goes from death to death," still caught in the wheels and cycles of karma. "Brahman can be apprehended only as knowledge itself," at least, in the beginning. For, at the pinnacle of illumination, this Brahmanself is Love. "Evil does not touch Him, for, in His divine knowing, all 'evil' is burned away."

To walk the Way to enlightenment comes down to basics: "Be selfregulated, be generous, be compassionate."

In the *Kaivalya Upanishad,* immortality is achieved by "indifference to the world." This is not, of course, apathy regarding human suffering, but it is realizing that the apparent state of the "material" world is not absolutely real, and is no viable master. This is called entering "the lotus of the heart," where Brahmanself dwells. "He is bliss." But by knowing Him, the deepest Self, "there is no other way to liberation." One "goes to Brahman" by "seeing this Self in all beings, and all beings in this Self."

Only "when He is in the state of dream that people call 'being awake' does He manifest as a personal self." He says, "From Me, all emerge, and in Me, all exist, and to Me, all shall return." Then, he says with greater clarity, "I am this manifold universe."

In the *Svetasvatara Upanishad,* the cosmos is said to be a "wheel." It consists of repeating cycles of "birth and rebirth." You are "stuck" to the wheel as long as you believe yourself separate from Brahman. The text says that you are "in bondage," and can be saved only through the "grace of Brahman."

Brahman is "the substance." All else is simply "the shadow." "The personal Soul forgets the Lord, and is thus bound to pleasures." In higher Reality, Mind, all matter, and all *maya* are equally "one with Brahman."

This deepest Self is the Observer and Recorder, but has no direct place in action that creates harmful karma. It acts only as Love. Thus, It is called the "Destroyer of ignorance."

"The truth is that You are always in full Union with the Lord, but you need to realize and know this." "Nothing further is there to know."

How is this gnosis discovered? "Control the senses and harness the Mind." "Prevent the senses from attaching themselves to objects of pleasure." "Be drunk with the wine of divine Love."

The Self so known "projects the universe, maintains it, and then withdraws it back into Himself." In other words, he dreams, lives in the dream for a while, and then, ends the dream. "Out of Himself" do all things come, and He "conveys bliss and wisdom upon all who are devoted to Him." This leads to selforgivness, which leads to joy: "He destroys their sins and sorrows."

"He envelopes the universe," yet resides in "the lotus of the heart." In the physical body, his interface is "ten fingers above the navel," at the heartchakra or Lovecenter. Through this Love, "He is the Friend ... of all." "Through His grace, a person ... transcends grief." He is a powerful inner Fountain of tranquility.

To Him, the Self, it is written, "Thou alone art...Thou art consciousness Itself." Again, "Thy Power divine projects this visible universe." Again, "Thou appearest as this universe, as evolution and as dream." "When Thou art seen, time and form disappear." This is "timeless" life.

REVIEW, CONCLUSION, AND ADDITIONAL NOTES

"Brahman" was the name given by these mystics to the cosmic Mind, especially that part known as the "Creator/Dreamer" of the world of "external, material" existence. This was, then, the deepest level of the Unconscious, the Core, the Spirit, or God. In the Upanishadic Writings, it is often called simply "the Self."

This Mind is also called the "*sat-chit-ananda Brahman*," which means "the Spirit of existence, knowledge, and bliss." It is also called the "*advaita* Brahman," meaning the "undivided Spirit." The separation of the cosmos into separate persons and things is ultimately illusion. All is unified, One, Brahmanmind projected or exteriorized. It is also called "*akanda* (indivisible) Brahman," implying that Mind is never really divided from Itself. (See the *Brahmanubhava Upanishad*.)

This Mind is also called, with fair regularity, "the One without a second," implying the final and ultimate unity of the one Mind behind all creation. It alone is Reality. It alone has unrelative or absolute existence. This is why other schools of mysticism have called this cosmic Mind the "Absolute."

It is said to be "subtle." In fact, none of the senses can detect this deeply Unconscious Mind. It is so very subtle, in fact, that the average person has no idea that It even exists, although It exists in her as fully as in the most enlightened sage or master. It is also recognized as "pure" (suddha), for this Mind intrinsically has not the faintest trace of contamination or pollution. It is stainless, completely flawless. It is unmixed, unadulterated, unalloyed Love, and Its purity is the most pristine, far beyond human comprehension.

It is also "immovable," for the Mind Itself does not have to move. Since It fills all things, It is already everywhere! Movement is tied in with spacetime, and It is spaceless and timeless. It dreams of movement, but Itself never has to move. It is found in pure stillness, and is itself both perfect and perfectly still.

It is said to be "eternal" (*nitya*), which is often mistaken for "everlasting," but which literally means something much closer to "timeless." That is, It is transcendental; it transcends time, which is simply one of Its canvases upon which it "paints" the world. Time is a medium for dreaming, but is also itself part of the dream. Time is like matter: Both are dreamed up simultaneously by Mind, and neither has any independent or absolute existence.

This Mind also "illuminates mind." This includes *buddhi*, "intellect." That is, the conscious mind is illuminated by the great Unconscious.

In the *Dicharabindu Upanishad*, this great principle is taught: The *atman*, or "Soul," can be known only by continuous inquiry, asking yourself, "Who am I?" Combined with the "practice of truth," penance, and selfrestraint, this question can lead the seeker to ever deeper levels of the Unconscious until she discovers, and touches, the Coremind. Try to redefine "I," so that it does not mean just the culturally, environmentally, or genetically formed ego. Try to see the Self as engulfing and including the cosmos, not as separate from it. For the Self partakes of Mind, and thus, is one with the Immeasurable and Illimitable. This means that your Self is not your body; it is also not your senses.

The true "I" is the *sat-chit-ananda atman,* the combination of existence, knowledge, and bliss. Getting stuck to, and believing that you are, a mere physical body, causes untold misery, and keeps the relentless wheel of karma spinning. This is a "cause of transmigration." To reidentify the Self, the senses must not be allowed to run amuck, or to dominate the mind.

For the senses are turbulent. They are always "running outside," distracting the mind, deluding it. They rob you of your interior focus on Spirit, and deluge you with delusion. The cure for this is the practice of moderate *dama*, or "selfrestraint."

A commentator on the Upanishads writes, "Not an iota of spiritual progress is possible without purity of thought." This means, among other things, speaking the truth under all circumstances. Monitor the mind. Some choose even to keep a daily record, diary, or journal of their mindflow.

In the *Jyotirbindu Upanishad,* it says that the Brahman is "selfshining (*svayam-jyotis*)." In other words, It is spiritually illuminated from within, and needs no other source of Light. It is described as "stainless," for It is not made impure by even the "impure world." It is the Essence of purity. It is not contaminated by either ignorance or Its "child," thoughts of harm and "evil." There is no evil, not a trace or hint, in the Creator/Dreamer, at the Corelevel of the Unconscious. It is also "undifferentiated." Although it dreams a world of billions of components, It is Itself one, single, living in harmony within Itself. Its potential cannot be limited by categories. It, like the enlightened Soul, is "timeless," or outside the timeflow altogether. Because of this factor, it is also "spaceless," which means that it does not exist in the cosmos of matter at all. Its existence is in the immaterial and real cosmos of Mind, where there is no time, no space.

This Mind is also "causeless." It is what has been called, in Christian theology, "the uncaused First Cause." Nothing and no one dreams It up. As it is selfshining, so It is also selfexistent, caused or created by no Mind external to Itself. Its being is intrinsic and inherent. It is absolutely selfsustaining.

"It is without destruction," which means that It cannot be destroyed by anything, ever. It is invulnerable, indestructible, invincible. It also is above the world of polarized opposites, such as "highness and lowness." Like the Tao, It has no "name," for anything that could attempt to classify It would be miserably insufficient, inadequate, and inaccurate. In Itself, again like Tao, It is "formless." Although It dreams into being all forms, It is wholly contained within none. Mind is immaterial, intangible, and without form. It is "allpervading" (*chidakasa*). Being beyond description, It is "above the reach of mind and speech." The finite has not a chance of encompassing the Infinite. But it can be grasped by pure, subtle, one-pointed Mind in an altered state of openness and lucidity. There are in fact four methods or approaches that make this possible: discrimination, dispassion, the "six virtues," and liberation-aspiration. These are all said to be boosted and reinforced by reflections on the Upanishads. A very popular reminder/mantra is *tat tvam asi,* "that thou art," or, "you are that." In this, "that" means anything that seems to be separate or apart from your Self. Another popular reminder is, "I am Brahman," used as a mantra.

Brahman is "spotless" (*niranjana*). Its stainless pristinity is beyond comprehension. In this purity, It is homogeneous through and through. Every micropsychon is stainless.

It is the inner and deepest Self, the *antaratma.* But it is not just "your" Self, but the inner Self of everyone and everything. It is Coremind, Lovemind, Spirit, or God. It is universal, for it is cosmic Mind.

In the "Text of Bliss," the *Anandabindu Upanishad*, the major and only characteristic that defines Brahmanmind is bliss. This Mind is called the "embodiment of," and is said to be "full of," bliss. This Unconscious Core is the sum total of all pleasures. In fact, all the joys and happiness of all the sentient worlds in all the galaxies is only a drop in the ocean of bliss that is Brahmanmind. By way of an aside, in the *Taittiriya Upanishad*, it is written, "This world has come out of bliss. It exists in bliss... He who knows the blissful Brahman is not afraid of anything." Why is this? The most horrific elements, the most monstrous, are mere paper tigers; they are dragons made of smoke. Nothing in this world can harm the Soul, and the Soul is the true Self. However nightmarish the world becomes, the enlightened can find comfort in the fact that none of it is absolutely real. As convincing as the "props" might be, the world is still a stage. As scared as people might become, the whole world is "virtual."

Also, as in Christianity, the Lovemind is the polar opposite of the fearmind, and so, both cannot coexist with equal power. In fact, to be completely literal, the fearmind has no intrinsic existence. Only Lovemind is absolutely, intrinsically, independently real. And Creatormind, Brahmanmind, emerges from and is a part of Lovemind.

Sensual pleasure can be great, and the mystic enjoys it too. But as a dominant master, it is catastrophic. It can be as sweet as honey, but its mastership in life laces the honey with arsenic. Some extremists, particularly of the Brahmanic ascetic variety, carried this principle to the absurd extreme of feeling that *all* sensual pleasure was dangerous or evil. This is not so. In fact, ordinary sensual pleasure is seen as a form of bliss (*ananda*), and is called *vishaya-ananda*. It is true that if your whole mind or mental pleasure arises only or exclusively from sensual stimulation, that can and does lead to big trouble. A particularly notorious and noxious example in our culture is the man who thinks with his "little head," instead of with mind. Many men, in fact, have turned their entire lives over to penis-dominance, until a few centimeters of tissue have become their god. For many, it is the center of the cosmos; they have no room for anything or anyone else in their lives or minds. They suffer from mega-ocd (obsessive-compulsive disorder).

Besides, the bliss enjoyed in Brahmanmind, intrinsic to It, not created by the environment, is hundreds of thousands of times as great as any sensual pleasure. In fact, the bliss of a *jnani* (mystic) resting in Brahmanmind is millions of times as great, and is "indescribable." Mystics call this "ecstasy" or "rapture."

Besides the form of mild "bliss" provided by the sensual cosmos, there are four other kinds of bliss: 1) *yogananda*, the bliss arising from yoga or mystical practices, 2) *atmananda*, the intrinsic bliss of the Self, which must be discovered and touched through meditation, 3) *advaitananda*, the bliss that arises from discovering nonduality, or oneness with all, and 4) *vidyananda,* the bliss of spiritual knowledge/understanding.

Brahmanmind is described as "a mass of bliss," or "dense bliss," meaning "concentrated bliss" (*anandaghana*). More, It is "eternal bliss" (*nityasukha*). This implies that it is timeless, untouched or unaltered, uninfluenced by the world changes inevitable in the timeflow. This bliss is also a continuous Flow. It is called "infinite bliss" (*anantasukha*). This bliss arises, is discovered, only when we return to our original Home, the Brahmanmind. No matter how many sensual pleasures that you provide for a fish that is on land, it will not be content until you return it to water. The land is an alien world to its nature. And so getting lost in materialism is as alien to our deepest Self, and we can never know happiness until we are submerged and immersed in this Lovemind. As mystics from all times and climes have reminded us like a mantra, you simply cannot find lasting or genuine happiness from mere material things.

***

End of *Luminous Jewels of Love and Light*, Volume 2.

Richard Shiningthunder Francis

About The Author

Richard Shiningthunder Francis was consultant to *Time*, *Newsweek*, and "60 Minutes." He is founder of the Institute of Agapology and Metaphysics, the Pneumarium, Love Ministries, Inc. (www.loveministries.org)

The author of *Jehovah Good-bye; Journey to the Center of the Soul; Luminous Ecstasies and Passions; Falling In Love With Yourself* and *The Mystic Gospels,* He has been the subject of three TV series: "Psychology of Spirituality," "Way of Universal Love," and "Spiritual Awakenings." He hosts two radioprograms: "Heartmind" and "Soulmind."

Francis has lived in Central America, and Appalachia.

Former editor of *Lovespirit* and *Cosmic Visions*, he was consultant for the Holistic Medical Center and the Center for New Age Studies. He lives in Liberty Township, Ohio, with his beloved wife of thirty-two years, Ada Maria.